£9.00

LUND STUDIES IN ENGLISH 96
Editors Marianne Thormählen and Beatrice Warren

CW01551414

LUND STUDIES IN ENGLISH 96
Editors: Marianne Thormählen and Beatrice Warren

The Fallen World in Coleridge's Poetry

Agneta Lindgren

Lund
University
Press

Lund University Press
Box 141
S-221 00 LUND
+46 46 31 20 00

Art nr 205 58
ISBN Lund University Press 91-7966-555-1
ISSN 0076-1451

Acknowledgements

No human endeavour is ever an island entire of itself, but an achievement carried out thanks to the good will and generosity of many people.

My list of acknowledgements begins with my thanks to Professor Emeritus Sven Bäckman, who admitted me to the graduate seminar in English Literature at Lund and assisted my initial efforts, and to the members of the seminar, especially Annelie Hultén, Björn Sundmark and Cecilia Wadsö.

A scholarship from the New Society of Letters (*Vetenskapssocieteten*) in Lund gave me the opportunity to do research at the Centre for the Study of Literature and Theology, University of Glasgow, 1996–1997. Among the seminar members of the Centre, I am indebted to Dr Kiyoshi Tsuchiya, Glasgow University; Dr. Andrew Hass, Houston University, Texas; Carmen Burkhalter, Faculty of Divinity, University of Lausanne; and Kay Carmichael and Ruth Dunster, University of Glasgow, for valuable discussions of ideas and parts of my text.

I am grateful to Professor Stephen Prickett who supervised my work during my stay in Glasgow, not only for his readings of and comments on parts of this book, but also for his generous help and many valuable suggestions.

I also wish to thank the Hjalmar Gullberg and Greta Thott scholarship fund for a grant which enabled me to finish this thesis, and Dr Eva-Maria Jansson of the Faculty of Divinity, Lund University, for helping me with the Hebrew.

Finally, and with special gratitude, I acknowledge my debt to Professor Marianne Thormählen, who, during the whole course of this project, not only kept me on the right track, but also encouraged me patiently, guiding me through to the completion of the book.

This list would not be complete without my thanks for the love and support of my children, Christian and Paula.

Sölvesborg, February 1999

Agneta Lindgren

Contents

Introduction

The complexity of Coleridge's work is manifested in the diversity of approaches to which he has been subjected. The fragmentariness of that work, and the contradictory elements within it, have sometimes been considered as merely a matter of taking refuge in ambiguities. The difficulty in making an assessment of Coleridge's intellectual position has been perceived as "wad[ing] into a morass [since] Coleridge is a writer almost unique in his special combination of allusiveness, fragmentariness of statement, complication of interests, and neurotic inability to attend to the demands of formal presentation", as McFarland says (1969, viii).

It has been claimed that a system of polarity, or an attempt to reconcile opposites, should be applied not only to Coleridge's criticism but to all his mental activity. It is moreover frequently stated that what has been called his vacillation between an "atheistic" Spinozan philosophy and the Christian's faith in a discernible, personal God should be seen as a conflict between a "philosophy of the head" and a "philosophy of the heart". There are critics who try to prove that his Christian faith functions as some kind of bridge between these antagonistic forces. It has furthermore been argued that Coleridge's practical criticism deals not with organic wholes but with fragments, that his writings produce contradictions which resist resolution, and that these discrepancies cannot be explained by the "dialectic" nature of his theory or by his tendency, "deriving from his religious education, to think in terms of the paradox of the incarnation (the poet 'incarnated' in his text and yet transcending it)" (Venuti 165).

Modern critics do not deny that Coleridge's literary theory was a sophisticated and functional instrument. However, they have maintained that some basic terms in his theory, essentially as they come forward in *Biographia Literaria* – such as "will", "reconciliation", "organization", "unity" and "identity" – are not clearly defined in his own writings but often developed in a contradictory way, obscuring similarities instead of resolving discrepancies. This state of affairs is fortunately changing. Profitable challenges against it have been voiced by for instance Thomas McFarland, in his books *Coleridge and the Pantheist Tradition* (1969) and *Romanticism and the Forms of Ruin: Wordsworth, Coleridge, and Modalities of Fragmentation* (1981), and by Kathleen Wheeler, in her book *The Creative Mind in Coleridge's Poetry* (1981). However, Stephen Prickett – one of the most prominent scholars in English Romanticism today – has produced a new awareness in our understanding of the Romantic period. His works, particularly *Words and The Word: Language, Poetics and Biblical Interpretation* (1986) and *Origins of Narrative: The Romantic Appropriation of the Bible* (1996) not only contain explorations and explanations of underlying fundamental philosophical and religious implications and contextual situations; they also provide instruments and approaches conducive to a better appreciation of the Romantic poets' positions and idiosyncrasies. Among other circumstances inherent in the Romantic period, he stresses the importance of the new way of reading and interpreting the Bible which came with Higher Criticism, as well as the impact of Robert Lowth on the English Romantic poets.

The tenderly nurtured idea that Romantic art should be a synthesis of the "I am" and the "it is", that is of subject and object, forming a kind of "reconciliation of opposites", is difficult to find in Colerige's work and particularly in his poetry (though there are a few exceptions). Coleridge's poetry juxtaposes or conflates "opposites"; but as we shall see these "opposites" are never reconciled, contrary to what has been said in the past. Instead something "new" is created out of something seemingly paradoxical; Coleridge "[links] apparently disconnected ideas (...) under tension, [in which he] combines opposite or discordant qualities in a creative unity" (Prickett 1986, 143). A neat synthesis of opposites or of conflicting discourses might lead to over-simplified and one-sided results, especially when applied to the variety of opinions and the apparently ambiguous or fragmentary statements that occur in Coleridge's works. We have a tendency to reduce chaos into patterns in our eager search for unity in construction and thought, thus overlooking the complexity and richness of a work of art. Unity and recognizable patterns are comforting. Past and present literary criticism has devoted a great deal of energy and ingenuity to the pursuit of such patterns. Critical works of relevance for this study will be introduced as a point of departure for each chapter.

Many sophisticated explanations could be presented concerning the Schelling element in *Biographia Literaria* , as well as in regard to the rather fragmented lines of argument in it. First and foremost, it should be borne in mind that the book is, among other things, an autobiographical statement, and a very personal one at that. The subtitle is, after all, "or Biographical Sketches of My Literary Life and Opinions". In his first chapter, Coleridge actually states:

> I have used the narration chiefly for the purpose of giving a continuity to the work, *in part for the sake of the miscellaneous reflections suggested to me by particular events*, but still more as introductory to the statement of my principles in Politics, Religion, and Philosophy, and the application of the rules, deduced from philosophical principles, to poetry and criticism. (5) (my italics)

Biographia Literaria is thus in part autobiographical.

In his fairly recent biography of Coleridge (1990), Richard Holmes covers the writer's life until his departure for Malta in 1804.[1] As late as 1971, Norman Fruman had pointed out that it was generally admitted that no adequate biography of Coleridge existed. He also acknowledged the difficulty of finding a biographer able to deal with the subject (iv). This, he explained, was partly the result of the fragmentary character of the material that all Coleridge's biographers had worked with, and partly due to the fact that Coleridge's letters and notebooks had not been available for inspection before. Fruman's opinion is not completely correct, though, as *The Notebooks of S. T. Coleridge* covering the years 1794–1804 were collected and edited by Kathleen Coburn and published as early as 1957–1961. Anyone writing on Coleridge and/or his work owes an enormous debt to her. There were, furthermore, *S. T. Coleridge's Collected Letters,* edited by Earl Leslie Griggs, in four volumes, covering the years 1785–819, published in 1956–1959. Besides, it was possible to consult many letters and notes to Coleridge, or about him, by his contemporaries. The problem has therefore not exactly consisted in the

---

[1] Richard Holmes's new book on Coleridge, *Coleridge: Volume II, Darker Reflections,* has not been included here, as, unfortunately, this study was in press when Holmes's book appeared.

lack of information but rather in the lack of an adequate biographer. Holmes fulfils this requirement; he approaches Coleridge without prejudice, but with sensitivity and inspiration.

Most critical discussions of Coleridge's philosophy have explored his relation to the German metaphysicians of his own time. Many of the ideas put forward and discussed by Coleridge were not new, but part of a wider Western philosophy and Christian heritage generally. His writings were intended to be read and understood by the intellectual public at that time. It is therefore strange that some critics have concentrated so much on his so-called plagiarisms, as Coleridge never aimed to be original when discussing philosophy or religion. He never claimed any originality in his philosophy or religion, only in his literary works.

The same circumstance adheres to concepts such as the "reconciling of opposites" or "organic unity", ideas which were current before Coleridge's time but which are sometimes referred to as if they had been invented by him, a claim he himself never made. He only used what was already there and seldom accepted anything without reservations. It is important to bear in mind that Coleridge also had certain objections against Kant, although he certainly admired him. In the following letter, he repudiates a suggestion that he had adopted Kant's philosophy:

> Of the three schemes of Philosophy, Kant's, Fichte's and Schelling's (...) I should find it difficult to select the one from which I *differed* the most – tho' perfectly easy to determine which of the three Men I hold in highest honor. And Immanuel Kant I assuredly do value most highly; not, however, as a Metaphysician but as a Logician, who has completed and systematized what Lord Bacon had boldly designed and loosely sketched out in the miscellany of Aphorisms, his Novum Organum. (*CL.* V, 1438, 8 April 1825) (Coleridge's italics)

As mentioned, Coleridge's relation to the German metaphysicians has been well documented; but as McFarland maintains, the differences between his philosophy and that of these German philosophers have never been explored. However, McFarland himself provides a full-length study of the complex relation between Coleridge and Schelling in the chapter entitled "The Problem of Coleridge's Plagiarism" (1969, 1–52), where he supplies an exposition of defenders and detractors of Coleridge's so-called "borrowings". McFarland writes:

I shall attempt to justify (...) that it is not Coleridge who 'has little insight into the incompatibility of different trends of thought' or 'lacks a sense for the subtle shades of terminological differences' or who is 'heterogeneous, incoherent and even contradictory', but rather Wellek and the other accusers who fail to penetrate to the real subject of Coleridge's discourse, who fail to realize the small number of genuine positions possible in philosophy, and who fail to understand fully the rules, pertinencies, and historical traditions of syncretistic thought. (1969, 13)

This is a bold statement, but McFarland pursues his aim convincingly. Another important scholar, not only on Coleridge but on Romanticism in general, M.H. Abrams, has this to say about Coleridge:

In criticism what [Coleridge] took from other writers he developed into a speculative instrument, which for its power of insight and, above all, of application in the detailed analysis of literary works, had no peer among the German organic theorists. (1953, 17)

Quotations, particularly from Schelling, in *Biographia Literaria* have been attributed as borrowings. There are also, however, as can be seen from the notes in the above-mentioned work, examples from other philosophers. Coleridge mostly admitted his obligations. In *Biographia Literaria,* ch. 9, he confesses his indebtedness to the Mystics (149–52) and to Kant (153–57), as well as to Fichte and Schelling (157–67). Though there are some parts – particularly from Schelling – which are almost literally translations and not accounted for by Coleridge, he expanded or developed ideas (in other works as well as in *Biographia Literaria*), sometimes creating new levels of understanding. Prickett, for instance, mentions Coleridge's substitution of Schelling's word 'intelligence' for "the more Kantian 'imagination' in line with [Coleridge's] insistence on the active function of the mind in perception" (1986, 143). Behind this way of borrowing lies a very human explanation. If there is something we are highly interested in or admire, we are apt to adopt or appropriate it. We make it part of our own intellectual life; it comes forward spontaneously, and in this process, we tend to forget about acknowledging our authorities, since what we have borrowed, we take for granted that our audience recognizes as well as we do. This is psychology of the simplest kind, and Coleridge is the first to acknowledge it, admitting that "[w]e insensibly imitate what we habitually admire" (*The Friend*, Ess. iii). A borrowing could of course be more sophistically explained as some kind of "appropriation", along the lines proposed by Prickett, who suggests that

> the very idea of 'appropriation' [is] *both* a quality of thinly disguised theft *and* a recognition that such a take-over is a necessary part of the way in which any person, or even society, makes an idea its own – that appropriation is, in other words, a normal condition of intellectual and cultural vitality. (1996, 32) (Prickett's italics)

In some curious way, then, we believe that what we have appropriated, others have appropriated too. We are in part entitled to believe so, since some ideas have the propensity to be embraced even, as Prickett writes, by "society". Hence we do not reflect on whether the "borrowing" might actually constitute a "theft." As Prickett points out, "the primeval tension between theft and creative acquisition is not an accident of the written word, but in some way endemic to it" (34). Appropriating something also implies that we claim something, a role, a position, as it were. The Romantics who "appropriated" from earlier tradition were very conscious of earlier conventions; but their "appropriation is immediately linked with its seeming opposite, originality, in such a way that it can be read back into a new interpretation of the past" (42). The Romantic writer was very well aware of his relation to and difference from tradition. It was only with knowledge of the other combined with self-knowledge that he was able to interpret and change tradition, transforming it into something new. Prickett provides examples of such an integration, that is of both "the dubieties of appropriation" (what we call cultural tradition, and the organic growth of 'aneignen') out of which comes richness, diversity: "The truly 'traditional' work is the one that is really new. The great poet or writer (...) is the one who can absorb and appropriate the works of the past and *then* create something distinctly different from them" (47) (Prickett's italics). A poet aware of a tradition is also able to "play" with appropriation, a phenomenon reflected in different kind of ironies, for example the ones employed by Coleridge in *Biographia Literaria* with its "unconventional mixed genres (...) its extended metaphoric situations [and] patchwork borrowings" (Wheeler 162).

Ideas come and go. Some are more persistent than others; some come back slightly transformed; some return more similar to the original; some turn up as allusions or echoes, and yet others only give us a hint of what could have been the original idea. Our culture was not exactly created ex *nihilo*.

Coleridge's work has lately been viewed from a hermeneutic point of view, which could be summarized in E.S. Shaffer's lines: "It is through his delicate art of quotation and reminiscence of quotation that Coleridge suggests a unique hermeneutic community within each poem, one in which the participants set up a subtext of dialogue" (1990, 220). Thus Coleridge's quotations, his allusiveness, his idea of literary communities, his vocabulary, as well as the religious connotations of his statements and his Miltonic echoes should be understood, according to Shaffer, as "a complex model of Romantic intertextuality in the service of a new secular hermeneutic dialogism" (222). Consequently, for an appreciation of Coleridge's work it is necessary to consider its affinity to "a body of thought" or to see it as a contribution to a literary fellowship. Such an approach will also help us to understand the presence of Milton, not as has been suggested as some undermining or debilitating influence or as the result of mere plagiarism, but as evidence that this older poet belongs to Coleridge's ideal community of hearers and readers. Coleridge's own idea of a reader or audience is to some degree manifested in his discussion of Wordsworth's "Immortality Ode" in *Biographia Literaria,* where he makes it clear that the common language of poetry is not a spontaneous unconscious growth from man in a natural state, but rather a highly self-conscious construction of poetic genius. Therefore, Wordsworth's definition of the vehicle of poetry as "the real language of man" is replaced by a justification of the poem as a more enigmatic phenomenon: "A poem is not necessarily obscure, because it does not aim to be popular. It is enough, if a work be perspicuous to those for whom it is written and, 'Fit audience find, though few' "(II ch. 22, 147). The same idea about the poet's audience can be found in Coleridge's answer to a letter from Thomas Poole. After *Religious Musings* had been published in April 1796, Richard Poole had complained to Coleridge that the poem was "too metaphysical for common readers". Coleridge answered that "the Poem was not written for common Readers" (*CL.* I, 124, 5 May 1796). There is a strong note of elitism in such a statement; but similar expressions were used by other Romantics as well. Shelley thus points out that "every poet writes only for the next generation of poets". Wordsworth is of the opinion that "an *accurate* taste in poetry (...) is an *acquired* talent which can only be produced by thought and a long continued intercourse with the best models of composition" (Preface to *Lyrical Ballads* 1802) (Wordsworth's italics). Coleridge's awareness of literary fellowship, his feeling of belonging to a "transhistorical community", is expressed in his text and is incontestable.

We should not forget, however, that apart from his literary theories and philosophical writings, Coleridge's disposition was, as Harding points out, "an intensely religious one" (1974, 28). It could hence be argued that Coleridge aimed at a political and moral system that was intricately cross-bred by a religious, eschatological view of life which only poetry could be adequate to express, and that the poet's interest lay in mingling poetry, philosophy and religion. In Coleridge's case, the outcome might be termed "religious philosophy". For anyone who sought an expression for such poetic impulses, Milton would provide the ideal model. In a letter to Thomas Wilkinson of 31 December 1808, Coleridge writes: "[T]rue philosophy rather leads to Christianity" (*CL*. III, 735) . In another letter, of 25 September 1816, he explains his future projects and informs H.J. Rose: "[M]y aspirations are toward the concentring of my powers in 3 Works. The first (for I am convinced that a true System of Philosophy = the Science of Life) is *best* taught in Poetry as well as most safely"(*CL*. IV, 1031) (Coleridge's italics).

Throughout his life Coleridge wrote and commented upon religious and theological problems and topics. These writings can be found in letters, notebooks and marginalia. Relatively late in life he wrote *Aids to Reflection*. It is generally asserted among critics that Coleridge, having been a Unitarian, became an orthodox Christian; scholars even mention the year 1802 as some kind of turning-point for his acceptance of the dogma of the Anglican Church. His prose writings, mainly from his later life, have been studied by James Boulger, who considers that Coleridge managed to advance "interpretations of orthodox doctrines which might take into account the emotion and will, without swamping the intellect and rational elements in religion in a deluge of sentiment" (1961, 3). Coleridge always stressed the importance of the emotional side of religion as well as the personal commitment of the individual when considering Christian faith and dogma. In *Aids to Reflection,* for instance, Coleridge wrote: "Christianity is not a Theory, or a Speculation, but a *Life*: not a Philosophy of Life, but a Life and living Process" (134) (Coleridge's italics). This statement implies the well-known paradox in faith between emotion and intellect and is important to bear in mind, not only when reading Coleridge's prose works but also when reading his poetry.

Boulger claims that Coleridge leaned towards Calvinistic positions, including doctrines such as justifying faith in which emotion plays a major role, and he adheres to the generally accepted idea that "before 1801–1802 Coleridge's chief speculative interests were philosophical materialism and religious Unitarianism" (12). Coleridge admitted his adherence to Unitarianism even though he later rejected it. About Coleridge's later poetry, Boulger writes: "While suggesting the understandable intrusion of the philosophical and religious interests in the late poetry, it reminds us of the inferior nature of this poetry" (196). This opinion of Coleridge's later verse is common, and critics who have trie¹ to trace some kind of development in his poetry have not gone beyond the year 1804 (the year of Coleridge's departure for Malta).

Robert Barth, however, looks upon Coleridge's so-called Unitarian period or connection as an "aberrant interlude in Coleridge's relationship with the Anglican church." He also points out the various attractions of Unitarianism for the young Coleridge. The Unitarian church was a fairly respectable form of dissent from the Established Church which attracted many intellectuals, then and later. In particular, the strong social concern of Unitarianism "made it an acceptable means of objecting to injustices in current social and political structures" (1990, 291).

Coleridge and the Seventeenth Century

Coleridge frequently returns to the distinction between "Reason" and "Understanding". This antithesis has been considered to be a borrowing from Kant, but Coleridge professed to have found it in other quarters, as Brinkley has shown:

> Coleridge sought to clarify the difference between the Understanding and Reason by reviving the ancient distinction between 'intuition' and 'discursive' reason. Here again he appeals to the seventeenth century. (1968 intr. xxxiv)

In *Biographia Literaria* I, ch. 10, 173–74, Coleridge refers not to Kant, but to his seventeenth-century authorities. He writes:

> I have cautiously discriminated the terms, the REASON, and the UNDERSTANDING, encouraged and confirmed by the authority

of our genuine divines, and philosophers, before the revolution [of 1688];

> both life, and sense,
> Fancy, and *understanding*, whence the soul
> *Reason* receives, and REASON is her *being*,
> DISCURSIVE, or INTUITIVE. Discourse
> Is oftest your's, the latter most is our's.
> Differing but in *degree*, in *kind* the same.
> (PARADISE LOST. V)

This quotation affirms Coleridge's affinity with Milton but also with the terminology of the seventeenth-century divines in his discussion of two key concepts in his philosophy, reason and understanding.

Louis Bredvold has pointed out that "the seventeenth century was [Coleridge's] spiritual home, and its controversies and idiosyncrasies, even more than those of German Romanticism, congenially reflected his own tastes, and his intellectual bent" (xxiii). The best proof of this is found in his extensive surveys of English writers from that century, notably the great divines and Milton. These writings have been collected by Roberta Brinkley, in *Coleridge on the Seventeenth Century*. Bredvold considers it "unfortunate that so little use has been made of Coleridge's comments on the writers of the Great Age" (xxi), and finds that though

> some few gems (...) get quoted, at second or third hand (...) it is not the custom for the student of Hooker, Jeremy Taylor, or even Milton, to consult Coleridge as a part of his task. The difficulties have perhaps been sufficient to discourage many who have made the attempt. (xxii)

Coleridge not only recognized the literary value of these writers but shows a true understanding of their various positions. What could there be in these writers that so attracted him? It is possible to argue that it was the doctrines over which seventeenth-century theologians argued with such heat: the Fall, free will, Original Sin, evil. He was also drawn by their style, conceits and imagery, as Bredvold has stressed:

> Their weight of quotation and reference and the Latinization of style

were no handicap to Coleridge; and the allusiveness was but an added source of enjoyment (...) He enjoyed the intellectual appeal of the artificial conceits which often appeared, and found a congenial mental exercise in the wordplay. But it was the imagery characteristic of the writing of this period which afforded him the greatest pleasure. (125)

Coleridge was himself aware of the fact "that his own style was consciously modelled on that of the seventeenth century" (Bredvold xxiv) and admitted it in letters and notes. In *The Friend,* he makes this clear in the following terms:

> We insensibly imitate what we habitually admire; and an aversion to the epigrammatic unconnected periods of the fashionable *Anglo-gallican* taste has too often made me willing to forget, that the stately march and difficult evolutions, which characterize the eloquence of Hooker, Bacon, Milton and Jeremy Taylor, are, notwithstanding their intrinsic excellence, still less suited to a periodical Essay. This fault I am now endeavoring to correct. (Essay iii, 20) (Coleridge's italics)

The religious and ontological dimensions of Coleridge's writings show a constant preoccupation with human suffering, evil, sin and guilt. Part of the answer to these eternal problems he tried to find in his own Christian faith. He found kindred spirits in some of the seventeenth-century writers who were concerned with religion and philosophy, and among these, Milton was his lodestar. These seventeenth-century writers presumably not only satisfied his emotional needs but also his intellectual ones. But here, again, while his own ideas were congenial with many of the theological and philosophical problems discussed by these writers, he never abandoned his critical attitude.

Brinkley also notes the similarity of the theological atmosphere of the seventeenth century to that of Coleridge's own day. She mentions components such as the diversity of beliefs, religious controversy and the development of materialistic thought that stirred the opposition of the religious leaders. In both periods there were thinkers who tried to find common minimum essentials of belief, and in both periods there was also a manifest interest in biblical criticism and the relation between Church and State (126).

A Short Comment on the Historical Background of the Two Ages: Milton (1608–1674) and Coleridge (1772–1834)

A very general view of the historical background of the two ages, of Milton (1608–1674) and Coleridge (1772–1834), will be attempted before concentrating on some characteristics that are of more specific interest in the context of the Fallen World motif.

Both periods were, of course, times of war: The Thirty-Years'-War and the Napoleonic Wars were both significant conflicts. Milton's lifetime also spanned the English Civil War. Both periods were characterized by social and economic distress as well as by social upheaval and disturbance. In both periods the political systems were under stress, and there was a common dread of civil disorder. In the early 1790s it was also commonly believed, particularly in dissenting circles, that the end of the world was near. Prickett points out that "[t]he French Revolution gave a new impetus to such movements, and from the 1790s onwards there were a whole series of millenarian outbreaks" (1981, 134). Priestley, also a Unitarian and mentioned in Coleridge's poem *Religious Musings,* took the acts of violence in France 1792–1794 to be the terrors described in the Book of Revelation as the harbingers of the Second Coming. Many people believed that Britain was on the brink of revolution. When the price of flour rose owing to a cold winter in 1795, bread riots began to break out in various places in England. At the end of October, the king was attacked on his way to open Parliament by a mob crying out "Bread! Peace!" Earlier that year Coleridge wrote: "We have reason to believe that a revolution in other parts of Europe is not far distant. Oppression is grievous, the oppressed feel and complain (...) the evil is great, but it might be averted" (*Lectures 1795 On Politics and Religion*).

The thinking of all Englishmen in both these periods was dominated by the Established Church, and in their search for an ideology or spiritual coherence in difficult times it was only natural that people turned to religion, i.e. to the Church or to various religious sects. Religious questions were often bound up with politics and there was a great demand for sermons in both periods. The Established Church enforced unity and conformity. There was a longing for some kind of illumination or revelation which the Establishment did not provide, a desire which seems to have fostered the rise of many different sects. This circumstance, together with economic motives, also took many emigrants to America in the 1790s. Priestley and his family, for instance, left England for

Pennsylvania in 1795. Coleridge's theoretical "pantisocracy" project in America is well known and should be regarded in this historical context.

The pre-revolutionary period in England during the seventeenth century is also known as "years of increasing national disillusionment" (Christopher Hill 1977, 21). Hill discusses the intellectual origins of the English revolution and considers England's intellectual crisis as part of a wider European economic and social crisis (1965, 4). These years in the seventeenth century were certainly marked by an intellectual crisis. It is reflected in late Jacobean and Caroline drama, which have often been labelled as "gloomy" and "introspective". The idea of the progressive decay of nature was more specifically expressed and asserted in these years than ever before. Hill looks upon the literature of the late Jacobean and Caroline periods as self-searching in character. This may in part also be due to the hard censorship of the pre-revolutionary period, as well as to the fact that authors voluntarily abstained from publication. A self-searching quality is arguably present in the literature of the late eighteenth century, too. The Prefaces to *Lyrical Ballads* demonstrate this quality, and so does Blake's Romantic manifesto, *The Marriage of Heaven and Hell* (1793), which – as Prickett points out – "is not often treated as being a work of literary criticism, as a manifesto for an aesthetic position, yet that (among other things) is what it is" (1981, 222). Shelley's "A Defence of Poetry" (1821) and Wordsworth's "Prelude" are also good examples of a self-exploring spirit. There seems to have been a need for critical theory as well as a questioning of the poet's own identity as an artist in this period.

In Milton's time, many people shared the hopes and dreams of a new society. These hopes were often expressed in prophecies. Millenarian beliefs were common, and it was widely believed that those were the latter days of the world, to be followed by the thousand-year rule of Jesus and the saints. According to Hill, Milton was a radical Millenarian. In 1641 Milton expressed his belief that Christ's kingdom "is now at hand". Milton thus had a vision of Christ as the shortly-expected King of a just society. His Millenarianism was also bound up with the sense of England as the chosen nation. Millenarianism was nothing new, but in revolutionary periods and hard times such beliefs come to the surface. Biblical prophecies, especially those in the Books of Daniel and Revelation, were interpreted as referring to present-day England. According to Downing & Millman,

Millenarianism provided the impetus for much of the radical religious debate of this period; combined with the utopian hopes of many of the religious sects, which were also shared by the more radical secular groups, it helped to fire the English Revolution. (106)

In Milton's time there was a demand for a preaching clergy that led to the appointment of lecturers outside the Established Church. These preachers were often appointed and paid for by wealthy merchants and town corporations. In both periods the dissenting chapels thus often competed with the Anglican Church. In the dissenting chapel "were to be found the radical shoemaker, the visionary, the millenarian, ready in the 1790s as they had been in the 1640s" (Brooks 47, 48). Milton came to advocate itinerant preachers, maintained by voluntary contributions. In 1659 he hoped to see the itinerant system backed up by local preachers.

In Coleridge's time Unitarianism was, as was pointed out above, a fairly respectable form of dissent from the Established Church. Having drawn attention to the powerful social conscience of the Unitarians, Prickett points out that though they were few in number at the end of the eighteenth century, the Unitarians "constituted a kind of intellectual élite amongst Nonconformity"(1981, 119). While Coleridge was writing *Religious Musings* and *The Destiny of Nations*, he was also composing his sermons. On his journey to secure subscriptions for the *Watchman* in 1796, he stayed in Unitarian homes and preached in Unitarian pulpits. Later on, in *Biographia Literaria*, he tells us:

> I argued, I described, I promised, I prophecied; and beginning with the captivity of nations I ended with the near approach of the millennium, finishing the whole with some of my own verses describing that glorious state out of *the Religious Musings*. (I, ch. 10, 181)

Finally, how do these short comments on the historical backgrounds relate to the Christian doctrine of the Fall of Man? An explanation might be offered along the following lines: In the seventeenth century, people looked beyond the literal level of a text in a way which seems to flourish in times of repression and strong censorship. It was generally assumed that the classical myths contained "true history". Classical myth and biblical narrative were often set alongside each other as containing the same truth. This manner of reading is, of course, also relevant to the typological interpretation of a text, as explained in the *Christabel* chapter below. According to Hill, London radicals during the revolution "believed that Revelation 8 and 11 – chapters on which Milton drew in *Paradise Lost* for his account of the war in Heaven – and Amos 8 and 9 gave an account of English history in the sixteen-forties" (Hill 1977, 341). For Milton, the Fall of Man was an historical event, and from the late 1650s it became more and more important in his thinking, being put to use in order to explain God's cause in his chosen nation.

In any discussion of the revolutionary theories of the seventeenth century, explanations of the origins of private property and social inequality should be kept in mind, as Hill reminds us: "If Adam had not fallen, men would have been equal, property would have been held in common; a coercive state became necessary to protect inequalities in property, which are the consequence of post-lapsarian greed and pride" (346). Radicals in the seventeenth century believed that with the abolishing of private property and wage labour humanity could be brought back to a pre-lapsarian state of bliss and innocence. There was a genuine hope of overcoming the Fall. These same ideas were also common in radical circles in the England of the 1790s. The Fall thus had social implications. The demands for equality and human rights became more insistent in both periods. This became more apparent with the collapse of censorship during the turbulent years of the Civil War, when the various sects seized the opportunity to publish their views. Hill mentions Diggers, Ranters, Arminians and Quakers in the seventeenth century as characteristically keeping up a continuous discussion about the Fall and about sin, a discussion which refers to the relation between the Establishment and the individual. Hill maintains that Milton accepted the social implications of the Fall and that "[a]ny revolutionary theory, therefore, had to take into account mid-seventeenth-century discussion of the Fall" (346). The Fall also more and more came to be a way of explaining why God's cause had failed in the nation of his choice.

After the Restoration of Charles II in 1660, Milton did not have the same high hopes for the English nation. He was, as Hill says, "still searching for an audience which would appreciate him, 'fit though few' " (348). In both *Paradise Lost* and *De Doctrina* we can read about the doctrine of the remnant, the few just men who will save mankind. These few just men were often referred to as the saints. Hill considers Milton to be the first to use the story of the Fall to account for the failure of a revolution.

The revolutionary ideas from the seventeenth century were an inspiration for Coleridge in the composition of *Religious Musings* and *The Destiny of Na-*

tions, where we also find the idea of the Millennium and the chosen nation closely bound up with the Fall as an explanation of contemporary social and economic inequality and oppression. Repressing its critics and ignoring the crisis, the Establishment of the 1790s was mindful not only of the French revolution but also of the Civil War in the seventeenth century.

Milton was not only the ideal poet for many Romantics; he was also a symbol, representing the man who fought for freedom and liberal ideas. Wordsworth's invocation of Milton is famous:

> MILTON! thou shouldst be living at this hour:
> England hath need of thee: she is a fen
> of stagnant waters: altar, sword, and pen,
> Fireside, the heroic wealth of hall and bower,
> Have forfeited their ancient English dower
> Of inward happiness. We are selfish men;
> Oh! raise us up, return to us again;
> And give us manners, virtue, freedom, power.
> Thy soul was like a Star, and dwelt apart;
> Thou hadst a voice whose sound was like the sea:
> Pure as the naked heavens, majestic, free,
> So didst thou travel on life's common way,
> In cheerful godliness; and yet thy heart
> The lowliest duties on herself did lay.
> ("London, 1802", comp. September 1802, publ. 1807)

Both Coleridge and Wordsworth looked back to Milton. They saw him not only as a poet, but as a man and the very model of a freedom fighter.

It is of course obvious that Coleridge had his own contemporary society in mind when writing *Religious Musings* and *The Destiny of Nations*. In these works he denounces social injustice, the war with France, and the abuses perpetrated by the British ruling classes who responded with effective repression to social unrest and to all demands from the lower classes. The two poems could therefore be seen as a picture of the Fallen World with a stress on contemporary evils. It is impossible to be mistaken about Coleridge's personal commitment and passion when denouncing the horrors and injustices of his time.

* * *

It should, furthermore, be remembered that Coleridge was brought up during a period of theological stagnation. Stephen Prickett speaks of it as "a spiritual vacuum", remarking that "[m]odern impressions confirm this contemporary feeling of spiritual and physical decay" in the Church of England (1981, 116–17). Especially after the French Revolution, few Englishmen wanted to call themselves sceptics. Even the so-called "pious deists" were afraid of being reminded that Robespierre had delivered an oration on the Supreme Being. It was even seen as a sign of "ecclesiastical healthiness" when problems of faith were no longer discussed, "when Christianity had so wrought itself into men's nature that it was no more in need of being debated than the movements of the planets or the changes of the seasons", as James Anthony Froude put it (qtd. in Stewart 18). The effort of apologetics during the Age of Reason had been to support and sustain the Christian mysteries with evidence. Thus the appeal of religion was deliberately intellectualized. The bad fortune of individuals was often traced to personal sins. The problem of the eighteenth century had been how to deal with the mysterious elements in the doctrine of revelation. The deists had claimed that genuine religious truth is wholly disclosed by the intelligence of man. Their opponents had replied that not everything in religion is compatible with intelligence, and that there is a body of dogma which even contradicts reason and must still be accepted. The deists supposed that the truth can always be "understood" by the human mind, and that to "understand" a statement is a prerequisite of believing it.

It is often argued that Romanticism could be seen as a protest against mechanistic theories of the mind, especially the empirical philosophy and the rationalistic thinking of the Enlightenment. Viewing English Romantic poetry as a whole, Harold Bloom considers it as "a kind of religious poetry" (1971, xvii). This is also Stephen Prickett's opinion when he discusses the religious context of the Romantic period:

> For evidence that Romanticism in both countries [England and Germany] was primarily a religious phenomenon we need to look not merely at contemporary changes in the emotional climate but also at the transformation of the whole way of understanding religious belief that underlay those changes. (1981, 143)

Prickett furthermore points out the sharp changes in human understanding that took place during the 1780s and the 1790s: "[T]he unifying factor in all these new ideas is to be found in a quite fundamental shift in the climate of feeling, and in attitudes towards emotion." He then again stresses that the origin of all these changes is a religious one (125).

One of the most popular ideas of Romantic poetry is the still current belief that it deals with the happy communion between man and nature; but there were certainly darker sides to Romanticism. Perhaps Kant was important for Coleridge here: in his semi-dualistic metaphysics, Kant can be interpreted as explaining the world as distinctly separated from transcendental reality, or God. Kant also stressed that there is no goodness in Nature as such, and that all moral values must be non-natural. This point of view differs from the philosophy of Berkeley, whom Coleridge read in the years 1795–1796. Berkeley's idealism is evinced in the idea that even "the very blemishes and defects of Nature are not without their use, in that they make an agreeable fort of variety, and augment the beauty of the rest of creation, as shades in a picture serve to set off the brighter and more enlightened parts" (*Principles*. Part I 93). Berkeley considered nature as purposive, as divine language, and confessed his belief in Providence (94). God's Providence emerges in *Religious Musings* and *The Destiny of Nations,* written in 1794–96; but later works do not propound this idea. Except in these two texts, it is hard to find any belief in the purposiveness of Nature or faith in Providence in Coleridge's poems.

There was, though, something which Coleridge did not find in Kant: the 'fact' of Original Sin. "This he found in his own experience, his everpresent sense of weakness, failure and defeat; his need of redeeming grace" (Willey 1971, 238). This may account for the stress he came to lay upon Will and Redemption, and the Original-Sin factor may contribute to explaining why he took to the seventeenth-century divines. Coleridge's belief that man is a "fallen creature diseased in his will" goes against the beliefs of the political radicals of his own time and also against those of the Enlightenment.

Two early essays by Coleridge, one written in September 1790 and the other in January 1791, demonstrate his early awareness of the Fall. However, these compositions deal not only with the Fall but also with another question connected with it, that of freedom or free will. They begin with an elaboration of the Plotinian thesis that the Fall in itself is an involuntary act; it is also inevitable, the result of the soul's contact with the world. On 10 March 1798, Coleridge makes the following affirmation concerning Original Sin in a letter to his brother George:

Of GUILT I say nothing; but I believe most stedfastly in original Sin; that from our mothers' wombs our understandings are darkened; and even where our understandings are in the Light, that our organization is depraved, & our volitions imperfect; and we sometimes see the good without *wishing* to attain it, and often *wish* it without the energy that wills & performs – And for this inherent depravity, I believe, that the *Spirit* of the Gospel is the sole cure. (*CL.* I, 238) (Coleridge's italics)

Coleridge thus not only accounts for Original Sin but also expresses his belief that fallen man's will is diseased. In *Aids to Reflection*, he writes:

I profess a deep conviction, that Man was and is a *fallen* 'Creature, not by accidents of bodily constitution or any other cause, which *human* Wisdom in a course of ages might be supposed capable of removing; but as diseased in his Will, in that Will which is the true and only strict synonyme of the word I, or the intelligent Self. (139–40) (Coleridge's italics)

The idea of man as fallen is also the topic in another letter to his brother George, of 1 July 1802:

I have (...) convinced myself, that the Socinian and Arian Hypotheses are utterly untenable. ... – My faith is simply this – that there is an original corruption in our nature, from which & from the consequences of which, we may be redeemed by Christ – not as the Socinians say, by his pure morals or excellent Example merely – but in a mysterious manner as an effect of his Crucifixion – and this I believe – not because I *understand* it; but because *I feel,* that it is not only suitable to, but needful for, my nature and because I find it clearly revealed. (*CL.* II, 443) (Coleridge's italics)

Kant's "sense of duty" does not exist in a Fallen World, since there is "an original corruption of nature". Coleridge furthermore relates the Fall of Man to man's moral history:

A Fall of some sort or other – the creation, as it were, of the Non-Absolute – is the fundamental Postulate of the Moral History of Man.

Without this hypothesis Man is unintelligible, with it, every phenomenon is explicable. The Mystery itself is too profound for human insight. (*Table Talk* 25 April 1830)

Coleridge's interest in man's fallen condition could have impelled him towards the study of religion with an emphasis on the will and Redemption. The belief in man's fallen situation could have aroused his interest in the seventeenth-century writers, for whom the Fall was not only something to be sincerely believed in, but was also regarded as a matter of supreme importance. These seventeenth-century writers considered the Fall as an actuality of individual life and thus gave the Fall an existential dimension. In "A Hymne to God the Father", Donne for one starts his poem by confessing his Original Sin: "Wilt thou forgive that sinne where I begunne, / Which was my sin, though it was done before". During the years when Milton and Jeremy Taylor studied in Cambridge, the Fall was a frequent topic of discussion there and elsewhere. Taylor himself wrote about a learned professor "whose ordinary lectures in the lady Margaret's chair for many years together, nine as I suppose or thereabouts, were concerning original sin and the appendent questions" (qtd. in Paul Elmen 139). For his discussion on Jeremy Taylor and the Fall of Man, Elmen informs us that he "call[s] to our aid the criticism of Samuel Taylor Coleridge" (139).

Coleridge shared his interest in human alienation and his view of man as fallen with other philosophers and writers of the Romantic era. Man's alienation, or separation from himself and others, was especially apt to be embodied in the form of the unrepentant, restless wanderer. This view reflects one of the dark sides of Romanticism as well as its interest in ontology. The poet as a visionary in a fallen world perceives "a divinely-appointed correspondence between language and the material world, which, however much it might have been dislocated and fractured by the Fall, nevertheless still endured as a kind of bedrock guarantee of reality" (Prickett 1993, 134).

* * *

Both M.H. Abrams and Stephen Prickett bring up the name of Robert Lowth in their discussion of Romantic poetry. Lowth's book *Lectures on the Sacred Poetry of the Hebrews*, which appeared in English in 1778, is a comprehensive critical examination of the Hebrew Bible. It is furthermore a collection of poetic documents, and it could be understood as a poetic manifesto. Abrams states that the book "was bound to have a radical impact on the accepted system of criticism" (1953, 76).[2] Prickett also stresses the importance of Lowth's book and is of the opinion that it "affected the whole development of English poetry" (93). Lowth's work is highly relevant not only to an understanding of Romantic literary theory, but also to a full comprehension of Coleridge's idea of the prophetic and visionary poet.

Lowth acknowledged the importance of the context of the biblical texts, i.e. he tried to recreate the biblical writers' minds as human beings in a social and historical context. For a modern reader this is a commonplace, but at that time it was something new. This consideration of the context also suggests a new kind of sensitivity to the appreciation of a text. That sensitivity is perhaps best illustrated in Lowth's own words:

> He who would perceive the peculiar and interior elegances of the Hebrew poetry, must imagine himself exactly situated as the persons for whom it was written, or even as the writers themselves; he is to feel them as Hebrews ... nor is it enough to be acquainted with the language of this people, their manners, discipline, rites, and ceremonies; we must even investigate their inmost sentiments, the manner and connexion of their thoughts; in one word, we must see all things with their eyes, estimate all things by their opinions; we must endeavour as much as possible to read Hebrew as the Hebrews would have read it. (113–114)

Wordsworth's discussion "What is a Poet?" in his Preface to *Lyrical Ballads* (1802) exhibits the same awareness of the context of a text. He states, among other things, that

> [i]t will be the wish of the poet to bring his feelings near to those of the persons whose feelings he describes, nay, for short spaces of time perhaps, to let himself slip into an entire delusion, and even confound and identify his own feelings with theirs.

---

[2] Robert Lowth was a theologian and a Hebrew scholar, who was elected to the chair of Poetry at Oxford in May, 1741. His book is a series of lectures, delivered in Latin between 1741 and 1750 and translated into English in 1778.

Wordsworth furthermore thinks that the poet should consider himself in the situation of a "translator". This implies some kind of identification with the literary protagonists, a personal involvement in the fictional characters, who are often taken from "real life" and "translated" into poetry. Lowth, however, points out the difficulty in identifying with the other. He writes that "in many cases it will not be easy to do; in some it will be impossible; in all, however, it ought to be regarded" (56). He is also very well aware of the gulf between the reader and the text, as well as of the discontinuity between one historical-cultural context and another.

Lowth's new concept of the prophet and poetry in the Old Testament also influenced the Romantics, especially Coleridge, Blake, Shelley and Wordsworth. Lowth explains that the Hebrew word 'Nabi' means a prophet, a poet, or a musician, under the influence of divine inspiration: "They [the Hebrews] considered poetry as something sacred and celestial, not produced by human art or genius, but altogether a Divine gift" (25).

Lowth's study led to the discovery of the construction of Hebrew verse itself. Among other things, he remarked on its difference from the traditional techniques of European verse. He claimed that Hebrew poetry was best translated into prose. Prickett claims that this observation had an effect of "blurring traditional distinctions between prose and verse" (95). This is how Wordsworth writes on the prose/poetry relationship in the Preface to *Lyrical Ballads*, 1802:

> (...) not only the language of a large portion of every good poem, even of the most elevated character, must necessarily (...) in no respect differ from that of good prose (...) some of the most interesting parts of the best parts of the best poems will be found to be strictly the language of prose, when prose is well-written.

In addition, Wordsworth asserts: "I have shewn that the language of prose, may yet be well adapted to poetry", concluding that "there neither is, nor can be, any essential difference between the language of prose and metrical composition".

The key conception of the poet as a prophet and a visionary is thus closely linked to this new way of interpreting the Bible, where the prophet has the status of a transformer of society as well as of a mediator and revealer of divine truth. This new reading of the Bible, inspired by Lowth, influenced Romantic literary theory, as Wordsworth's statements suggest.

The following lines from *The Prelude* will serve as a characteristic example of the Romantic presentation of the visionary poet:

> ... Dearest Friend [i.e. Coleridge],
> Forgive me if I say that I - (who long
> Had harboured reverentially a thought
> That poets, even as prophets, each with each
> Connected in a mighty scheme of truth,
> Have each for his peculiar dower a sense
> By which he is enabled to perceive
> Something unseen before) forgive me, friend,
> If I, the meanest of this band - had hope
> That unto me had also been vouchsafed
> An influx, that in some sort I possessed
> A privilege, and that a work of mine,
> Proceeding from the depth of untaught things,
> Enduring and creative, might become
> A power like one of Nature's.
> (Book 12, 298-312)

Though British biblical scholars and poets took up the new critical methods of studying the Bible, they left the development of what was called the Higher Criticism almost entirely to German scholars. According to Willey, the "first thirty years of the nineteenth century in England a barren and reactionary bibliolatry was prevalent" (1964, 47). If Christianity held its ground in a century of biblical criticism and scientific agnosticism, by discovering a firmer foundation in the specific religious experience, this was, as he states, "the debt of modern theology to Coleridge" (40). Coleridge is both a literary critic and a theologian and as such partakes of both worlds. He "sits uneasily at a key point in the historical separation of what we now think of as two separate academic disciplines" (Prickett 1993, 123). It is difficult for the late twentieth-century scholar, thoroughly secularized and acclimatized to this academic division between literary and biblical studies, to recapture a mental framework in which they did not require separate ways of thinking. This also means that "much of what Coleridge has to say in certain contexts is truncated, shorn of meaning, or even liable to misinterpretation" (123).

Coleridge's Relation to Higher Criticism

Lowth's importance not only to biblical criticism but also to Romantic literary theory is evident. Biblical criticism may be said to have had a bearing on literary criticism; indeed, literary criticism arguably influenced biblical exegesis. However, as Prickett shows, the typological mood prevailed in literature well into the Victorian era:

> Lowth's stress on the literal meaning of biblical texts arising within a particular historical context was not, in fact, so much an endeavour to get rid of traditional polysemous typological and mystical interpretations of the Bible as to put them on a sounder scholarly basis in response to Deist attacks on its historical authenticity. (1991, 182-83)

The approach of Higher Criticism differs both historically and literally from the typological method. It may be summed up in Lampe's words:

> In place of the unhistorical attitude which saw the Bible as a vast harmonious complex of prophecy and fulfilment, type and antitype, allegorical picture and spiritual reality, fused together by the uniform inspiration of the Holy Spirit, Biblical criticism sought to recover the true and original meaning of the literal sense, and to set the various documents comprising the Bible in their proper context in history instead of seeing them as pieces fixed unalterably in a divinely planned mosaic pattern of Holy Scripture. (15)

This shows that the typological conception of the Bible as a unity is beginning to break down in the nineteenth century. Biblical passages could not be taken out of their setting in history and formed into a unifying typological pattern. The belief in a divine activity behind the correspondences in historical events was abandoned. Christianity was looked upon as a myth with components in common with other oriental myths. Higher Criticism thus applies a mythological approach to the Bible.

Coleridge's relation to Higher Criticism has been well documented by E.S. Shaffer in her book 'Kubla Khan' and The Fall of Jerusalem: The Mythological School in Biblical Criticism and Secular Literature, 1770–1880 (1975). She claims that no study has been devoted to "Coleridge's interest in, and contribution to, the higher criticism" (7). However, as Shaffer also remarks, Coleridge had many objections against J. G. Eichhorn. This resistance is illustrated in the notes Coleridge made in his own copy of Eichhorn's *Introduction to the Old Testament*. Prickett considers Coleridge's marginalia in Eichhorn's book to be an illustration of the basic difference in sensibility between these two critics (1991, 201).

Coleridge's biblical criticism is fragmentary and unsystematic; but, as Prickett indicates:

> Unlike Eichhorn, Coleridge brought to his biblical criticism a sensibility formed by a prolonged exposure to *both* biblical *and* secular literature. He is, for instance, overwhelmingly conscious of writing within a culture so steeped in biblical assumptions and patterns of thought that it was no longer possible for someone within that system fully to grasp the extent of that influence or the ways in which it has come to condition his perspectives on the world. (202) (Prickett's italics)

Coleridge had a comprehensive knowledge of the Bible and of its typological potential, as well as insights into Higher Criticism. As Prickett recapitulates, Coleridge had "an acute historical awareness [but also] a poetic sensitivity to the literary nuances of the text" (203). It is thus perfectly possible to envisage the poet operating at two distinct levels, using the typological method as well as the new way of reading the Bible, in creating his poetry.

Finally, though the differences between the typological approach and Higher Criticism are notable, it may, in practice, sometimes be difficult to distinguish between them. A quotation from Shaffer demonstrates this problem:

> Coleridge, then, in advancing into the critical school of Biblical studies, was indeed at the fine point of consciousness of his age. He was so far from being an antiquarian that he became an adherent of that school of history which abolished antiquarian research into 'evidences' of the truth of each separate event, whether Christian or secular, in favour of a '*new notion, both exacting and comprehensive, of human development*' in which '*history is a reinterpretation of the past which leads to conclusions about the present.*' (33–34) (my italics)

This is not an interpretation of history according to the new Higher Criticism; rather, it closely resembles the typological approach to history.

* * *

Looking back on this short introduction to Coleridge criticism, and on the main issues associated wih this poet and his work, one is struck by the impression that "a comprehensive study of Coleridge's poetry remains to be done" (Fruman xii). But that is not all. Coleridge's extensive comments on and relationship to the seventeenth-century writers and divines, and particularly their view of man as fallen, have not been given adequate attention. His relation to Milton and *Paradise Lost* has not been fully explored. Nobody has, as far as I am aware, studied Coleridge's poetry drawing on a typological approach aimed to show that many metaphors occurring in his poetry are in fact of biblical origin and typological in character. Nor has any previous critic clarified the extent to which these elements in Coleridge's work adhere to a tradition in English literature.

Therefore, the aim of this work is to study ideas and motifs in Coleridge's poetry which bear a relation to the concept of the Fallen World. *Paradise Lost* will be used as a foil when reading Coleridge's poetry. In any discussion of Fall poetry, it is natural to include Milton and his epic poem. Taking into consideration the concept of a Fallen World, Milton could even be called *the* Fall Poet. Furthermore, there will be a typological reading of the events, characters and concepts displayed in the poem *Christabel*. An explanation of the nature of typological reading, with its corresponding metaphors, will also be provided in that chapter.

As was pointed out above, Coleridge shared his admiration for Milton with other poets from his own time. His early readings of Milton also made Miltonic quotations and allusions come naturally. Milton played a considerable part in the Romantic revival; indeed he has been called "the priest of poetry during the Romantic period". For the Romantics, that is, he was not only an ideal man but an ideal poet. They commented profusely on him; but his contribution to and influence on their thought has not been exhaustively studied. *Paradise Lost* was published over a hundred times between 1705 and 1800, and there was an affection for it which even led to special editions being prepared for children. Moreover, various devices were employed to popularize the poem, to make it intelligible to people without any formal education. There were even prose versions of it. The highest ambition of the abundant religious poetry of the eighteenth and the beginning of the nineteenth century was to imitate Milton in language and diction. Referring to this kind of religious poetry, R.D. Havens points out that we who think of the first third of the nineteenth century as the period of Byron, Wordsworth, Shelley and Keats are likely to be disconcerted when we find what the people of the time read. The most popular reading matter at the time consisted of sermons and other religious-moral writings which were supposed to be of an edificatory character (403, 404).

The Grim View of the Fall

To comprehend Milton and *Paradise Lost* we must not only attempt to understand the contemporary context; we must also try to perceive the connection between culture and textual tradition. This is also in line with Lowth's ideas, which were discussed earlier, and with Coleridge's stress on knowledge both of the poet as a man and of the time in which he lived, and its corresponding values. Coleridge writes in his "Lecture on Milton and the Paradise Lost", 4 March, 1819:

> Tho' it was and is my intention to defer the consideration of Milton's own character to the conclusion of this Address, yet I could not prevail on myself to approach to the Paradise [Lost] without impressing on your minds the *conditions* under which such work was producible, the original Genius having been assumed as the immediate agent and efficient cause – and these conditions I was to find in the characer of his time and in his own character. (*Lectures 1808–1819 On Literature*, Lecture 4)

The above quotation illustrates Coleridge's awareness of the need for a contextual understanding of a text. The same insistence on context can be detected in the following statement: "The man who reads a work meant for immediate effect of one age with the notions and feelings of another, may be a refined gentleman, but must be a sorry critic" (*Marginalia* 571).

Since the concept of a Fallen World scarcely forms part of the present-day reader's normal frame of reference, a general exposition of it and its concomitant articles of faith will be attempted. The ensuing commentary will serve as an introduction to the concept, as well as to the pertinent doctrines attached to the idea, with an emphasis on aspects of particular relevance to the present study.

The Fall was considered as, essentially, a separation between man and the divine order. This involved moral degradation and a corruption of both man and nature. The separation or corruption does not only involve man's relation to God, but also to other men (broken relationships, war) and to nature itself. Nature's involvement in the Fall was a common literary theme. When Sin and Death invaded the created order, nature also reacted adversely. The most important consequence of the Fall was the introduction of sin, evil, death and corruption into the world. Corruption was understood as both real and metaphysical. Sin is not only the concept of Original Sin but also a term related to evil in all its forms, such as death, war, murder and disease.

There are sets of abstract properties attached to this separation or alienation from God. The state of being cut off from him is sometimes called the "inner hell", or the "hell within". The feeling of being an outcast from God and his love and affection instils in man a feeling of isolation, of guilt, remorse; it causes a diseased will and creates confusion, which could be referred to as "the wandering quality" (vanity) and the inability to perceive error as such. The final state of the "inner hell" is total egoism and a resorting to "satanic" despair, hate and guile. This "inner hell" is thus a state of mind. There is another concept which is also used in *Paradise Lost,* "Paradise within"; this expression represents man's experience of God's grace. Thus, Hell and Paradise are places, but also states of mind.

The doctrine of the Fall therefore implies a grim view of a sinful and corrupted world where man's will is diseased. The harsh conceptions of a Fallen World are partly redeemed by the idea of regeneration through grace, or justification *sola fide*. This idea of grace is connected with predestination, the doctrine of the aristocracy of the elect. Orthodox Reformation doctrine was predestinarian (it was restated intrinsically in the Confession of Westminster in 1647). The 39 Articles of the Anglican Church are in many ways full of Calvinistic concepts; thus "the infected will" means that "the will is depraved to the extent that it is likely to refuse to obey reason" (Calvin, *Institutes* II, ii 2-4, qtd. in Sinfield 31). Hence the belief that man is so wretched as to be incapable of good choices. The idea of predestination also implies that God is the cause of everything. That means that human wickedness is equally part of the Divine scheme, which in turn leads to the conviction that Providence determines everything. The paradox of human suffering and divine goodness could thus be resolved. To explain evil by means of such a paradox also suggested God's foreknowledge, i.e. the idea that God knows the behaviour of man in advance.

Paradise Lost is the result of Milton's poetic intent to deal with the myth of the Fall and its consequences, one of which is evil in all its forms. Evil can be perceived in Milton's epic in the forms of concrete events such as war and murder; but there are other serious consequences of the Fall which are manifest on psychological, epistemological and ontological levels.

Fallen man's understanding and knowledge are considered as fragmentary, separated from unity and perfection. Article IX of the Anglican Church asserts that "[m]an is of his own nature inclined to evil and incurs the wrath of God and damnation." This implies that man, if not wholly evil after the Fall, still inherits a "loss of Heaven" or "banishment from the presence of God", according to the above-mentioned Article. This loss was often mentioned in connection with the concept of the "inner hell", though "the former is far broader than the latter, for once the alienation between the Creator and the creature has occurred, the loss may be subordinated to the sinner's total commitment to evil, but the inner hell persists none the less" (Patrides 1964, 217-27). This quotation relates to the idea that "sin means suffering for the sinner, a well-known classical and Christian thought" (Schaar 1982, 185).

John Donne exposes two traditional aspects of hell in a sermon of 1620; there are, he writes; "two sorts of torments in hell, 'Paena damni' and 'Paena Sensus' [the Pain of Loss and the Pain of Sense]". A brief summary of Robert Boulton's views on hell should assist in gaining a comprehension of these concepts:

> About HELL, Consider I. *The Paine of losse*, Privation of GOD's glorious presence, and eternell separation from those everlasting joyes, felicities and blisse above, is the more horrible part of hell, as Divines affirme. There are two parts (...) of hellish torments; I. *Paine of losse*; and 2. *Paine of sense*: but a sensible and serious contemplation of that inestimable and unrecoverable losse, doth incomparably more afflict an understanding soule indeed, than all those punishments, tortures, and extremest sufferings of sense.
>
> It is the constant and concurrent judgement of the ancient Fathers, that the torments and miseries of many hels, come farre short, are

nothing, to the kingdom of heaven, and unhappy banishment from the beatificall vision of the most soveraigne, only, & chiefest Good, the thrice-glorious *Iehovah* ... The farre greatest, and (indeed) most unconceivable griefe would be, to be severed for ever from the highest and supreme God ...

2. *The Paine of sense.* The extremity, exquisiteness and eternity whereof, no tongue can possibly expresse, or heart conceive ... [The] severall paines of all the diseases and maladies incident to our nature [are] nothing to the torment which for ever possesse and plague the least part of a damned body! And as for the soule: let all the griefes, horrours and despaires that ever rent in peeces any heavy heart; and vexed conscience: as of Iudas, Spira, &c. And let them all bee heaped together into one extrement horrour, and yet it would come infinitely short to that desperate rage and restless and restless anguish, which shall eternally torture the the least and lowest faculty of the soule! (*Of the Foure Last Things*, 1639) (qtd. in Patrides 1964, 220–221)

The exposition of these different "Paines" is traditional. If we were to describe both the Paine of Loss and Paine of Sense in one word, it would be alienation. The Paine of Sense is a mental description of despair, similar to a "vexed conscience", which makes hell a condition rather than a place. Milton was of course also aware of these traditional views; in his *De Doctrina Christiana* there is a summary statement of the 'poena damni' and the 'poena sensis'. The idea of the "inner hell" was expounded by numerous thinkers, and Patrides mentions several of them. Patrides's article shows that Milton's interpretation of all the different dimensions of hell reflects the views of his contemporaries. This "inner hell" is also present in Coleridge's poetry, as will be shown below.

In *Paradise Lost* Milton made it clear that he regarded hell both as a condition and as a place. The poem defines the location of hell. The "inner hell" or "hell within" is first described in the state of the fallen angels, and most remarkably in the portrait of Satan. Having put forward the concept of inner hell in connection with Satan, Milton demonstrates its applicability to fallen man as well (Patrides 229).

Satan in *Paradise Lost* is banished both from Heaven and from God, and is tormented by "the thought / Both of lost happiness and lasting pain". The "pain of loss" is soon subordinated to the expulsion "from bliss". The other fallen angels suffer as well. Milton concisely expresses the position of the hell within:

> A mind not to be changed by place or time.
> The mind is its own place, and in itself
> Can make a heaven of hell, a hell of heaven.
> (I. 253–55)

From the following lines we learn that the "inner hell" is a mental enclosure, which ironically lacks the freedom that Satan in the first two books of *Paradise Lost* so boldly aspired to:

> The hell within him, for within him hell
> He brings, and round about him, nor from hell
> One step no more than from himself can fly
> By change of place[.]
> (IV. 20–23)

Another very intense mental picture of the despair and anguish of the "inner hell" is the following one:

> Me miserable! Which way shall I fly
> Infinite wrath, and infinite despair?
> Which way I fly is hell; my self am hell;
> And in the lowest deep a lower deep
> Still threatening to devour me opens wide,
> to which the hell I suffer seems a heaven.
> (IV. 73–78)

Milton develops the concept of the "inner hell" and its dimensions in other works as well, most notably in *Samson Agonistes*. Samson recognizes: "Myself, my sepulchre, a moving grave", and the chorus clearly perceives, as they put it to him, that: "[t]hou art become O worst imprisonment the dungeon of thyself". This is commented on by R.A. Shoaf in these terms: "Sundered from unity (...) with his Maker, which alone makes unity in the self, Samson must suffer a 'living death', living as the grave in which he is dead – brutal confusion" (175).

The final consequence of the "inner hell" is Satan's resolution:

> So farewell hope, and with hope farewell fear,
> Farewell remorse: all good to me is lost;
> Evil be thou my good[.]
> (IV. 108–10)

The last cords binding him to God and nature are broken when he bids farewell to remorse, i.e. his conscience, which was confused or "vexed" before and which he now totally abandons, as from now on his only transcendental creativity will reside in doing evil and working destruction. At this point, his alienation is irrevocable.

Felix Culpa or the Fortunate Fall

The Fall has also been interpreted as a "fortunate" event. The idea of a fortunate fall was, however, rejected from Reformation iconography and also removed from the English liturgy by the compilers of the Book of Common Prayer. The idea of a *felix culpa* is a reading practice which does not take into consideration the context of the text. With such a reading, the critic will understand and engage with *Paradise Lost* as an ambiguous text. The traditional notion of a *felix culpa* is as old as the previously discussed view of the Fall. C. Hill traces it back to St. Ambrose (1977, 346) and says that it was often associated with radicals and heretics. It implies that without the Fall, that is without sin, the grace of God would not have been manifested: so in this sense sin is actually a *felix culpa*. In modern literary criticism, the reading of a *felix culpa* has become, as Danielson puts it, "an unfortunate cliché of Milton criticism" (1989, 125). It could be argued that it does not correspond with the ways in which artists, poets and composers have understood the God of Genesis or the Fall for centuries. Milton and other poets of his time regarded neither the Fall nor the suffering that results from it as fortunate. To them, the idea that sin was the cause of redemption lacked pertinence. Sin and Death were not thought to have increased man's bliss, and the suffering that sin causes to guilty and innocent alike was much discussed.

Diane Kelsey McColley discusses the *felix culpa* as follows:

> I do not think Milton and other seventeenth-century English writers

subscribed to the idea that the Fall was fortunate; and Dennis Daniel-son has so cogently and learnedly refuted it that it scarcely seems nec-essary to revive the question. I do so partly in response to the implicit invitation in Danielson's recognition that 'it is hard to conceive of a more important question in the study of Milton than whether the Fall is fortunate or unfortunate'. (154)

The concept of a Fortunate Fall is, as was pointed out above, as old as the grim view of the Fall. The term Fall in itself presupposes a standard from which one has been separated downwards, that is a fall from one condition to another. It means a change from a static to a dynamic state, a change from unity to fragmentariness, a displacement.

Both the grim conception of the Fall and the idea of a Fortunate Fall will be applied in my interpretation. It could be argued that the idea of a Fortunate Fall may be considered as a demythologizing of a tradition. However, if we wish to demythologize a tradition we also need to be in command of the given (traditions, conventions, codes, different contextual circumstances). A fuller understanding of the range within which the Fall concept operates in this study will emerge as the book progresses. What should, however, be borne in mind when dealing with a myth is its inherent repeatability. The Fall thus does not obviously involve a historic account of a supposed first sin (though this is the belief of some people); but it is essentially "concerned to give a representative account of what may be held to be repeatedly occurring in the life of man". Thus the "first" Fall anticipates and symbolizes "a recur-rent situation for individuals" (Smith 149); or, in other words: man, being fallen, has the propensity for re-enacting the Fall. Most Fall stories tend to deal with favourable elements in man's fallen state, too, such as grace and redemption.

This work will be divided into three chapters: the first on *The Rime of the Ancient Mariner*, the second on *Christabel*; and the third on *Kubla Khan*. At the start of each chapter there will be an introductory section in which the poem's relation to the Fallen World motif will be presented and to which my examination will refer back.

Versions and Editions

It is only natural for a literary work to exist in different versions, and only more so in the case of a text which is two hundred years old. *Christabel* provides a salient example: Coleridge began writing it in 1798 and expanded it in 1800, and it did not go into print until 1816. Before publication, the poem had circulated widely in manuscript copies; it had been read by Wordsworth, Scott and Shelley, among others. Alterations in the different versions are made by Coleridge or close friends and relatives or, as J. Stillinger points out: "Many, probably most, of the unique readings in the transcripts are explainable as misreadings, or copying errors" (87).

What is more important, though, where Coleridge's poetry is concerned (and this is particularly applicable to *Christabel*) is the fact that "the significant differences among the manuscripts – that is, the variants most likely to have originated with Coleridge – are, in the overall view, few in number and not very important critically" (Stillinger 88).

I will use and refer to Ernest Hartley Coleridge's edition *S. T. Coleridge : Complete Poetical Works* on the following grounds. The 1912 text is based on the 1834 edition, which as a later edition includes the revisions that continued up until the end of Coleridge's life. I will, however, focus on differences among different versions when there is sufficient reason for the purposes of this work to do so. For my reading of *Paradise Lost,* I have chosen Alastair Fowler's edition from 1971, which supplies extensive and useful comments on the poem.

Other Works Dealing with the Fallen World

Coleridge's literary output during the years 1797–1804, and particularly during his *annus mirabilis* (1797–1798), has often been compared to his earlier poems, such as *Religious Musings* and *The Destiny of Nations*. During this time his concern with the Fallen World motif intensified and was especially focused on the study of evil. The concern with the problem of evil is also manifested in the poet's notebooks and letters from this period. While poems written before these years present and explain evil from a viewpoint with Calvinistic implications, the poems from the years 1797–1804 often deal with crimes of some kind – a circumstance which may entail some moral perplexity for the reader, since they display evil as being victorious and innocence as betrayed. The themes of isolation, separation, loss of love and affection and broken relationships are inherent in these poems. Several of the poems from these years develop the theme of wandering. All these themes are central to the Fallen World motif. For an understanding of their full intensity and import in Coleridge's poetry, some general discussion is called for. Before entering into a more detailed analysis of *The Ancient Mariner, Christabel* and *Kubla Khan,* which are almost invariably held to be Coleridge's most important poems, I will therefore start with a general comment on some poems from about the same period (1797–1798) which also reveal a preoccupation with the Fallen World motif.

One of these poems is "The Raven" (1797). This poem tells the story of innocent people perishing on a ship. The origin of their fate is an acorn left by swine, which was picked up by a raven and buried. This acorn grew into a tall oak tree where the raven was to build his nest, which is destroyed when the tree is cut down. The acorn, which symbolizes evil and revenge, was left randomly. In this poem, moral coherence seems to be deceptive when the raven rejoices in the death of those who had nothing to do with the bird's loss of mate and nestlings. Instead the raven thanks Death "again and again" for the killing of innocent people, and the last words of the poem are written in block letters, "REVENGE IT WAS SWEET". The subtitle of the poem reads: "A Christmas tale, told by a schoolboy to his little brothers and sisters", which associates the story with nursery tales. In a way, the moral difficulty here lies in innocence betrayed; the deaths of the raven's mate and nestlings and of the men on the ship are the result of the actions of an indeterminate source of evil. Interestingly, though, the woodman who cuts the tree has eyebrows like a "pent-house" hanging over his eyes. He does not see what he is actually doing; he only looks at the ground and not up at the sky. This woodman acts like the Ancient Mariner. They both bring about evil consequences as a result of one single unthinking, seemingly careless act.

Another work from this time is the prose fragment *The Wanderings of Cain* (1798), which also deals with the themes of isolation, loss of love and affection, broken relationships and wandering. It was composed in the same year as *The Ancient Mariner* and the first part of *Christabel.* Coleridge often added prefaces to his poems such as the one to this fragment, which was written in 1828 and contains the following lines: "Alone by night, a little child,- / In place so silent and so wild- / Has he no friend, no loving mother near?" The forsaken child who has to face a hostile world recurs in *Christabel.* A rough draft of a continuation or alternative version of *The Wanderings of Cain* was found among Coleridge's papers at his death. In the preface he says that he is drawing a picture of "the birth, parentage, and premature decease of *The Wanderings of Cain*". *The Ancient Mariner* was written instead.

In *The Wanderings of Cain* both Cain and Abel are victims in some sense, and both are miserable and restless. Enos is mentioned as "the innocent little child" who is trying to bring his father to the cake and pitcher. These objects could be seen as symbols of the Eucharist, hence representing forgiveness. Cain feels persecuted by "'The Mighty One'", who, as he explains, "'pursueth my soul like the wind, like the sand-blast he passeth through me; he is around me even as the air!'" He feels a strong death-wish: "'O that I might be utterly no more! I desire to die'" (33–36). This prose fragment has several affinities with *The Ancient Mariner*. Cain's agony could be compared to that of the Ancient Mariner and his shipmates when undergoing the affliction of the polar spirit's revenge. Cain's physical appearance is similar to the Ancient Mariner's, and it tells us of his suffering: "his countenance told in a strange and terrible language of agonies that had been, and were, and were still to continue to be" (67–69). The endless repetition of evil's restlessness and torment, and the appearance of the afflicted character, conform to traditional usage for depicting evil in the Fallen World.

The setting of *The Wanderings of Cain* is a desolate landscape, which is a commonplace in apocalyptic-millenarian imagery.[3] The desolation of an apocalyptic desert can also be found in *The Destiny of Nations* from 1796: "And first a landscape rose / More wild and waste and desolate than where / The white bear, drifting on a field of ice, / Howls to her sundered cubs with piteous rage / And savage agony" (470–74). In the landscape of *The Wanderings of Cain* we can "discover nothing that acknowledged the influence of the seasons"; there are "hot rocks and scorching sands" (74, 77). A bird and a serpent image appear here too, as in *Christabel*, this time it is a vulture caught within the coils of a serpent, which is described as follows: "the huge serpent often hissed there beneath the talons of the vulture, and the vulture screamed, his wings imprisoned within the coils of the serpent" (78–81). Fallen nature

---

[3] The Book of Enoch is often an inspiration for apocalyptic-millenarian writings dealing with the problem of evil. Furthermore, it is – rather than the Paradise story of Genesis – the earliest basis for popular Jewish speculaton as to the origin of the general sinfulness of the world. The Book of Enoch uses, as F.R. Tennant remarks, "the legend of the watchers not necessarily with the full intention of thereby accounting (...) for the first sinful act, but for the origin of widespread depravity. The fall of the race and the beginning of the unsatisfactory moral condition of humanity as a whole seem there to be traced to the lustful invasion of the world by these fallen celestial visitors" (236).

in the stark image of a serpent torturing another animal figures in *Religious Musings* as well: "Or serpent plants his vast moon-glittering bulk, / Caught in whose monstrous twine Behemoth yells, / His bones loud-crashing!" (274–76) The picture of a serpent crushing a large animal's bones while the victim howls is one of the most terrifying images of a Fallen World one can imagine. In *The Wanderings of Cain* there is a mention of "the groan which the Earth uttered when our first father fell" (87–88), which is a reference to Nature's involvement in the Fall. By a rock, like some kind of altar raised in the wilderness, Enos finds "the pitcher and cake" (91–92). (The rock here might be a symbol of Christ.) As Cain and Enos advance, before reaching the rock, they see a human shape smiting his breast and crying aloud: "Woe is me! woe is me! I must never die again, and yet I am perishing with thirst and hunger" (95–97). This lamentation comes from the shape which is identified as Abel, the victim, who later falls down at Cain's feet and cries out bitterly: "'Thou eldest born of Adam, whom Eve, my mother, brought forth, cease to torment me!'" (117–18) Cain raises up the Shape and says: "'The Creator of our father, who had respect unto thee, and unto thy offering, wherefore hath he forsaken thee?'"(126–28) To this Abel answers: "'The Lord is God of the living only, the dead have another God'" (140–41). And at this "Cain rejoiced secretly in his heart" (142).

The answer to evil's restlessness comes at the end of the canto, when Cain again begs for the God of the dead, as he longs for peace and asks: "'what sacrifices are acceptable unto him? for I have offered, but have not been received; I have prayed, and I have not been heard; and how can I be afflicted more than I already am?'" (169–72). Here lies the central theme of this prose fragment: evil trying to find peace. Cain suffers extremely in his restless wanderings and is, as he says, "dried up"; he makes sacrifices and prays without result. The futility of his efforts can be explained by the fact that he feels sorry for himself instead of feeling compassion for his victim. He has not yet reached the point of repentance, hence Abel's answer to his self-pity: "'O that thou hadst had pity on me as I will have pity on thee'" (172–73). When Cain does feel pity for Abel and repents, he will be on his way to his much desired peace and death.

According to Coleridge's prefatory note, this work was planned in three cantos. What remains is canto II. Though only a part of a larger scheme, it can be read as something completed, since the main point is clearly made in the depiction of evil as a restless wanderer trying to attain peace. Cain, like the

Ancient Mariner, will go on telling his fearful story. By their mere presence, and by narrating their experiences, they torment people they meet, killing joy. One typical victim of this evil influence is the Wedding-Guest in *The Ancient Mariner*, who "cannot choose but hear" the Ancient Mariner's story and will never be the same person again:

> The Mariner, whose eye is bright,
> Whose beard with age is hoar,
> Is gone: and now the Wedding-Guest
> Turned from the bridegroom's door.
>
> He went like one that hath been stunned,
> And is of sense forlorn:
> A sadder and a wiser man,
> He rose the morrow morn.
> (618–25)

Another poem from this period that is worth mentioning in the context of the Fallen World is "The Three Graves", with the subtitle "A Fragment of a Sexton's Tale" (1797–1809), which features "a maid forlorn". In this poem evil kills joy and love, as indicated in the last line: "And never she smiled after."

It is noteworthy that even some of the so-called conversation poems from the same period suggest the theme of separation and loneliness, the fundamental predicament of these poems being that of the poet musing in solitude. It is true that this solitude is partly a Romantic trope, but the insistence on the separation theme is still striking. In "This Lime-tree Bower my Prison" (1797), the poet is left behind while his friends are strolling in the woods and fields.[4] In "Frost at Midnight" (1798), the poet sits alone at midnight in a sleeping house where his "cradled infant slumbers peacefully" (7). His thoughts are focused on his loneliness as a boy at school. The same theme appears in "To the Rev. George Coleridge" (1797), where the emotional consequences of being uprooted from one's family are made explicit, as in the lines:

---

[4] This is one of the very few poems where nature is described as prelapsarian, as something pure and inspiring: "Henceforth I shall know / That nature ne'er deserts the wise and pure"(60–61). It is also interesting to note that most of Coleridge's nature poetry and notebook descriptions of outdoor scenery were written when he was living close to Wordsworth.

Me from the spot where first I sprang to light
Too soon transplanted, ere my soul had fix'd
Its first domestic loves; and hence through life
Chasing chance-started friendships.
(17–20)

Other work-titles from this period announce the central idea of separation from one's fellows: "Fears in Solitude" (1798), "Separation" (1805), "The Blossoming of the Solitary Date-tree" (subtitle "A lament") (1805). The preface of the last poem speaks of the Fall, and in the second passage the "ache of solitariness" is referred to. In "Ode to Tranquillity" (1801), the isolation of the poet is explained in these terms:

Aloof with hermit-eye I scan
The present works of present man -
A wild and dream-like trade of blood and guile,
Too foolish for a tear, too wicked for a smile!
(29–32)

Finally, one of the poet's most famous poems, "Dejection: An Ode" (1802), is organized as an extended series of extremely solitary musings. This emphasis on separateness can also be related to the Romantic cliché of the solitary poet, as well as to Coleridge's biographical background; but the fact remains that all these themes, developed in the above-mentioned poems, are also part and parcel of the Fallen World.

The preceding brief review of works, chiefly poems, from approximately the same period that saw the composition of *The Ancient Mariner, Christabel* and *Kubla Khan* thus reminds us that the characteristics of the Fallen World were very much to the fore in Coleridge's writings throughout the period in question.

The Rime of the Ancient Mariner

General Critical Comments

The attitude of the earliest critics of *The Ancient Mariner* was frustration, "because", as John Spencer Hill points out, "it defeated expectation" (152). Since the poem could not be filed under any neat heading in a system of ballad classification, "the easiest solution was simply to invoke custom and convention to declare the work incomprehensible" (153). What differs from our preconceptions is always a threat. The critical responses to the first editions are, however, also understandable; the work clearly went against what was traditionally conceived of as poetry. The archaic language used in the edition of 1798 was a challenge, too. The rich allusiveness and the metaphoric language of the poem could, while inviting interpretation, give rise to confusion. The poem's power to resist reductionism can be appreciated in the wide variety of interpretations it has elicited. Hill indicates that "the most popular approach holds that *The Ancient Mariner* is, by design and intention, a spiritual allegory depicting human life as a sort of Pilgrim's Progress on the sea". Along these lines, the poem is looked upon as if " *The Ancient Mariner* – who is at once himself, Coleridge and all humanity – having sinned, incurs punishment and seeks redemption" (155). Both the words "pilgrim" and "progress" – carry strong connotations of Christian design. Usually, however, a pilgrim – such as Bunyan's – finally arrives in his Jerusalem, and this certainly is not the case in *The Ancient Mariner*.

In view of the diversity of opinions and positions in the interpretative history of *The Ancient Mariner*, a certain temerity is required in anyone who wishes to contribute something new to this story. Here, the main task will consist in examining certain aspects which might have been overlooked, and which have bearings on the Fallen World motif. The all-too-common conviction that this poem should be read as a simple paradigm of sin-penance-redemption will be addressed in this chapter. It seems that whatever approach or paradigm is applied in the interpretation of *The Ancient Mariner*, it tends to leave an impression of overdetermination. The term *aporia* can be made to indicate overdetermination, translated as the "impassable path" (Cuddon 55). The use of the word *aporia* could be viewed as an admission that the interpretation has reached a point where it can go no further. It implies an awareness of hermeneutic difficulty and conflict in the interpretation; one admits to being at a loss. Even though *aporia* could be viewed as a kind of awareness of a Fall, it may at the same time open up a kind of freedom in the 'playfulness' it offers the reader-interpreter, so long as it is understood that the interpreter's comprehension is allowed to prevail. The reader can thus respond by accepting a Fall and the impassable path. This might lead to dogmatic assertions or to a passive acceptance of a lost case, or it could engender a wilful 'playfulness' which I would like to call *diaporia* or a Fortunate Fall: in spite of, or even thanks to, the "impassable path", the interpreter cannot resist venturing into dangerous territory.

The ensuing analysis begins with a discussion of the relationship between the gloss and the verse, a relationship which cannot be ignored. This matter is discussed at length, as it has bearing on the issue of morality in poetry in general and in *The Ancient Mariner* in particular. It will also be relevant in the examination of a symbolic reading of the poem, supported by the familiar paradigm of sin-penance-redemption. One of the most influential studies to present such a symbolic reading will be used as an example: Robert Penn Warren's essay "A Poem of Pure Imagination". This will be followed by an attempt to explain why certain judgements operate when interpreting a text, and how appropriation is achieved in a Fallen World. Distantiation or alienation will be seen as necessary, though admittedly not stable, stages in any interpretation. The idea of "inner hell" will be discussed in relation to the Mariner. There will be a short presentation of the poem's relation to the Cabbala, an issue which has been brought up by Tim Fulford, who ties the Cabbalistic elements to a Christian interpretation. In this connection, concepts such as 'tradition' and 'archetype' will be briefly addressed. It is contended that there is no adequate or simple response to *The Rime of the Ancient Mariner* (from now on called *AM*). The concept of disconfirmation might help the essential "newness" of this poem to emerge. The chapter ends with a discussion of the notion of *diaporia* in connection with the Fallen World concept.

The Gloss – Verse Relationship

Any interpretation of the poem has to consider the relationship between the verse and the gloss which was added in the edition of 1817.[5] Hill considers that "the gloss provides a running commentary and summary of the poem's narrative action (...) a translation of the poem's substance into prose" (121). The gloss, however, possesses more than an explanatory function. The gloss and the verse present two different narrative levels or two different kinds of narrative logic; they elicit two different psychological, moral and philosophical responses. These two levels do not cohere. Besides, there is the voice of the balladeer which begins and ends the story. All these different levels demand a response. There is an uneasy feeling of uncertainty as to which level the critic or the reader should respond at when faced with this diversity of voices and their interaction. What further complicates the interpretation is the highly emotional force of the poem, which might be felt as a threat. The reader might therefore be inclined to choose simplicity, opting for either the gloss or the verse or even confounding them.

Since the gloss runs through the poem from beginning to end, it is undoubtedly a very important part of it. Critics have discussed whether the gloss is there to explain certain obscure or ambiguous incidents in the poetic narrative, a circumstance which illustrates the need to rationalize poetry. Hill also mentions those who regard the "the gloss as a 'parasitic growth' that must be removed before the poem can be properly appreciated or understood" (122). Such anxious statements speak for themselves, but the main impression they evoke is that of the meddler who cannot resist setting things in order. Hill, however, points out that "the gloss achieves a semi-autonomous status and functions dramatically as a kind of choric commentary on the poetic narrative" (122). Such a comment, though helpful to some extent, does not explain or interpret the dichotomy between the narrative of the gloss and the narrative of the verse.

---

[5] "With only minor revisions and corrections the 1817 version of 'The Ancient Mariner' was reprinted in all later lifetime editions of Coleridge's poems (1828, 1829, 1834); and, although the 1834 version has become the *textus receptus*, the 1817 text was the last to incorporate significant alterations and so stands effectively as the final redaction in a complex series of revisions and rewritings stretching over nearly two decades" (Hill 122).

Kathleen Wheeler has made an excellent collation between the verse and the gloss. She has consistently furnished general views, particulars bolstering her case. Her interpretation of the 'Argument' as an embryo gloss seems highly warranted. She starts by showing that the gloss offers "a typically unimaginative reading: it depicts an overlaying of a facade of conventional meanings to explain the tale and incorporate it into a body of accepted belief" (47). She then proceeds to make a penetrating and clear exposition of the gloss's relation to the poem, and of the discrepancy between them. The gloss frequently seems to veer dangerously towards a moralizing allegory. It names and generalizes, which leads – as Wheeler points out – to a kind of depletion of "the energy and intense openness of the verse" (56). She is of the opinion that

> *[t]he gloss moralizes by interpolating guilt, blame, remorse, superstition, omens, cause and agency, sin and retribution into the action of the poem, while in the verse moralizing is specifically and markedly excluded.* (59) (my italics)

This statement should put us on our guard when we attempt to distinguish between the moral, psychological and philosophical levels of the gloss and the verse respectively. Furthermore, the above quotation leads us inexorably into one of the most intensely debated issues connected with this poem, namely that of its moral. In this context, Coleridge's own account on the moral in *AM* should be recalled, since it is also relevant to the ensuing discussion:

> Mrs Barbauld told me that the only faults she found with the Ancient Mariner were – that it was improbable, and had no moral. As for the probability – to be sure that might admit some question – but I told her that in my judgement the chief fault of the poem was that it had too much moral, and that too openly obtruded on the reader as a principle or cause of action in a work of such pure imagination. It ought to have had no more moral than the story of the merchant sitting down to eat dates by the side of a well and throwing the shells aside, and the genie starting up and saying he must kill the merchant, because a date shell had put out the eye of the Genie's son. (*Table Talk* 31 March 1832)

The revenge of the genie belongs to the (im)probabilities of imagination, and as such it cannot harness any moral power. There is, at most, a cause and an effect in that story. However, when Coleridge is of the opinion that the poem *AM* had too much moral and that this fact was, as he saw it, its chief fault, it should be borne in mind that we do not know exactly what 'moral' he was referring to. It has generally been agreed that the moral of the poem should be the Mariner's statement in lines 610–17, which have been called his "farewell stanzas":

> Farewell, farewell! but this I tell
> To thee, thou Wedding-Guest!
> He prayeth well, who loveth well
> Both man and bird and beast.
>
> He prayeth best, who loveth best
> All things both great and small;
> For the dear God who loveth us,
> He made and loveth all.

Beside these lines, the gloss reads: And to teach, by his own example, love and reverence to all things that God made and loveth.

The lines above from the poem sound rather like a set of clichés, "too openly obtruded on the reader", to use Coleridge's expression. As will be shown, these two stanzas are in fact highly disconfirmative. The moral confirmed by a character in a poem can be quite different from the moral of a poem. The moral stated by the Mariner in his "farewell stanzas" could be regarded, as Coleridge points out, as an "obtrusion (...) in a work of such pure imagination". The conclusion that the mentioned stanzas constitute *the* moral of the poem has been drawn by readers/interpreters. Coleridge's general idea of moral in poetry comes out in a letter to Southey, written in 1802. Describing the faults in William Lisle Bowles's poetry, Coleridge writes:

> There reigns thro' all the blank verse poems such a perpetual trick of
> *moralizing* every thing – which is very well, occasionally – but never to
> see or describe any interesting appearance in nature, without connect-
> ing it by dim analogies with the moral world, proves faintness of Im-

pression ... They are 'Sermoni propiora' which I once translated – 'Pro-
perer for a Sermon'. (*CL.* II, 459) (Coleridge's italics)

It cannot be said more explicitly: poetry can stand and speak for itself without
the crutches of an externally applied moral. The idea of poetry as a means in
itself of conveying a moral also emerges in Robert Lowth's *Lectures on the
Sacred Poetry of the Hebrew,* a book which was essential for Romantic literary
theory. He is of the opinion that poetry "contributes not only to pleasure, but
to magnamity and good morals, [and] it is deservedly supposed to participate
in some measure of Divine inspiration" and that it "insinuates or instils into
the soul the very principles of morality itself" (9, 17). This is to say that
poetry is itself able to activate moral feelings without impositions similar to
those that occur in the gloss or in the clichés of the farewell stanzas.

It is important to bear in mind that it is the gloss that introduces concepts
such as 'justification', 'crime' and 'accomplices' into the drama. As Wheeler
points out, these words are "charged with cultural significance"; similarly,
they connect the gloss "with the second version of the 'Argument' [*Lyrical
Ballads,* ed. 1800] [which] mentions 'cruelty' 'contempt', 'Judgements', and
'laws of hospitality'"(61). The gloss also introduces concepts such as
'avenged', 'vengeance', 'horrible vengeance', 'penance for life'. The verse does
not make such connections. Arguably, the gloss uses the verse to confirm its
own unimaginative conclusions. What emerges, then, in Wheeler's study is
the existence of different psychological levels of reading this poem, an aspect
which had not been given due attention before. The gloss-maker's comments
are essentially conventional; preoccupied with time sequence, causality and
spatial determinations, they name and generalize. However, as Wheeler says,
the most striking characteristic of the gloss is its moralizing and superstitious
tone. The essential moral, if any, has to be understood as poetic moral conveyed by poetry *per se.* The issue of the moral in *AM* will be further addressed
in the concluding remarks.

Symbolic Reading – the Paradigm of Sin-Penance-Redemption

As was mentioned before, symbolic interpretations of the poem abound, particularly as regards the paradigm sin-penance-redemption. A classic example
of a symbolic interpretation of the poem is Robert Penn Warren's "A Poem of

Pure Imagination", which, it will be contended, stands as an illustration of self-fulfilling prophecy: fallen man, lacking an assurance of wholeness, easily embraces idiosyncrasies conducive to personal epiphany or revelation. Warren looks upon the shooting of the albatross as a re-enactment of the Fall and argues forcefully for establishing the "criminality" of the act of shooting the bird:

> The crime is, symbolically, a murder, and a particularly heinous murder, for it involves the violation of hospitality and of gratitude (*pious* equals *faithful* and the bird is "of good omen") and of sanctity (the religious connotations of pious, etc). This factor of betrayal in the crime is re-emphasized in Part V when one of the Spirits says that the bird had "loved the man" who killed it. (229) (Warrens italics)

In order to prove that the shooting of the Albatross is in fact a murder, and even a "particularly heinous" one, a link between deliberate intention and action must be established. There is no such link in the poem. The Mariner shoots the Albatross, but we are not informed of any purpose or aim behind his action, nor of any express intention to kill. The verse does not convey the purpose or intention of the act, nor does the gloss. This is what Wheeler writes about the killing:

> It is not at all clear from the verse that the killing is a 'crime'; the event of killing is kept in the verse utterly mysterious and unexplained. There is no hint of motivation or intention whatsoever. An inability to appreciate the distinction between killing as an event and killing as a crime only exposes the thickness of the moral spectacles through which the world is interpreted. (61)

There is thus no active will behind the shooting. The verse offers no basis for the use of phrases such as "the violation of hospitality and of gratitude". In the Argument of 1800, however, something along those lines is articulated: "how the Ancient Mariner cruelly and in contempt of the laws of hospitality killed a Seabird". Furthermore, the verse does not establish the attributes of "good omen" and of "sanctity", which are the gloss-maker's words (the gloss speaks of the bird of "good omen" and of the "pious bird of good omen"). The gloss-maker shows his superstition in the same way as does the crew: "Ah wretch! said they, the bird to slay, / That made the breeze to blow!" (95–96). The poem is, after all, as Coleridge himself pointed out, a poem of "pure imagination", where there is no need for logical consequence in terms of cause and effect.

Warren tends to take on a moralistic tone when establishing the concept of "criminality":

> There is (...) a third way in which the criminality is established. We can get at it by considering the observation that if a man had been killed, we could not have the 'lesson of humanitarianism', which some critics have taken to be the point of the poem. But we must remember that the humanitarianism itself is a manifestation of a deeper concern, a sacramental conception of the universe, for the bird is hailed "in God's name" both literally and symbolically, and in the end we have, there-fore, in the crime against Nature a crime against God. (229)

Warren is thus sure of the "criminality" inherent in the shooting of the albatross, though such a belief charges the poem with cultural-moral judg-ments which it cannot be clearly seen to convey. Besides, he lacks an aware-ness of the dichotomy between the verse and the gloss. The bird, the alba-tross, appears "as if it had been a Christian soul"(65) in the verse. Wheeler points out:

> [T]his simile and the mystery surrounding its appearance in the icy, lifeless realm makes it possible to focus on the symbolic and poetic function of the albatross, at least until the gloss intrudes with 'Till a great sea-bird, called the Albatross'. 'Seabird' directs the attention to a literal, external animal, and then depletes the symbolic aspect, whereas in the verse the thing which comes is first and only an 'Albatross', *like* a Christian soul, and not a sea-bird at all. In the gloss it is first a sea-bird, and only *called* an albatross. But the gloss thus calls attention to its method by this line, when it calls the thing, that is, names it. (56) (Wheeler' italics)

This is one example of how the gloss interferes with the verse. It is difficult to establish with confidence what the Albatross stands for. The verse seems to confound its poetic connotations, while the gloss only names it. As Paglia puts it: "This albatross is the biggest red herring in poetry. Its only significance is as a vehicle of transgression" (324). Admittedly, though, so was the apple. Even so, it is possible that Coleridge wished to convey a suggestion of a Fall of some sort by means of a sense of mystery, in this case letting the vehicle of transgression be a big sea-bird. But it is uncertain whether we can establish a "crime", let alone a "heinous" one, and it follows from this that there is no linking of it to a "crime against Nature and [then] against God." This is not, in other words, a conclusion we can draw from the poem; it is a cultural-moral tag invented by the interpreter.

The idea of the shooting of the albatross as an analogue of the Fall also occurred to W.H. Auden:

> But for the Fall (the shooting of the Albatross), Adam (The Ancient Mariner) would never have consciously learned through suffering the meaning of Agape, i.e., to love one's neighbour as oneself without comparisons or greed (the blessing of the snakes), so that the Ancient Mariner might well say in the end, *O Felix culpa*. (72–73)

Auden's book can be recommended to anyone who wants to study Romanticism; but with regard to this particular aspect of the poem, one wonders how tenable such a moral interpretation will be. It is difficult to find any *felix culpa* in the poem. Warren's comment is relevant in this context: "He [the Mariner] gets home, in the moonlight, which, we recall, is the light of imagination, and in the end he celebrates the chain of love which binds human society together, and the universe" (255). The idea of a "celebration of love" seems taken out of the blue, since the Mariner remains an outsider, a lurker at thresholds. Warren's reading of the poem is strong; but his interpretation, though beautifully expressed, is questionable in its emphasis on a providential salvation-and-redemption theme, connected with a final "celebration of love". Ultimately, he sees Part V as "The moon of imagination and the storm of creative vitality here joining triumphantly to celebrate the Mariner's salvation" (244). Warren's study will be referred to again below; suffice it to say here that if one interprets the poem as a simple paradigm of sin-penance-redemption, other serious issues that emerge in the poem are certainly avoided, such as the Mariner's suffering, his feeling of guilt and his isolation, which are left unresolved.

Other critics, for instance Bostetter, have protested against what they see as Warren's rigidly symbolic interpretation and his view that "the poem dramatizes fundamentally Christian statements of sin, punishment, repentance, and redemption". Bostetter's basic rejection of a symbolic interpretation of the poem and the theme of the sacramental vision is expressed in the following terms:

> They [the critics] have an uneasy fear that to admit that a poem is an expression of attitudes which may not be rationally defensible is to concede some fatal weakness which robs it of greatness. The need for the poet to believe that he has been granted special moral insight is almost irresistible – otherwise of what ultimate worth is his eloquence? When he turns critic, therefore, the temptation is strong to justify poetry on moral grounds. This is the temptation to which Warren succumbs. He simply cannot believe that a poem so authoritative in vision, so powerful in symbolism as The Rime, is not morally meaningful beyond our fears and desires. *As a result, he is led ironically into imposing the moral laws of what Coleridge called the reflective faculty upon a universe of pure imagination.* (77) (my italics)

The italicized words in Bostetter's lines pin down one of the problems of *AM* : Warren and others have imposed upon a work of imagination a moral and a symbolic interpretation which is, as has already been maintained, difficult to find resolved in the verse itself; its main or even sole basis is in the gloss, which moralizes and draws conclusions from a limited perspective. Moreover, Bostetter's observation points to the tendency to fear and anxiety in reading or interpreting when confronted with attitudes which do not cohere with our preconceptions.

Distantiation

The following pages, which deal with the concept of distantiation, will look into the ways in which we seem predisposed to come up with a certain response to a text. Paul Ricoeur's discussion of the problematics which arises between "alienating distantiation and participatory belonging" may be helpful in this regard. Ricoeur points out that *Verfremdung* (distantiation) is not only what understanding must overcome; it conditions interpretation, too. His optimistic stance is reflected in his statement that we are "prepared to discover a relation between *objectification* and *interpretation* which is much less dichotomous, and much more complementary, than that established by the Romantic tradition". He, moreover, trusts our ability to take "distantiation by writing and objectification by structure seriously", linking it to the "notion of the world of the text" (140) (Ricoeur's italics). It is true that Romantic hermeneutics and Romantic literary theory admit that perception and knowledge arise from "being". The context, historical and psychological, as well as the endeavour to render a text contemporary was emphasized by the Romantics. There is, of course, as Ricoeur points out, no common situation to the writer and the reader; that is, you cannot retrieve the past. He therefore tries to establish the autonomy of the text; this is certainly desirable, but it is doubtful whether it is entirely achievable. It seems to me, however, that Ricoeur is thinking of the Romantic idea of self-understanding when recalling Heidegger's suggestions concerning the notion of *Verstehen*, which he (Ricoeur) brings up and explains in the following terms:

> [T]he theory of 'understanding' is no longer tied to the understanding of others, but becomes a structure of being-in-the-world. More precisely, it is a structure which is explored after the examination of *Befindlichkeit* [state of mind]. The moment of 'understanding' corresponds dialectically to being in a situation: it is the projection of our inmost possibilities at the very heart of the situation in which we find ourselves. I want to retain from this analysis the idea of 'the projection of ownmost possibilities', applying it to the theory of the text. For what must be interpreted in a text is a *proposed world* which I could inhabit and wherein I could project one of my ownmost possibilities. That is what I call the world of the text, the world proper to *this* unique text. (142) (Ricoeur's italics)

This has been quoted at some length, as the Romantic notion of self-understanding is involved here too, in the sense of "Befindlichkeit" as part of understanding. Ricoeur confesses his faith in the autonomy of the text. The text in itself is, of course, the assignment. We are, to use Ricoeur's words, "prepared to discover a relation between objectification and interpretation"; but the final outcome of our interpretations is always conditioned by our existential mode or self-understanding, our perception of "being in a situation". We can at most be aware of the overlapping between our assignment, the text, and our "being-in-a-situation" by means of a dialectic discourse between ontology and epistemology; but the result will always show our participatory belonging. Such discourse does not arrive at a synthesis in Coleridge's poetry in any kind of Hegelian manner ("the reconciliation of opposites"). Instead, a new fact or condition, a *tertium aliquid*, is born out of the impossibility of such overlapping (the point is raised below with reference to *Kubla Khan*). Finally, Ricoeur stresses that "[a]t all (...) levels of analysis, distantiation is the condition of understanding" (144).

With this in mind, it is time to return to Warren's study. The hermeneutical confidence with which Warren imposes a Christian paradigmatic interpretation of a sin-penance-redemption theme, and undertakes a symbolic reading of the poem which leaves a sense of overdetermination, should warn us against a reductive reading of it. He ignores, for instance, the different levels of the verse and gloss. His way of gaining access to the poem is, however, interesting in another respect. As was argued above, we approach a text with a sense of "participatory belonging", that is, with our collection of internal, existential moods, expectations and preconceptions. Fallen man will not possess a perfect understanding, and his judgements are fragile. Warren even points out that "[f]or whatever it may signify, I may say that my basic interpretation of *The Ancient Mariner* was arrived at before I had made a systematic study of Coleridge's idea of symbolism" (283).

This is an honest affirmation which says something about Warren's preunderstanding of the poem; but "for whatever it may signify", it tells us that even if we set out with a whole formula of both theoretical and ideological assumptions, by this very regulation the result of our exploration has been conditioned from the beginning. The absence of the idea of distantiation or alienation is a deficiency in Warren's analysis; self-understanding lies even at the very heart of the dialectic between distantiation (alienation) and understanding (interpretation) which might make an "objectification" of the text possible, helping us perceive "its structures, its sense and its reference" (Ricoeur 144). Warren has travelled directly from his own being-in-the-world, but without an ontological awareness of self and without realizing the dialectics between alienating distance and interpretation. Self-fulfilling prophecy or personal epiphany lies in the very nature of criticism, particularly when we are confronted with a work that invites participation as insistently as *AM*. Hermeneutical confidence produces an illusion of order and neatness. Closed metaphysical and moral systems can be comforting; this may be regarded as a yearning for prelapsarian order and perfection, a kind of "home-sickness".

When reading Warren's interpretation of the symbolism in *AM*, it is thus as if we were provided with a reading strategy of Warren's own fabrication, one of whose main themes is Original Sin, defined as a "contamination implicit in the human condition (...) the sin of use, exploitation, violation" (ed. 1958, 69). Marshall Walker writes: "From Coleridge's *Aids to Reflection* Warren derives the view that Original Sin is not hereditary Sin; it is original with the sinner and is of his will" (194). One of the main characteristics of Warren's literary characters is their recoil from identity, their repudiation of the definition of themselves. In *Heaven's Gate*, for instance, false identity appears in the abundance of images of decay and deformation. In *All the King's Men*, some of the "most pervasive imagery (...) enforces the redemption-rebirth theme (...) and the related Eden-fall-knowledge motif to which the title obliquely refers" (Longley 9). Warren's characters struggle with their failure of moral will, which not only separates them from themselves but from community with others. There is often a movement from sin to redemption in his works. One of Warren's best known poems, *Audubon: A Vision,* is interesting in the context of *AM. The Norton Anthology* informs us:

> In his book-length poem *Audubon: A Vision,* Warren's version of the historical John James Audubon must enter what Yeats once called 'the abyss of the self' to create an heroic selfhood at the center of the poetry. Warren imagines a man launched into his true vision after an encounter with a violence at the heart of experience (...). But reverence demands the heart's total response to the beauty of existence itself. This is why Warren commands his hero and himself; 'Continue to walk in the world. Yes, love it!' (2397–98)[6]

Against such a background, Warren's interpretative strategy could be looked upon as almost confessional. Though his interpretation of Coleridge mirrors his own work, as a framework or system for reading other poets' works, it is still a creative re-enactment of the poem *AM* and as such a contribution to the critical story of *AM*.

Warren's interpretation has been discussed at some length, as it is a good

---

[6] "He slew them, at surprising distances, with his gun / Over a body held in his hand, his head was bowed low, / But not in grief. / He put them where they are, and there we see them:/ In our imagination. / What is love? / Our name for it is knowledge." (From *Audubon: A Vision*, VI 11–17) The historical John James Audubon (1785–1851) was an ornithologist and painter of birds.

example of how our being-in-the world prepares us in our perceptions of a work of art. It is also a good example of the idea of appropriation. There is no innocent reading, since in interpreting something we interpret ourselves, a statement which could be formulated in Coleridge's words: "When a man is attempting to describe another's character, he may be right or he may be wrong – but in one thing he will always succeed, in describing himself" (*Notebook* I 74 G. 68 1796–97).

According to the Romantics, perceptions and the forming of judgement are to be assumed as active processes anchored and filtered through our self-image. That sounds like a truism for a modern reader; but according to Basil Willey, the "great struggle and victory" of Coleridge's life was "his triumph over the old tradition of Locke and Hartley, which had assumed that the mind in perception was wholly passive" (1964, 22). Man's forming of judgement as filtered through his self-image was also considered by Lowth:

> [as] shadow or image of himself which man beholds when the mirror is turned inward towards himself, he is enabled in some degree to contemplate the souls of other men; for from what he feels and perceives in himself, he forms conjectures concerning others; and apprehends and describes the manners, affections, conceptions of others from his own. (57)

Lowth, as well as Coleridge, moves from ontology to epistemology; they are hence both fundamentally aware that their judgements are anchored in self-understanding.

By way of recapitulation, then, the apparent restrictions in a symbolic reading place a kind of obligation on a work of "pure imagination" which it can hardly support. How can we deem *AM* to be a poem about redemption? Whatever attributes we invest in our notion of redemption, be it Christian or not, that would imply some kind of spiritual growth, which is a very uncertain condition in the text. It speaks more of some inscrutable fate. A spiritual world that demands a submission to confusion and guilt emerges, where the Mariner acts like some kind of scape-goat. *AM* depicts, as Bostetter puts it, an authoritarian universe which is despotic and unpredictable and where the factor of caprice is decisive (66). Bostetter is of the opinion that the poem "throws into question the moral and intellectual responsibilities of the rulers of the universe" (68). Moreover, the Mariner's fate, including his life-long penance, is administered by a set of spirits. His doom to death-in-life is the result of a game of dice. The Mariner's punishment, implemented by spirits of different kinds, might be an instance of a Christian reading of Cabbalistic elements, as Fulford suggests; but on the other hand, spirits of all sorts abound in Romantic literature. One good example of this is Shelley's *Prometheus Unbound*. In any case, the themes of isolation and guilt which the poem depicts so vividly do not come to rest within a narrow reading along the lines of a sin-penance-redemption paradigm. We are apparently faced with something where our instinct to organize and make whole does not meet with the mystery, and the many questions raised in the interpretative story of this poem are left unresolved.

Coleridge and the Cabbala

In his interpretation of *AM,* Piper is of the opinion that Coleridge's vision was modified by his readings of apocalyptic literature. As an example, he brings up Thomas Burnet's *The Sacred Theory of the Earth,* which gives an account of the last days:

> The great Force of the Sea will be broken, and the mighty Ocean reduc'd to a standing Pool of putrid waters, without vent and without recruits. But there will remain in the midst of the Channel a great Mass of troubled Liquors, like dregs in the bottom of the vessel; which will not be drunk up till the Earth be all on Fire. (qtd. in Piper 1987, 52)

However, it would have been more consistent in this case to look at a quotation from Burnet's *Archaeologiae Philosophicae,* since it figures as an epigraph to the poem. The passage from Burnet in *AM* is taken from one of his sources of Cabbalistic lore. As Fulford informs us, this passage was already annotated by Coleridge in a notebook of 1801, and in 1817 it helped to form the newly added gloss to the poem. According to Fulford, Coleridge had read Jacob Brucker's *Historia Critica Philosophiae,* a work which discussed the Cabbala in detail, as early as 1797. Coleridge read *The Zohar* (The Book of Brightness) while in Germany for the first time. Furthermore, he knew Burnet's discussion of the Cabbala in his *Telluris Theoria Sacra* as early as 1795 (Fulford 65).

Fulford is of the opinion that Coleridge was developing some kind of

Christian symbolism by way of a Cabbalistic interpretation of Hebrew scripture, and that in so doing he was

> indirectly acknowledging what had always been present in 'The Ancient Mariner' – a 'seraphic philosophy', developed directly from detailed kabbalistic sources – whilst removing any questions which would hinder it from harmonising with the other reinterpretations of the 'Image of God' present in his text. (65)

According to Fulford this 'seraphic philosophy' links "the names of fire, seraph and angels to the doctrine that the divinity latent in God's spoken word was available for every man's redemption if he could comprehend its presence" (65–66). The ensuing statement has affinities with the idea of grace: "Once the mariner has interpreted the dead men as seraphim, he is able to discover in them renewal of spoken community on a spiritual level" (66). There is a hint at a redemption theme in this suggestion; but as Fulford is very well aware, this is not in itself enough to turn the poem into a "smooth juxtaposition of interpretative discourses" (66–67).

As was pointed out above, *AM* resists readings intent on making it a paradigmatic redemption story at any cost. If we concentrate on the idea of redemption or grace in this poem, we forget "the desperation, isolation and crisis that it renders so strongly", as Fulford points out (67). The feelings of desperation, isolation, crisis and loss of community that feature so prominently in *AM* are present in *The Wanderings of Cain* as well. Cain, as Fulford puts it, is "deprived of his ability to interpret the spiritual presences which fill the world" (67). The lack or deprivation of an interpretative faculty could be seen as a consequence of a Fall, which also deprives Cain and the Mariner of the possibility of understanding their fate. The Mariner as well as Cain is left with his guilt and with the inability to comprehend his situation.

As we have seen, the poem has resisted criticism for 200 years. Coleridge himself admitted that the poem did not fit in with conventional ideas, as this comment in *Table Talk* illustrates: "The 'Ancient Mariner' cannot be imitated, nor the poem 'Love'. They may be excelled; they are *not imitable*" (359) (Coleridge's italics). The poem's different sources of references and authorities are difficult to adapt to an interpretative resolution. As was pointed out above, the verse and the gloss represent different discourses.

Dissimilar traditions and authorities seem to conflict in the poem. As it is so powerful and so allusive, it offers endless opportunities of discussions purporting to secure *the* "meaning". Fulford is of the opinion that the poem should be read in the context of disconfirmation. (As he tells us, he uses the concept of disconfirmation as discussed by Prickett in *Words and the Word* 149–95, 168.) In his examination of *The Wanderings of Cain,* Fulford arrives at the conclusion that

> [i]t signals a break in the hermeneutic circle of reinterpretation of spiritual texts, and a break out from preconditioned mentalities, as its inconclusive identification with Cain's continuing isolation refuses to exhibit Cain as a moral lesson. (...) It might be called a work of disconfirmation, and for that reason one of the first English Romantic texts, since, in seeking to confirm the moral authority of scripture by creative reinterpretation, it succeeded rather in questioning it by an intensity of investigation into a potentially heroic rebellious psyche. The resulting tension was unresolved and the work left unfinished, as was to become common in Romanticism. (68)

The above comment could be applied to the Mariner as well. As we proceed in an attempt to arrive at something that might be called an interpretation of the poem, problems crop up at every turn. When tracing complex references from different sources – be their origin Cabbalistic or Christian-apocalyptic, neo-Platonic, or biblical-mythical – we have to find out what authority all these references possess in relation to the text. It would, for instance, be helpful to be able to establish the nature and extent of Coleridge's use of supernatural elements in the poem; but we lack a paradigm for it. It could be argued, of course, that the supernatural is used for poetic reasons and should not be regarded as part of a closed religious, metaphysical or moral system. Previous studies and interpretations of this poem have often raised these difficulties.

Any attempt to establish a static reading of *AM* is bound to undermine its integrity to some extent, and any reliability we might find would be very fragile. We may even be tempted to behave like the gloss-maker, applying moral and meddlesome comments to a poem which the poet himself considered to be a product of pure imagination. Different critical approaches to the poem tell us how we, as individuals, approach such a product. Ultimately, they teach us that the supernatural, the mysterious, can only be known as it presents itself; and that in the endeavour to define "Imagination" we describe ourselves. However, in our longing for wholeness and a comprehensive solution we are bound to go on trying to get beyond/behind the Fall, looking for clues and patterns, so we can put the Mariner to rest and go home.

Disconfirmation

Bringing the concept of disconfirmation to bear on *AM* might be one way of coming to understand it. There is no simple cause-and-effect sequence in the poem. As was argued before, reading it symbolically according to a sin-penance-redemption rationale deprives *AM* of its richness; it neglects both the dissimilar discursive levels and the theme of suffering, guilt and isolation.

Generally speaking, it could be asserted that disconfirmation both affirms and denies a tradition, as well as our conventional expectations or explanations. It has to do with similarity and difference – that is, it is not neither-nor but both-and. Disconfirmation is not a matter of rewriting or support; it involves a transformation of tradition. In this it both affirms, contradicts and disconnects tradition. Rewriting tradition, it creates something new which could be considered, in Coleridge's words, "not imitable". The following Coleridgean dictum is also relevant to the concept of disconfirmation: "In philosophy equally, as in poetry, genius produces the strongest impressions of novelty, while it rescues the stalest and most admitted truths from the impotence caused by the very circumstance of their universal admission" (*The Friend* Essay xv 110). [7]

Stephen Prickett uses the story of Elijah in the Bible as an example of disconfirmation which could be summarized in the following words: "Elijah had come expecting one thing and found another – entirely different" (ed. 1989, 14). A preconception of something already taken for granted is confounded as a result of encountering something "where there is no equivalence, because what is being said is strange and without parallel"(32). There is a tension between what is familiar and expected and what is unfamiliar and

---

[7] Existing works of poetry, according to T.S. Eliot, already "form an ideal order among themselves, which is modified by the introduction of the new (the really new) work of art among them ... [t]o conform merely would be for the new work not really to conform at all; it would not be new, and would therefore not be a work of art". "Tradition and Individual Talent", *Selected Essays 15*.

disturbing. What is new also breaks through boundaries. Disconfirmation could briefly be defined as an overthrow of expectations.

The Figure of the Mariner

The idea of disconfirmation can be studied in the character of the Mariner. Bloom looks upon the Mariner as an

> archetype, the Wanderer, the man with the mark of Cain, or the mocker of Christ who must expiate in a perpetual cycle of guilt and suffering, and whose torment is in excess of its usually obscure object and source. This archetype figures in Blake and in Keats, but is more basic to Wordsworth and Clare and Beddoes. In Coleridge, Byron and Shelley it becomes something more, a personal myth so consuming that we hardly know whether to seek it first in the life or in the work. (1971, 206, 207)

If we allow with Coleridge that "[w]e judge by comparison"(*The Friend* Ess. vi 47) , the Mariner could be defined in terms of differences from and similarities to a conventional archetype, both as it emerges in Bloom's short comment and with reference to something that could, in general terms, be labelled a "Romantic archetypal hero". It is true that the use of the 'archetype' concept could be regarded as a literary convention, and the expression "Romantic archetypal hero" may be too general a term to cover such a broad spectrum of heroes as Romantic literature contains. The difficulty lies, of course, in the establishing of a criterion for the term 'archetype'. The word is translated as "original pattern" (see for instance Cuddon 58); but this term implies that all originals would produce exact copies, which is only possible in a Platonic sense, since "[t]he formation of a copy is not solved by the mere pre-existence of an original; the copyist of Rafael's Transfiguration must repeat more or less perfectly the process of Rafael", which is an improbability (*Biographia Literaria* I, 137). A copy will always be a modification of the original.

It seems from Bloom's quotation that he understands 'archetype' in a Freudian fashion, suggesting that the kind of archetype that occurs in different Romantic writers should "become something more, a personal myth". In any discussion of the term 'archetype', the Jungian connotations of the word spontaneously spring to mind. The Jungian model implies that the archetype is unconscious by its very nature and cannot become conscious. However, it tends to create images or visions that correspond to aspects of conscious experience. Maud Bodkin's Jungian interpretation of mankind's inherited collective archetypes, as defined in her book *Archetypal Patterns in Poetry*, is in line with this perspective. Inherent in the Jungian interpretation lies the belief in a commonly shared experience, which could be expressed in Bodkin's words: "When examining a certain image-pattern (...) it is suggested [that we] discern a corresponding pattern of emotion" (114). Such a statement supposes that there are symbols and imagery which could be recognized and accepted "by a group or by a cultural tradition, as universally valid" (115). It is, of course, comforting to believe that in the process of inquiring "concerning the emotional patterns activated in response to the poem" we will be able to "inquire into the poem's meaning" (26). However, this "inquiring" rests on the hypothesis that we should share the same emotional patterns and furthermore respond to them in the same manner as generations before. This seems to me very uncertain. Perception changes according to contextual positions, and we do not respond emotionally collectively. In his study of the archetype, Northrop Frye stresses the aspect of the conventional; "we do not ordinarily notice [the use of an archetype] unless we are unaccustomed to the convention" (1957, 96). His idea of an archetype is more intellectual than the emotional approach which appears in Bodkin and other Jungian interpreters. Following Frye, the archetype can be perceived as "associative clusters" with "complex variables", which are expanded by associations. At one extreme, according to him, there is pure convention (the pure variable); at the other there is "a deliberate attempt at novelty or unfamiliarity, and consequently a disguising or complicating of archetypes" (102, 103). If the archetype were to be communicated at all, in the sense that Frye proposes, we would need to be very educated readers indeed, recognizing, enlarging and expanding on the archetype. It could even be debated whether we would in that case be dealing with an archetype at all. Literary terms are, of course, evoked and used for convenience and custom, granting a measure of compromise in the employment of a conventional meaning of a term. With these reservations, I adopt the idea of an archetype as embodying various manifestations or modifications of a central concept.

Having said this, one may well ask in what way the Mariner may be said to constitute a representation of an archetype in a broader sense. One archetypal characteristic in the Romantic hero is the feature that both "object and source of [his] crime" are obscure. His background and the nature of his transgression are often barely hinted at, which emphasizes the casual and the mysterious. This is also the case in *AM*. The belief that obscurity is an important part of the sublime – that is, what is concealed is as impressive as what surfaces – was popularized by Burke. Likewise, as pointed out by Stock, "anthropomorphism, elusiveness, and obscurity [were] defended by Lowth as stimulating religious wonder" (314). Lowth explains the use of obscurity in poetry. In his lecture on "The Didactic Poetry", where he discusses the parabolic style, he makes the following points:

> This obscurity is not indeed altogether without its uses; it whets the understanding, excites an appetite for knowledge, keeps alive the attention, and exercises the genius by the labour of the investigation. The human mind, moreover, is ambitious of having a share in the discovery of truth: excessive indolence or dulness only requires a very open and minute display, or prefers a passive inertness to the exercise and praise of perspicacity and discernment; and that knowledge is ever most delightful, which we have compassed by our own efforts. (268)

Obscurity invites interpretation; it excites our longing to know and understand. In this connection, Auden's comment on the Romantic hero is appropriate: "Something catastrophic has happened in the past to all of them" (111). However, the true origin of these heroes' past and mysterious crimes is usually withheld from us, as was pointed out above. Furthermore, they are wanderers sharing traits with mythical figures such as the Wandering Jew and Cain. They are often depicted with satanic overtones. As is well known, Satan in *Paradise Lost* (henceforward referred to as *PL*) – a traveller and tormented trespasser – has lent characteristics to many of these heroes. They set themselves apart from family and society. They are solitary figures, and in their relationship to others contacts are superficial and temporary. Their sin and origins are as obscure as those of the hero-villains in the Gothic genre. Mrs Radcliffe's Schedoni's background is as obscure as Ambrosio's in Lewis's *The Monk*. Another of these heroes is Emily Brontë's Heathcliff. As Stock tells us, when discussing Schedoni and the Gothic genre, there were "legions of daemonic hero-villains" (293). With these general attributes, the Mariner may be said to represent an archetype in a wide sense of the word. It is important, though, to realize that 'archetypes' may differ within the work of the same author. Byron's heroes are often self-sufficient, self-willed, glamorous and ironic, like Manfred and Don Juan. Both works show what Stock calls a "jux-taposition of ironic iconoclasm and serious Romantic drama" (296). Byron's drama *Cain,* on the other hand, brings up the consequences of the Fall and the problem of knowledge, among other things; Shelley's heroes are often rebellious, provocative and in search of knowledge and liberty. They are all possessed by some kind of self-destructiveness. Regardless of whether we con-sider an archetype as something stable, or as a conventional term, or whether we regard the concept itself as a variation of an archetype – that is, consider-ing it as embodying various manifestations or modifications – the Mariner still differs from an archetype in several ways.

The Mariner is dissimilar to other Romantic heroes in his physical appear-ance, which is stressed again and again: Even though the Wedding-Guest calls him a "grey-beard loon" from the beginning (and who listens to such a per-son?), he "cannot choose but hear". The Mariner is a compulsive story-teller, who to expire his own torment "stoppeth one of three" (2), holds them with his hand or with "his glittering eye" (13), and always has his will; and it seems that his hearers/victims, after listening to his story, are both sadder and wiser, like the Wedding-Guest. After telling his story, the Mariner has no further use for his interlocutors. His very presence and story bespeak terror rather than grace and redemption. He is presented in words suggesting a malign visita-tion, moral helplessness, and a foreordained fate. He has a "skinny hand" (9); he is "that ancient man" (19), the "bright-eyed Mariner" (20). According to the Wedding-Guest he is "long, and lank, and brown, / As is the ribbed sea-sand" (226–27). He leaves an impact on people he meets. The Wedding-Guest after hearing his compulsive story "went like one that hath been stunned" (622). The Pilot only needs to see him and "shrieked / And fell down in a fit" (560–61); "The holy Hermit raised his eyes, / And prayed where he did sit" (562–63); "(...) the Pilot's boy, / Who now doth crazy go, / Laughed loud and long, and all the while / His eyes went to and fro. / "'Ha! ha!'" quoth he, "'full plain I see, - / The Devil knows how to row'"(564–69). The Hermit, though "scarcely he could stand", puts the question: "'Say quick, (...) I bid thee say- / What manner of man art thou?'"(573, 576–77) All this suggests that not only his story but his mere presence are objects of awe. As Paglia points out: "If one accepts the Christian interpretation of the poem, how explain this peculiar reaction? The Wedding-Guest is not morally strengthened by the Mariner's exhortations. He is plunged into gloom and severed from society" (328).

The Mariner lacks a name, a particularity which pertains to the other characters in the poem as well. This is in itself a significant fact; according to Judaeo-Christian tradition, a name not only harbours information about a person's identity but about his origin, and thus it always has something to tell us about the bearer.[8] According to this traditional view, it was also felt that knowing someone's name gave you certain power over the person in question. In this respect the Mariner eludes us.

In a letter to Cottle of 24 June, 1799, Wordsworth pointed out, as a defect of the poem, "that the principal person has no distinct character, either in his profession of mariner, or as a human being who having been long under control of supernatural impressions might be supposed himself to partake of something supernatural." The remark "his profession of mariner" sounds strange, as if we were supposed to expect a realistic story of a mariner's profession and life. The Mariner does not have a name; that is, he is in a sense without origin or family, he has no established identity and he does not act in his capacity of a sailor. Could not these facts indicate that he might be understood as anyone or everyone, or that the reader is free to name him according to his/her perception of him? The Mariner is anachronic in the sense that he is ancient, as it were; but at the same time he has both synchronic and diachronic dimensions. He moves in and out of time as a timeless character, turned into a stereotype of himself, exclusive and indeterminate. He is a poetic abstraction. His non-identity aligns him with every man or collective mankind, but also with the fallen angels in *PL* who lack identity when stripped of their God-given names. In these ways the Mariner transcends his anonymity, and his distinct character resides in that aspect. The Mariner's experience can thus be regarded as an abstraction, or as a general statement on fallen man's predicament.

In *Biographia Literaria*, Coleridge discussed the defects (but also the merits and beauties) of Wordsworth's poetry, commenting on what he considered to be poetic truth. The relevant passages tell us something about his idea of poetry which might help us in our understanding of the Mariner. Referring to the "the second defect" in Wordsworth's poetry, Coleridge expressed his opinion in the following terms:

---

[8] Coleridge's punning on names has been demonstrated by Tim Fulford in his chapter "Coleridge's Punning Signatures" in *Coleridge's Figurative Language* 28–32.

There is, I should say, not seldom a *matter-of-factness* in certain poems. This may be divided into, *first*, a laborious minuteness and fidelity in the representation of objects, and their positions, as they appeared to the poet himself; *secondly*, the insertion of accidental circumstances, in order to the full explanation of his living characters, their dispositions and actions; which circumstances might be necessary to establish the probability of a statement in real life, where nothing is taken for granted by the hearer, but appear superfluous in poetry, where the reader is willing to believe for his own sake. (II,Ch. 22, 126) (Coleridge's italics)

This quotation has to do with poetic truth, where the poet "should paint to the imagination, not to the fancy" (127). Coleridge argues that this kind of pedantry often "occasion[s] in the mind of a reader, who is determined to understand his author, a feeling of labor, not very dissimilar to that, with which he would construct a diagram, line by line, for a long geometrical proposition" (127). He furthermore objects to Wordsworth's choice of characters and to a "*matter-of-fact* in character and incidents; a *biographical* attention to probability, and an *anxiety* of explanation and retrospect" (129) (Coleridge's italics). This anxiety in explaining biographical backgrounds in poetry intrudes on poetic faith, as does a moralizing tone. In the same context, Coleridge writes: "The praise of good men be his! In real life, and, I trust, even in my imagination, I honor a virtuous and wise man, without reference to the presence or absence of artificial advantages" (130). The ensuing quotation articulates his main objections to moralizing in poetry:

First, because the object in view, as an *immediate* object, belongs to the moral philosopher, and would be pursued, not only more appropriately, but in my opinion with far greater probability of success, in sermons or moral essays, than in an elevated poem ... For the communication of pleasure is the introductory means by which alone the poet must expect to moralize his readers. (130–31)

In view of this last statement, we realize how very disconfirmative the Mariner's moral statements sound as they come out in the farewell stanzas. It is a moral which punctures the whole poem. Indeed, it works rather like the displacement of a moral. It seems that "[t]he Mariner's farewell stanzas are a poetic non sequitur. They contradict everything that is great in the poem"

(Paglia 327). In the quoted section from *Biographia Literaria*, Coleridge proceeds to give examples of Wordsworth's poetic characters, for instance the chimney-sweeper whom Wordsworth, according to Coleridge, makes into "at once [a] poet, philosopher, and sweep! Nothing but biography can justify this" (133). The result of this "biographic" anxiety and the conversion of chimney-sweepers, pedlars, and leech-gatherers into great moralists and philosophers create the impression that in spite of all attempts,

> the fiction *will* appear, and unfortunately not as *fictitious* but as *false*. The reader not only *knows*, that the sentiments and language are the poet's own and his own too in his *artificial* character, *as poet*, but by the fruitless endeavours to make him think the contrary, he is not even suffered to *forget* it. (133) (Coleridge's italics)

To Coleridge it was vital for the images in a literary work to operate by their own force. Poetic faith is rendered impossible if a text is invaded by parasitical value-statements, such as for instance moral ones, and facts outside the poem itself.

In the letter to Cottle mentioned above, Wordsworth concluded that "*The Ancyent Mariner* has upon the whole been an injury to the volume, I mean that the old words and the strangeness of it *have deterred readers from going on*". His initial response was therefore to propose that if *Lyrical Ballads* were to appear in a second edition, Coleridge's ballad should be excluded and replaced by, as he wrote, "*some little things which would be more likely to suit the common taste*"(my italics). This last quotation shows Wordsworth's own perplexity before the poem, but also his contempt for the reader who would, he believed, be better off with trifles. His concern about the edition may have been due to economic reasons; still "the strangeness" he found in *AM* did not elicit any other response from him than dismissal. The Mariner certainly acts. He stops and holds "one of three" – if not by his hand, then by his "glittering eyes" – and forces his confessional story on one of them. He rows; he passes, as he says, "like night from land to land"; and he knows of his "strange power of speech" (586–87). He even floats: "My body lay afloat" (553) – this does not of course suggest anything in his favour, though. Two other, and crucial, actions of his seem to be undertaken without deliberation or intent: he shoots the Albatross and blesses the watersnakes – "unaware", as he says.

The Mariner also has affinities with Adam, to whom in the final Books of

PL a divided cosmos is presented, one where "[h]e has lost the direct availability of sun and meaning and sees only a world of apparent confusion and disorder" (Simpson 83). Book X tells us about the alterations in the relationship of heaven and earth and the division between God and man. In *PL*, however, redemption is foreshadowed. The character of Adam must be brought into any discussion of Fall and Redemption, but the Mariner's namelessness is relevant to Adam in a special way. In *Aids to Reflection* Coleridge extensively expounds his ideas of the Fall, Original Sin and the doctrine of redemption, maintaining "that in respect of Original Sin *every* man is the adequate representative of *all* men" (289). He then enlarges on the name Adam:

> Even in Genesis the word, Adam, is distinguished from a proper name by an Article before it. It is *the* Adam, so as to express the *genus*, not the Individual – or rather, perhaps, I should say, *as well as* the Individual. But that the word with its equivalent, *the old man*, is used symbolically and universally by S. Paul, (1 Cor. xv. 22. 45. Eph. iv. 22. Col. iii. 9. Rom. vi. 6.) is too evident to need any proof. (290)(Coleridge's italics)

Adam, like Satan, is a generic name in the Old Testament. The "ancient" Mariner could be seen as analogous to the "old man". However, St. Paul's "old man", which stands as a symbol of man before he has turned to God, is redeemed. Coleridge's emphasis on and belief in the doctrine of redemption, which he calls "the Remedy of the Disease" (291), do not apply in *AM*. The Mariner's experience is a dark one. He is denied death, and a dice-game sentences him to death in life, further "penance" looming ahead. To him life is more of a punishment than a gift. He is a guilt-ridden outsider, obsessed by his experiences, and still he pronounces the following lines which could be seen not only as a paradoxical statement considering his situation, but also as a disconfirmation of it, since he himself has no part in it. That is, as Paglia tells us: "[t]he Mariner illogically goes on to celebrate communal churchgoing under the kind gaze of the 'great Father' and ends his message" (327):

> O sweeter than the marriage-feast,
> 'Tis sweeter far to me,
> To walk together to the kirk

With goodly company! —
To walk together to the kirk,
And all together pray,
While each to his great Father bends,
Old men, and babes, and loving friends
And youths and maidens gay!
(601–09)

The cliché flavour of these stanzas was mentioned above. They both confirm and disconfirm the Mariner's own situation. For what we know, he might indeed be "[celebrating] communal churchgoing"; but the fact is that he does not enter into the community, lurking outside the church. There are other apparent disconformative characteristics in his behaviour. For instance, why did he bless the watersnakes? This is how they appear:

Beyond the shadow of the ship,
I watched the water-snakes:
They moved in tracks of shining white,
And when they reared, the elfish light
Fell off in hoary flakes.

Within the shadow of the ship
I watched their rich attire:
Blue, glossy green, and velvet black,
They coiled and swam; and every track
Was a flash of golden fire.

O happy living things! no tongue
Their beauty might declare:
A spring of love gushed from my heart,
And I blessed them unaware:
Sure my kind saint took pity on me,
And I blessed them unaware.

The self-same moment I could pray;
And from my neck so free
The Albatross fell off, and sank

Like lead into the sea.
(272–91)

Warren refers to these lines in the following manner:

> And in the light of the moon we have the stages of the redeeming process: first the recognition of happiness and beauty; second, love; third, the blessing of the creatures; fourth, freedom from the spell. The sequence is important (...) In it the theme of sacramental vision and the theme of imagination are fused. (244)

If a redeeming process is involved here at all, it would certainly be a novelty: in what other literary work do we find such imagery denoting a redemptive process with – as has been suggested – Christian connotations? It is hard to see it as illustrating the "theme of sacramental vision". The Albatross falls from the Mariner's neck; this should, in a rigorous symbolic reading, be a sign of redemption, but the horrors go on. In this he acts as some kind of scapegoat. It must be the first time in literature, as far as I know, that nature's "beauty" is described in the image of watersnakes, and moreover that their presence would make someone react with a "spring of love", blessing them "unaware".

Two acts seem especially significant when exploring the poem: the shooting of the Albatross and the blessing of the watersnakes. These two crucial events in the story do not involve any will or deliberate intent on the part of the Mariner; they are thoughtless actions. There are indications suggesting that the shooting of the bird could be regarded as a Fall. However, some circumstances should be borne in mind when arriving at such a conclusion. Inherent in all myths lies their repeatability even in our way of interpreting them; that is, we are prone to perceive analogues or likeness where there are differences instead. As Milton expressed it: "Who would claim that things which are analogous must correspond to each other in every respect" (*Complete Prose Works of John Milton* VI 547, qtd. in C. Hill 1977, 343). We are thus led to interpret "facts" in a myth in terms of earlier explanations of it. The Fall, as it is narrated in *PL,* takes place in a God-ordered, stable, Edenic world; whereas in *AM* the world is displayed as already fallen. Aside from demonic-apocalyptic imagery, instances of fallen nature emerge, for instance in the image of the Hermit's "cushion plump" covered with moss which "wholly hides / The rotted old oak-stump" (520–22), or in the picture of the animals, "the owlet whoops to the wolf below, / That eats the she-wolf's young" (536–37). The Fall was a wilful act of disobedience, the apple figuring only as a vehicle of the transgression. As this study repeatedly affirms, the Fall contains the embryo of grace and redemption; this is also foreshadowed in *PL*. The shooting of the Albatross is, conversely, an unconscious act; we are not told of any will or purpose. The bird comes for company and food. Its behaviour reveals its innocence, trustfulness and playfulness. The Mariner shows a total lack of will in the shooting of the bird, which trusted and loved him. In this act something is broken, and he is thrown into a capricious and vengeful Cosmos, separated from order, into a state of confusion, isolation and guilt. The other event which is performed on him – or which, as he says, he experiences "unaware" (repeated twice in the stanza) – is the blessing of the watersnakes:

> O happy living things! no tongue
> Their beauty might declare:
> A spring of love gushed from my heart,
> And I blessed them unaware:
> Sure my kind saint took pity on me,
> And I blessed them unaware.
> (282–87)

This seems to be a description of a moment of grace, and as such it is no wilful act either. This momentary glimpse of beauty and love comes to the Mariner while he is "unaware"; it happens as a gift, which does not involve any will. While this is certainly a novel description of grace, it supports the traditional view of grace as something given for free, read in a context of words with favourable connotations such as "happy", "beauty", "love", "[bless]", "kind saint", "pity". The Mariner, however, does not properly understand and receive the idea of grace, since he tries to explain it as being the result of his saint taking pity on him; therefore he is once more thrown into his own confusion and guilt. There is no redemption. He even seeks out the Hermit who will, he believes, shrive him from his experience and agony.

> It is the Hermit good!
> He singeth loud his godly hymns
> That he makes in the wood.

He'll shrieve my soul, he'll wash away
The Albatross's blood.
(509–13)

This stanza seems to suggest that the Mariner believes that a formal confession – the Hermit acting as a confessor – would wash away his sin, "[t]he Albatross's blood". But a formal admission of sin does not help as his only answer to guilt is centered around his own suffering and agony. True, there is some sort of acknowledgement of sin in the following lines:

And I had done a hellish thing,
And it would work 'em woe:
For all averred, I had killed the bird
That made the breeze to blow.
Ah wretch! said they, the bird to slay,
That made the breeze to blow!
(91–96)

As the above stanza shows, though, even his realization of sin is blurred. He admits a "hellish thing"; but this statement is not focused on the shooting itself, that is, on the the killing of something innocent which trusted him. Rather, it seems to emphasize the consequences of that act, namely the "change in the weather". Like the rest of the crew, the Mariner is not only superstitious but unfeeling, as he seems to regard the slaughtered bird as a mere purveyor of a useful wind. Lacking moral insight, he does not display any pity for the Albatross but only for himself, and there is no sign of real contrition. Feeling guilty, having a vexed conscience, does not lead to redemption: without awareness of sin and a will to be redeemed, no redemption can take place. The Mariner stays an outcast from God, telling selected hearers of his own torments and revealing his lack of awareness. In point of fact, the Mariner suffers from both "Pain of Loss" and "Pain of Sense". These concepts, explained in the general introduction to this study, could be expressed in one word: alienation. The poem suggests the relevance of another term: the Mariner is living a "LIFE-IN-DEATH" (193). As long as he does not strive for forgiveness with the true penitent's wholehearted dedication, he is not redeemable.

Inner Hell

The Romantics' vision and conception of man's fallen state moved "towards the study of the state of mind" (Smith 15). In so doing, they presented the Fall as a repetitive event. Wordsworth's visionary gleam perceived in solitude could be viewed as a sort of conception of the redemptive powers in nature, implying that the love of nature could redeem man and lead him to love his fellows. This old notion had been elaborated by William Godwin, who felt that when man participated in an act against nature, she takes her revenge on those who offend her. It has been commonly asserted that the Mariner's penance could be seen as some sort of retribution for having violated nature, symbolized by the albatross. But as was argued above, this explanation is too narrow to explain the Mariner's suffering, not least in view of the fact that its extent and his understanding of "sin" are blurred. The Mariner's alienation and sense of guilt can be held to suggest an "inner hell", a consequence of what he has done. This condition of essential alienation may be expressed in Kyoshi Tsuchiya's terms. He maintains that Coleridge's concern in *AM* was "to depict the figure of an outcast who is deprived of his personal character and action, and thrown into a chaotic, meaningless 'supernatural' ocean (...) his departure results in the 'fall' into his own internal depth, he now seeks for a recovery which must be from within himself. In this the Mariner fails" (90).

One of the first to perceive the "newness" of the poem was Charles Lamb, who pointed out that the disconnectedness of the *AM* imagery constituted a deliberate exploration of a mental state (Fulford 69). Man's internal darkness can be defined with reference to the concept of "inner hell", which was presented in the general introduction. The Mariner exhibits all the characteristics of someone suffering from separation, not only from God but from himself and from any sense of community with others. In fact all the themes pertaining to this concept can be found in the Mariner's psyche: the feelings of guilt, perturbation, despair, confusion of thought, and loss of context in his wandering homeless state. However, he lacks the satanic characteristics of rebelliousness and resoluteness, which are inherent in a great many Romantic heroes. He can be regarded as a representative of fallen man, "the old man", the unredeemed outcast, an isolated state expressed by Coleridge in other poems: "Pale Roamer through the night! thou poor Forlorn! "("The Outcast" 1), "Heaven's poor outcast – Man" ("Lines on a Friend" 2) and "A sordid solitary thing, / Mid countless brethren with a lonely heart" (*Religious Musings* 149–50). All the quoted poems were published in 1796.

As I have tried to argue throughout, there is no one adequate response to *AM*. Different responses in the critical literature only seem partially acceptable. The idea that it should be read as a paradigmatic example of sin-penance-redemption is difficult to assimilate, at least in a Christian sense. The conclusion that the poem is "about" the educative redemptive powers of Nature has been arrived at, without making it clear what kind of nature is actually present in the poem. Reading certain stanzas against the concept of disconfirmation can, at most, serve to emphasize the "newness"of this creation. The trouble with all these different approaches to the poem is that they leave readers with a sense of overdetermination. Too much is left out of account. It is also a poem which leads us into the unknown, the mysterious, even vengeful Cosmos. Therefore, finally, some aspects of the Cosmos in *AM* will be considered.

Concluding Remarks: Cosmology – *Diaporia*

> Solicit not thy thoughts with matters hid,
> Leave them to God above, him serve and fear.
> (*PL.* VIII 167–68)

The following lines are part of Lowth's introduction to his lecture on the Book of Job:

> I pretend not to any new discoveries; I presume not to determinate the subtle controversies of the learned; I scarcely venture to indulge the hope of being able to illustrate any obscurities. My sole intention is to collect, from such passages as appear the least intricate, the most probable conjectures: and what I conceive to have any tolerable foundation in fact, that I mean to propose, not as demonstration, but as opinion only. (Lecture XXXII 352–53)

I have quoted Lowth at some length, partly in order to show that the apologetical style in the presentation of a work is not peculiar to Coleridge – it was to be common in the context of Romantic art – and partly as a way of signalling that the following discussion is to be regarded as purely critical. That is to say, the theological implications of what follows should be considered as "opinion only". Finally, I wanted to demonstrate Lowth's awareness of subjectivity in interpretation, shown in phrases such as "probable conjectures" and in his declaration that his study was to be regarded "not as demonstration, but as opinion only". Subjectivity and self-knowledge are inherent in the idea of *diaporia*, which was discussed in the introduction to this chapter.

This last section on *AM* brings up the issue of *diaporia*. The discussion does not presume "to determinate the subtle controversies of the learned", to borrow Lowth's expression, but to collect certain strands from *AM* which seem to call for further comment. It aims to do so in the awareness of, on the one hand, the playfulness of *diaporia* and, on the other, of the perils involved in dissenting from the judgement of others.

The Fall did not only bring about changes in Nature but in the whole of the Cosmos. In *PL*, however, even before the Fall, Nature and the Cosmos are described in a somewhat confusing way, as the following lines bear witness:

> Only to shine, yet scarce to contribute
> Each orb a glimpse of light, conveyed so far
> Down to this habitable, which returns
> Light back to them, is obvious to dispute.
> But whether thus these things, or whether not,
> Whether the sun predominant in heaven
> Rise on the earth, or earth rise on the sun,
> He from the east his flaming road begin,
> Or she from west her silent course advance
> With inoffensive pace that spinning sleeps
> On her soft axle, while she paces even
> And bears thee soft with the smooth air along,
> Solicit not thy thoughts with matters hid,
> Leave them to God above, him serve and fear.
> (VIII. 155–68)

We could maintain that there is even a hint of a Fall in this passage from *PL*. Swaim has commented on these lines in the following way:

> Even confusion of the syntax evidences the point that God moves in various and mysterious ways. The speech is thus a kind of equivalent

of the voice of the whirlwind to Job, humbling Job by its questions and suggestions of his relative insignificance even while ratifying Job's highest vision of the glory of God's power and creativity. (8)

There is one book in the Bible which attempts to explain the origin of suffering and the idea of retribution, and that, of course, is the Book of Job. In *Biographia Literaria* there is a much-quoted passage where Coleridge discusses his own religious development and the idea of God: "For a very long time indeed I could not reconcile personality with infinity: and my head was with Spinoza, though my whole heart remained with Paul and John". In this context, he poses the following question and provides a con-cessionary answer:

> And what is this more than St. Paul's assertion, that by wisdom (more properly translated by the powers of reasoning) no man ever arrived at the knowledge of God? What more than the sublimest, and probably the oldest, book on earth has taught us. (There follows a translation of the German verse paraphrase by Jacobi ULS 248–9, which supplies verses 1–3, 12, 14, 20–8 of the book of Job.) (201–02)

Obviously, there are several major differences between the two stories that form the nucleus of these remarks (the Book of Job and *AM),* and some of them should be borne in mind from the beginning. One is the establishing of Job's virtuous character. He affirms his blamelessness ("God who has deprived me of justice"). Job is, as I see it, spiritually proud, and he possesses some kind of personal dignity. Feeling guiltless, he rebels, whereas the Mariner is guilt-ridden. There is thus no hint of virtue being brought to trial in *AM.* Another important difference is the reader's knowledge that Job's suffering is planned to test him; no such circumstance emerges in the poem *AM.* Yet another difference is that the Book of Job ends in mutual reconciliation: Job is restored to his material and social position, whereas the Mariner is doomed to "penance for life". Job complains; "In language suffused with legal terms, Job denounces God's disregard of his right" (Greenberg 289). No rebellion is to be seen in the Mariner, who is morally helpless. Job has "friends" and the Mariner has none; instead, he is cut off from any community.

There are, however, two important themes that the Book of Job and *AM* have in common: both tales attempt to explain the origin of suffering, and they both discuss the doctrine of retribution. In addition, both stories have a frame-story and a cosmology. The relationship between the gloss and the verse in *AM* could be seen as a counterpart to the interaction between Job and his friends.

As was pointed out above, the gloss in the poem moralizes and brings in the idea of a crime and of moral justice. Job's friends moralize, too, trying to explain Job's suffering as some kind of retribution conforming to orthodox Jewish tradition. For instance, Eliphaz, who preaches the doctrine of distributive justice, argues that "no innocent man was ever wiped out". He goes as far as to describe suffering as "God's benign discipline". Moshe Greenberg comments on Job's friends in the following terms:

> Eliphaz's carefully modulated reply sets the pattern for all subsequent speeches of the Friends: a prologue, demurring to Job, followed by a multithematic advocacy of the conventional view of God's distributive justice. Most of the themes of the Friends' argument are included in Eliphaz's speech: man's worthlessness before God; man's ephemerality and (consequent) ignorance; a call to turn to God in penitence; praise of God; the disciplinary purpose of misfortune; the happiness of the penitent; the claim to possess wisdom greater than Job's. (287)

Job suffers, and his life is a hopeless agony: night brings him only the terrors of his dreams and night visions. He vents his death-wish with passion, thus becoming "the spokesman of all the wretched of the earth" (287). The Friends, hurt by Job's challenge to their conception of the moral order, turn from comforters to critics, each harsher than his predecessor. Eliphaz implies that Job is a sinner; Bildad openly proposes that his children died for their sins. Therefore they look for some hidden sin or evil in Job, or in his children. The shooting of the Albatross is almost as obscure a crime as the idea of Job's children blaspheming in secret. Job is truly humbled into his insignificance when faced with the mystery of God's power and creativity. The moral of the Book of Job seems to be this: "Behold, the fear of the Lord, that is wisdom; and to depart from evil is understanding" (Job 28.28)

In *PL*, the Book of Job and in *AM*, man's insignificance in the Cosmos is displayed. However, in *PL* and in the Book of Job, God's power and creativity are established. Redemption is foreshadowed in *PL*. Job is also restored.[9] There is no restoration or redemption in *AM*. One may well ask whether the wisdom of Job might be the "moral"of the poem *AM*, as it appears in Coleridge's translation of the verse paragraph from Jacobi mentioned above: "The fear of the Lord is wisdom for THEE! / And to avoid evil, / That is thy understanding". If this idea is seen as workable, the moral of the poem would be different from the moral drawn in the Mariner's farewell stanzas or from the one articulated in the gloss, a "deliberate over-simplification to secure the full effects of distancing and perspective" forming a "tale-within-a-tale-within-in-a-commentary", as Smith also understands it (144).

The cosmology in *AM* also tells us about an encounter with the unknown and the mysterious. In his discussion of differences between Coleridge and Kant, Tsuchiya summarizes: "For the meeting point on which the human mind meets the unknown can be defined and described in human terms [according to Kant]. For Coleridge this meeting is a mystery" (212–13). Whereas Kant believes that we cannot solve the unknown itself, he is confident that it is possible to solve the way the mystery meets the human mind; that is, "'the concept of this connection must be capable of being determined and brought to clarity ('so muss doch der Begriff von dieser Verknüpfung bestimmt und zur Deutlichkeit gebracht werden können')" (Kant qtd. in Tsuchiya 213). As Tsuchiya rightly points out, "Coleridge sees this 'connection' as a mystery" (213).

Finally, Coleridge does not rewrite the different elements in the poem, irrespective of whether they derive from biblical, Cabbalistic, or neo-Platonic sources; he creates something new out of the given, something which does not possess the authenticity of a rewritten tradition but the authority of disconfirmation. That is, the poem defeats any expectation of the traditional, and it does not attempt to reconcile itself to any established textual convention or authority. If there is a fall or crime of some sort in the poem, there is definitely no murder-case. There is no redemption or recovery whatsoever, since there is no will to or awareness of it. There is, at most, the hint of a yearning towards it. There is certainly no rebirth pattern, as Bodkin suggests, no "descent into darkness and depths of the earth, followed by ascent" (254). The Mariner's voyage is circular; it may be interpreted as a non-spiritual pil-

---

[9] "The name of JOB, too, which, in Arabic, means returning to God, and loving him, and hating whatever is contrary to him, is so adapted to the character of his latter years, that we can never suppose it a name given to him by his parents, but invented by the author of the story" (Lowth 360).

grimage. His alienation speaks the language of "inner hell". Guilt, isolation and penance for life prevail. Destruction of unity between the Cosmos and society, and between man and society, becomes apparent. Moreover, the two levels of gloss and verse confirm the absence of a harmonious resolution. The poem is both a diagnosis and a doom of fallen man, "the old man". Here, that "old man" is unredeemed. There is, then, no assurance in the face of the mystery, nor in the face of imagination. There is, at most, the voice of the whirlwind.

Christabel

Criticism

Much has been written about what has been called Coleridge's "failure" to complete *Christabel* (from now on referred to as *CH)*. We know that this poem was in his mind until the end of his days. As late as one year before his death he declared:"I have, as I always had, the whole plan entire from beginning to end in my mind" (*Table Talk* 6 July 1833). Naturally enough in the circumstances, the poem is generally regarded as unfinished. Most scholars believe 1798–1800 to be the date of its composition. Coleridge himself told Lord Byron in a letter of 22 October 1815 that it was composed in the year 1798, but that it was not till after his return from Germany in 1800 that he finished "the second and a part of the third Book". Byron not only praised *CH* in his letter to Coleridge on 18 October 1815, but sent his copy to the publisher Murray with a letter of 4 November saying: "I think most highly of it [*CH*] and feel anxious that you should be the publisher; but if you are not, I do not despair of finding those who will" (*Byron Letters and Journals* vol. III, 246). The poem was then published through Byron's influence, in May 1816, in a collection entitled *Christabel and Other Poems*. The collection ran into three editions by the end of the year.

The first review of *CH* is the notorious one that appeared in *The Edinburgh Review* of September 1816.[10] The anonymous author of this piece saw no merit in the poem, which he considered so ridiculous as not even to deserve serious criticism. The sarcastic review also expressed contempt for the whole

---

[10] " *The Edinburgh Review* was founded in 1802 by Brougham, Jeffrey, Horner and Sidney Smith, its views were Whig and liberal. (...) *The Quarterly,* founded in 1809, was a Tory publication. The two together at the time of Waterloo had a circulation of over 20,000" (Byatt 203).

closing lines. The author of the review wrote that the production "is (...) utterly destitute of value. It exhibits from beginning to end not a ray of genius; and we defy any man to point out a passage of poetical merit in any of the three pieces which it contains" (i.e. *Christabel, Kubla Khan* and *The Pains of Sleep)* (qtd. in Schneider 1955, 424). The review has been ascribed to William Hazlitt; but as Schneider points out, this ascription rests mainly on Coleridge's assumption (1955, 420). It seems that Coleridge was unsure about the real originator of the article, and he returned several times to the abusive review. On 9 February, 1819, he wrote that Hazlitt

> against his own knowledge set about the report, that the GERAL-DINE in my Christabel was a man in disguise, and that the whole Poem had an *obscene* purpose, referring to me at the same time with a shrug of malicious anticipation – *Curse him*! how *he'll stare*! – And one of his clan has had the effrontery in a published Pamphlet to declare the Christabel '*the most obscene Poem in the English Language.*' At Sir George Beaumont's at Coleorton I found a Tract in which Milton is described as 'the blind monster who has newly dared put in print an *obscene* Poem, called Paradise Lost.' So you see, I am every way in most unexpected good company. (Coleridge's italics)

In another article, published in 1962, Schneider convincingly arrives at the conclusion that the abusive review of *CH* in *Edinburg Review* could have been written "only by Moore" (76). In *The Quarterly* of 1834 E.H. Coleridge, the poet's nephew, coined the expression "witchery by daylight" for *CH* by writing: "The thing attempted in 'Christabel' is the most difficult of execution in the whole field of romance – witchery by daylight." The label prevailed for a long time, even in twentieth-century criticism. Another famous, though now somewhat obsolete, approach was applied in Lowes's *The Road to Xanadu* (1927). Lowes refrains from writing about *CH*, but tells us in a footnote:

> I have not included 'Christabel' for the reason that 'Christabel' has failed completely to include itself. Wherever the mysterious tracts from which it rose may lie, they are off the road which leads to 'The Ancient Mariner' and 'Kubla Khan'. And we are following only where known facts lead. I wish I did know in what distant deeps or skies the secret lurks; but the elusive clue is yet to capture. (4)

Lowes's contention that "the elusive clue" of *CH* is still to be captured remains true. Few works of English literature have eluded critical consensus as successfully as *CH*.

The poem's resemblance to a Gothic romance was noticed even before its publication. An anonymous parody with the title "Christoball: A Gothic Tale" appeared in the *European Magazine* in 1815. As late as 1966, Watson was of the opinion that "the essential purpose of 'Christabel' (...) does not seem mysterious at all: it is a poem of Gothic terror" (114). The Gothic elements are easily recognizable, such as the gloomy medieval atmosphere with a nightmarish touch and the supernatural qualities with their corresponding sense of imbalance on the part of the rational order. There is also the motif of the persecuted maiden, who finds assistance neither inside nor outside the castle. Intrinsic to the Gothic pattern is the motif of an innocent person who, accused of some crime, suffers alienation while not being able to prove or even understand what is really going on and whose experiences thus foster a sense of mystery, fear and terror. To these Gothic elements one could also add the suggestion that some sort of mysterious crime has in fact been committed, under the influence of some evil power. According to Praz, it is only natural that "Coleridge in his turn was influenced by Gothic fiction; there is a [sic] air of family relationship between *Vathek* and *Kubla Khan*, *The Castle of Otranto* and *Christabel*" (1986, 31 n. 32). But it is obvious that *CH*'s affinities with the Gothic genre "do not provide a sufficient basis for the understanding of the poem" (Harding 1983, 329).

To these Gothic elements Coleridge added both the spirit and the form of the popular ballad, which further heightens the mood of the poem. The ballad mood by association invokes strong passions, evil and the possibility of tragic events.

In view of its status as a central poem in English literature, it is curious that "[t]he corpus of commentary on *Christabel* is very small" (Paglia 331). Paglia's reading of *CH* is perspicacious, and although I cannot agree with her on all points, at least she clearly understands the poem as "an epiphany of evil" (331). She furthermore declares that "[p]robably no poem in literary history has been so abused by moralistic Christian readings" (331). I have not found this to be the case. Modern criticism of *CH* could be summed up by Piper's statement: "Where [the poem] has not been seen as a story of evil triumphant, it has been seen as an essentially psychological treatment either of sexuality or the transition from childhood to maturity" (1987, 75). The critics who regard *CH* as a poem of sexual initiation tend to rely on reader-response theories, often linked to psychoanalysis. Most of this kind of criticism is concentrated on the two female characters in the poem. Christabel is considered to be on the threshold of adulthood and sexuality, and when innocence is shattered we need not necessarily see this as an evil process. One example of this kind of interpretation is Lucy Newlyn's presentation of *CH* as a Fall poem. While Newlyn's starting-point has affinities with the one adopted in the present discussion, she understands and presents the Fall as some kind of necessary and beneficial stage of growth; that is, she considers the Fall in *CH* as fortunate. I do not think the Fall in *CH* can be viewed in those terms; it is, rather, a matter of restating the traditional grim view of it. In *CH* there is no question of liberation in any sense of the word. Instead it "seems to offer no catharsis, no release from the intense suffering it so vividly depicts, the fear it seeks to arouse" (Bloom 1971, 217). Readings which incorporate a kind of sexual awakening related to the Fall and to Eve's encounter with Satan do not seem sufficiently anchored in the text. Surely, sexuality is not the issue. Calvin and most other Reformation writers directly refuted that interpretation of the Fall. Moreover, interpreting and presenting the Fall metaphorically, as some sort of sexual awakening experience, is to ignore contextual circumstances inherent in the idea of the Fall, be they philosophical, theological, social or historical.[11]

The seventeenth-century poets who held the stern traditional view of the Fall did not regard the matter of sin and virtue as the same thing; that is, they did not see righteousness and virtue as coming out of the Fall. There is no ambiguity here. As Milton said, evil is "impossible to mix / With blessedness" (VII. 58–59). He did not believe that in order to know good we have to know evil. Furthermore, arguing that the serpent stands for the source of some awakening of human potentialities, or as a symbol of transi-

---

[11] It is surprising that so much interest has been devoted to equating the Fall with, or "metamorphosing" it into, sexual awakening and pleasure, when in fact Milton describes prelapsarian "bliss" thoroughly in *PL* Book IV. It is true that he follows the Christian tradition of married love, but Book IV contains some of the best lyrical parts of *PL*; it is full of sensuous imagery. Placing the first intercourse of Adam and Eve before the Fall was a frequent feature in Protestant hexametrical panegyrics on married love. A very informative, sound and scholarly book on the subject of prelapsarian love, including the way in which it is depicted in visual art, is Diane Kelsly McColley's book *A Gust for Paradise, Milton's Eden and the Visual Art*. There is still another point which should be kept in mind. Though it can be argued that as a result of the Fall, sexual love would also be corrupted, it is nevertheless important to know that "on the whole (...) sixteenth-and seventeenth-century accounts of the Fall and its consequences do not feature the debasement of sensual pleasure as the most important result of man's transgression"(Thormählen 402).

tion into a higher consciousness, would be wrong according to this view. The serpent is in fact one of Satan's many disguises, and ironically he is finally turned into that animal. Satan is not a Prometheus;[12] his plot is "all pleasure to destroy, / Save what is in destroying" (IX. 477–78). It is true that some Romantics, but *not* Coleridge, viewed Satan's rebellious and seemingly bold fighting spirit as the attribute of some kind of revolutionary character claiming his rights in the face of repression. This view of Satan was more of a pose than anything else. Unfortunately, a position interpreted literally and without irony easily turns into a "truth". It is, however, possible to defend such an interpretation after reading the first two books of *PL*, since they do not deal with Satan's progressive moral deterioration. Another explanation why readers have felt compassion or empathy with Satan could be that Milton presents him entirely as a human being. Yet another reason would be Milton's emphasis on "Satan's apparent fortitude, strength, and noble determination (...) [which] conceal inward traits of a very different sort: moral viciousness as well as vacillation and confusion due to his dissociation from the divinely ordered world" (Schaar 1982, 205). In fact, the temptation to pity and sympathize with evil is one of the great problems in a Fallen World. It is not easy to look through evil's manipulations, its lies, its spell, and its fascination. Evil is an unreliable narrator and has its own particular rhetoric, as we shall see. The ensuing quotations from Coleridge have been extracted since they are relevant to what follows in this chapter. In 1818, Coleridge writes:

> The character of Satan is pride and sensual indulgence, finding in self the sole motive of action. It is a character so often seen *in little* on the political stage. It exhibits all the restlessness, temerity, and cunning which have marked the mighty hunters of mankind from Nimrod to Napoleon. The common fascination of men is, that these great men, as they are called, must act from some great motive. Milton has carefully marked in his Satan the intense selfishness, the alcohol of egotism, which would rather reign in hell than serve in heaven. To place this lust of self in opposition to denial of self or duty, and to show what

---

[12] "Remarkable contrast between the religion of the tragic poets and the popular ones of Greece. The former are always opposed to the Gods. The ancients had no idea of a *fall* of man, though they had of a gradual degeneracy. Prometheus was Jesus Christ and the Devil together" (*Table Talk* 8 May 1824, 58).

exertions it would make, and what pains endure to accomplish its end, is Milton's particular object in the character of Satan. (*Lectures 1808–1819. On Literature.* Unassigned Lecture Notes, App. A. II, 427) (Coleridge's italics)

This quotation is germane to the ensuing discussion. As Coleridge points out, restlessness, temerity and cunning are characteristics in the satanic personality. Another pertinent trait is, as he writes, that these "mighty hunters (...) must act from some great motive". This will be seen in the discussion of "the tyrant's plea" below. Inherent in a satanic character lies, as Coleridge says,

> remorseless despotism relatively to others; ... in short, by the fearful resolve to find in itself alone the one absolute motive of action, under which all other motives from within and from without must be either subordinated or crushed.
>
> This is the character which Milton has so philosophically as well as sublimely embodied in the Satan of his Paradise Lost. ... the same ingredients have gone to its composition; and it has been identified by the same attributes. Hope in which there is no Chearfulness; Stedfastness within and immovable Resolve, with outward Restlessness and whirling Activity; Violence with Guile; Temerity with Cunning; and as the result of all, Interminableness of Object with perfect Indifference of Means. (Appendix C *The Statesman's Manual, Lay Sermons* 65)

Here, evil is displayed as completely egotistical and arrogant; all means are subservient to its despotism, as Coleridge puts it, "with perfect indifference of means" to accomplish its objective. Evil's pride, temerity, and activity might be misinterpreted as strength and noble determination. With such an interpretation, however, we overlook the concealed moral viciousness in evil, since "behind the giant and the heroic leader lurk the ugly and revolting monster and liar" (Schaar 1982, 233). Evil is the great problem in the Fallen World, and it does not disappear or become less horrible if we rationalize or trivialize it, which is a way of defending ourselves against its grimness. When it appears as part of a literary performance with a powerful fascination, it may even – as will be argued below – lead us to romanticize the idea of it. Our inability to look evil in the eye would go some way towards accounting for the view of *CH* as an example of a Fortunate Fall.

Thus, in the following interpretation of *CH*, the grim view of the Fall will be applied. The contention put forward in these pages is that *CH* constitutes an anatomy of evil; it embodies a gloomy narration which describes preying evil as victorious in a Fallen World.

It is apparent that Coleridge makes use of Christian tradition and of a Fallen World motif in *CH*. The section below called "A Typological Reading of Christabel" examines the way in which Coleridge brings juxtapositions of different biblical components (e.g. the Fall with the Crucifixion) into play. An introduction to the concept of typology heads this section. Furthermore, since the essence of typology is metaphorical, attention is focused on the inherent characteristics of religious metaphors. The liturgical elements in the poem are commented on. However, the poem presents its biblical-religious metaphors as well as its liturgical elements in terms of their demonic counterparts, something which again indicates that we are concerned with the motif of the Fallen World, where evil, sin and death are triumphant. In the examination of these metaphors, Robert Lowth's discussion on "mystical allegory" will also be considered.

There is no redemption whatsoever in the poem; even the speaker loses his innocence, as will be discussed below. The poem does not satisfy our expectations of an ending, something which has given rise to a great deal of speculation. As was stated above, most *CH* critics regard the poem as a fragment or as an unfinished composition. There will be an attempt to approach this issue below by means of examining the poem's different rhetorical figures, such as exclamations, rhetorical questions and aposiopesis, which were also used by seventeenth-century religious poets. The outcome of a typological reading of the poem will be considered, too.

As was already mentioned in the general introduction, *PL* is used as a foil for my interpretation. The textual approach could be designated as a close reading with *PL* as an intertext. The texts, both *CH* and *PL*, form the core from which the religious-philosophical-ontological dimensions have been drawn.

A General Description of Time and Place in the Poem – Disorder – Time and Nature Out of Joint

The general mood of the poem is manifest already in the opening lines: " 'Tis the middle of night by the castle clock, / And the owls have awakened the crowing cock." From these two lines we understand that something sinister is about to happen: from folklore we know that the auroral cock, when he crows in the middle of the night, heralds even greater harm than his nocturnal counterpart, the owl, which is a conventional symbol of death. The "toothless mastiff bitch", an animal of vigilance, "maketh answer to the clock, / Four for the quarters, and twelve for the hour; / Ever and aye, by shine and shower" (9–11). There is something strange about this counting, as well as about the reaction of the animals of vigilance. We are introduced into a silent world, where sounds seem to be muted, with the exception of the deathbells and the "sleepy" noises of the animals. In the wood the only things to be heard are sighs from Christabel, "The sighs she heaved were soft and low" (32) and the sound of her beating heart, "Hush, beating heart of Christabel!" (53) conveyed by the speaker of the poem. The psychological atmosphere of the poem is one of chilly expectancy.

The awareness of silence, insisted upon throughout the whole poem, is very well exemplified in the following lines, which describe how Christabel and Geraldine enter into the castle:

> Sweet Christabel her feet doth bare,
> And jealous of the listening air
> They steal their way from stair to stair,
> Now in glimmer, and now in gloom,
> And now they pass the Baron's room,
> As still as death, with stifled breath!
> And now have reached her chamber door[.]
> (166–72)[13]

The "beating heart of Christabel" could be linked to the idea of time by way of a juxtaposition of *CH* and *PL*. One of the main characteristics of the Fallen World is disorder, including the sense that time is out of joint. The time

---

[13] Coleridge is a master in transmitting a sense of silence and stillness, as in these lines from "The Eolian Harp" (1795): "The stilly murmur of the distant sea / Tells us of silence" (11–12).

aspect in *CH* is interesting and revealing but has received almost no attention at all. One Coleridge critic states that "the time dimension in Coleridge's poetry is exceptionally full in its variety and perhaps unique in its deliberation" (Watson 37), but unfortunately Watson seems to be satisfied with this comment, as he does not provide any further discussion or development of his statement.

In *PL* Edenic time is in balance and in harmony with the rest of the creation. Before the Fall Eve is "due at her hour prepared"(V. 303), and there is a rhythmic recurrence of days and nights; but after the Fall, as Fowler remarks, "time's 'measure' falters, and Eve is late"(275).

This aspect is not in evidence until Book IX, which narrates the final temptation and Fall. Here Eve is away and Adam is "[w]aiting, desirous her return" (IX. 839). But at her being so long delayed, he feels that something is wrong: "Yet oft his heart, divine of something ill, / Misgave him; he the faltering measure felt" (IX. 845–46). He goes out to look for her and finds her at the Tree of Knowledge. Fowler comments on "the faltering measure" and writes that it "may also be nature's 'signs of woe'" (IX. 783) (487). Leslie Brisman in his article "Edenic Time" comments on this passage and claims that the description of Adam's waiting for Eve "so long delayed" points to "the new, fallen sense of duration in time as a bane. Suddenly the clock ticks too slowly" (152).

In Coleridge's poem, we cannot of course understand Christabel as being "late" in the above sense. However, she feels the "faltering measure" of time; it is revealed in her "beating heart", which in the context would mean, and very naturally so, that she is anxious. She feels that something is wrong, possibly with her lover, but she is also herself aware of doing something which is not right. As the speaker puts it, "What makes her in the wood so late, / A furlong from the castle gate?" (25–26) This echoes Adam's comment on Eve's strange desire to wander, "I know not whence possessed thee" (IX.1137); later on he accuses her of "wandering vanity" (X. 875). Therefore the repression of sounds signals a deficient or impaired awareness of time, and is a reminder of the incipient Fall. Like the suppression of sounds, Eve's and Christabel's troubled sleep and sense of anxiety are forerunners of the Fall. Both act as if they were in some kind of trance, which could be the result of a satanic dream (a point addressed below).

The discussion of the time aspect should include mention of the poem's numerous tense shifts from the historical present to the past. Some of these shifts can be explained by the exigencies of rhyme, but most of them occur within lines. There are furthermore six shifts from modern to archaic verb forms (in lines 7, 9, 44, 70, 76 and 92). Chambers has noted this, concluding among other things that "the accumulative effect of these shifts is to suggest that what is being depicted in 'Christabel' is timeless and cyclical: it happened, it is now happening, and it will continue to happen" (13). This makes a valid point. In the Fallen World concept lies the belief, depressing as it is, that the fallen condition in itself determines a repetition of the Fall. That is the case in *CH:* evil, embodied in Geraldine, does not shatter any Edenic bliss; she enters into a world that is already fallen.[14]

In Eden there had been eternal spring with the harmonious recurrence of day and night, but the Fall heralds the coming of seasons. As a consequence of the Fall, nature and mankind became mortal. No longer will trees blossom and bear fruit all the year round. In *CH* there is a temporal vagueness, and it seems that there is even some difficulty in telling us the month of the year: "Spring comes slowly up this way" (22) states that it is springtime, though it seems more like autumn. The season is pointed out again: "'Tis a month before the month of May" (21), i.e. April, which is generally conceived of as a spring month, with associations such as the rebirth of nature, bird song and flowers, verdure and fertility, signifying joy instead of gloom. It is curious that the month is not mentioned directly. There is also something sinister in the counting of the quarters of the hours of day and night. It creates a sense of suspense.

The moon, though full, yet "looks both small and dull" (19). The moon has many contradictory interpretational dimensions. In *CH*, it could be regarded as a literary convention employed to create atmosphere, or it could simply be associated with the Gothic genre. However, viewed in the context of the poem, where the Virgin Mary and a mother figure are repeatedly alluded to, it might be related to divine light and grace, which do not penetrate the clouds; thus it stands as a symbol of some hidden mystery. At the same time, the moon wraps the setting in a mysterious and melancholy grey light. It is very far from the prelapsarian, motherlike moon in *PL,* which in a night when "Silence was pleased ... o'er the dark her silver mantle threw" (IV. 604, 609).

The idea that the castle is exposed in the chilly night is illustrated by the

---

[14] The idea of juxtaposition of past, present and future events can also be found in Milton's "Nativity Ode", where the shifts in tense seem to include present, past and future, sometimes simultaneously. This is a feature characteristic of typology.

fact that although the gate of the castle is "ironed within and without" (127), there is no protection for Christabel to be found among the worldly powers. The line "[w]here an army in battle array had marched out"(128) has similar implications, and the murky shield hanging on the wall bespeaks decay in the power to guard and protect.

The only things that are green in the month of April are the moss and the "rarest mistletoe", the latter a parasitic plant on the broad-breasted oak tree. This tree is emblematic and important for an understanding of the poem. Symbolically, it represents the theme of man's rupture with nature, the paralysis of life forces. The mistletoe is a slow-growing but persistent plant; its death is determined by the death of its host. The oak tree is regarded with reverence in most mythologies and looked upon as a symbol of strength, representing protection and consistency. The oak may of course be interpreted in different ways, but this emblematic tree seems to comprise the idea of something which is ordinarily thought of as standing for strength, but is in this context attacked by other organisms that feed on it. The oak tree is, like everything else in the castle and its surroundings, in a state of decay and contributes to the oppressive setting.

It might be interesting to compare this particular oak tree with other oaks in Coleridge's poetry. "The Raven" begins with "UNDERNEATH an old oak tree," while the "Hermit good" in *AM* prays upon a "rotted old oak-stump", which is covered with moss (522). Christabel kneels to pray in the wood "beneath the huge oak tree"(35), which – as we saw – is covered with moss and invaded by a parasitical plant. The abandoned boy in "The Foster-mother Tale" is found, wrapped in mosses, beneath a big tree (23–24); Bethlen, abandoned royal orphan, is discovered "in the hollow of an oak tree" (*Zapolya* II. 347). Fruman also registers these passages and comments: "Whatever the ultimate significance of this repeated image, it is notable that it is (...) often connected with the theme of the abandoned child, the personal significance of which to Coleridge can hardly be doubted" (1971, 545). This is true of Christabel; she is abandoned by her lover, who is "far away", by her mother, who is dead, and in the end by her father, who rejects her. The trees in the above-mentioned works actually appear to stand for refuge and security; but the "stump" in *AM* as well as the oak tree in *CH* is in decay. The "wood" and the "forest" are said to be bare, but the emphasis is on the oak, which is more like the remains of a tree than a powerful living organism.

Death

Evil, Sin and Death were the main consequences of the Fall. Death is always present in *CH*, and in Part II the tone is set by the church bells, which not only mark out the time towards death; they also reflect the community's celebration of mourning, a reminder of man's fallen condition, born to death and decay:

> Each matin bell, the Baron saith,
> Knells us back to a world of death.
> (332–33)
>
> ....
>
> Between each stroke – a warning knell,
> Which not a soul can choose but hear
> From Bratha Head to Wyndermere.
> (342–44)[15]

By the Baron's decree, the ritual of death is imposed upon the castle and the neighbourhood outside ("So let it knell!", 345). The death-bells' ringing is the only sound really heard in *CH*, and nobody seems to be able to escape hearing it. As was pointed out above, other sounds are hushed, and silence is insisted upon.

The theme of death is strengthened in the following lines:

> Three sinful sextons' ghosts are pent,
> Who all give back, one after t'other,
> The death-note to their living brother[.]
> (353–55)

It is a death mass both for the living and for those already dead.

To this mass the devil provides an echo:

> The devil mocks the doleful tale
> With a merry peal from Borodale.
> (358–59)

---

[15] knell : "A sound announcing the death of a person or the passing away of something: an omen of death or extinction. Also, allusively, in phrases expressing or having reference to death or extinction. knell, v.c. fig. To sound ominously or with ominous effect. Also said allusively in reference to death or extinction" (*OED*, Vol. VIII, 489).

The merry peal is sinister in the true sense of the word and should be looked upon as a warning: it makes Geraldine rise "lightly from the bed", dress and "[trick] her hair in lovely plight":

> The merry peal comes ringing loud;
> And Geraldine shakes off her dread,
> And rises lightly from the bed[.]
> (361–63)

The devil's mocking note comforts her; it is her "tune", and there is a hint at her connection with evil.

Wandering – Rest – Sleep – Dreams – Confusion – Broken Relationships

The Fall implies a separation or corruption of man's relation to God, as well as of man's relation to nature and to other men. Man's alienation or separation from God creates what is called an "inner hell" or the "hell within", concepts mentioned in the general introduction to this study. It entails the feeling of being an outcast from God, a state characterized by a diseased will and a sense of confusion. It is closely linked with the motif of restless wandering as well as with loss of virtue.

It is of course traditional for evil to be depicted as an outcast and a wanderer. As Isabel G. MacCaffrey points out, "The word *wander* has almost always a pejorative, or melancholy, connotation in *Paradise Lost*. It is a key word, summarizing the theme of the erring, bewildered human pilgrimage, and its extension into the prelapsarian world with the fallen angels" (26). The three females in Coleridge's poem, Christabel, her mother and Geraldine, have one common characteristic: they are all wanderers. In the following discussion of the theme of wandering in *CH*, references will be made to *PL* with a view to illuminating Coleridge's ideas.

Restlessness in creation enters with Satan, who is warned by the archangel Michael not to trouble "Holy Rest". The situation in *CH* is quite different. There is no "Holy Rest" to disturb. Christabel informs Geraldine that her "father seldom sleepeth well" (165), though ironically this night he does, in contrast to the bard Bracy who is having what amounts to a nightmare. The spirit of the dead mother is anxious, and she is addressed by Geraldine as "wandering mother". The "wandering quality" is also hinted at in Leoline's advice to the bard Bracy: "And over the mountains haste along, / Lest wandering folk, that are abroad / Detain you on the valley road" (490–92). This restlessness in *CH* points to an already fallen world.

In *PL* rest is associated with ease of mind, but after the Fall Adam and Eve suffer its loss:

> ... their shame in part
> Covered, but not at rest or ease of mind,
> They sat them down to weep, nor only tears
> Rained at their eyes, but high winds worse within
> Began to rise, high passions, anger, hate,
> Mistrust, suspicion, discord, and shook sore
> Their inward state of mind, calm region once
> And full of peace, now tossed and turbulent[.]
> (IX. 1119–26)

In *CH* there is never any ease of mind at all. Christabel is uneasy about "the weal of her lover that's far away"(30); the dead mother's spirit is troubled; and Leoline's unrest is associated with a melancholy obsession with death. Melancholy was regarded as an especial characteristic of the corruption that followed after the Fall and is expressed thus in *PL:* "in thy blood will reign / A melancholy damp of cold and dry / To weigh thy spirits down" (XI. 543–45). The bard has a nightmare. The only one who finally seems to be at ease is Geraldine, who "Seems to slumber still and mild, / As a mother with her child" (300–01). She is like Sin (who in her perverse way is a mother figure), and Death, to whom Satan in *PL* promises a place where they "[s]hall dwell at ease" and where "all things shall be [their] prey" (II. 841, 844).

Milton prefigures Eve's fall by a devil-inspired dream, where the devil corrupts her imagination: Eve dreams of "offence and trouble" (V.34) and tells Adam in the morning:

> Close at mine ear one called me forth to walk
> With gentle voice, I thought it thine; it said,
> Why sleep'st thou Eve? Now is the pleasant time[.]
> (V. 36–38)

Eve goes on to describe how she arose in her dream and began to move about:

> (...) alone I passed through ways
> That brought me on a sudden to the tree
> Of interdicted knowledge; fair it seemed,
> Much fairer to my fancy than by day:
> And as I wondering looked, beside it stood
> One shaped and winged like one of those from heaven[.]
> (V. 50–55)

Just before Eve meets the serpent, the idea of rest is expressed: "Thou never from that hour in Paradise / Found'st either sweet repast, or sound repose" (IX. 406–07). It has been argued that Satan needs the dream to instil into Eve an "evil motion".

With regard to dreams in *CH*, different versions of the poem should be consulted. There are two lines in particular between 28/29, which I would like to draw attention to, as they deal with the theme of dreams: "Dreams, that made her [Christabel] moan and leap, / As on her bed she lay in sleep." Jack Stillinger states that these lines "appeared in 1816 (and never again)" and that they "could have been cancelled simply because of the ridiculous picture it creates of a person *leaping* while asleep; but it is also possible that it was read as too overtly sexual, since Christabel is moaning and leaping in bed while dreaming of her lover" (88) (Stillinger's italics). Fruman refers to the cancellation of these lines as an example of "Coleridge's extreme sensitivity to anything resembling an admission of personal sensuality in his poetry" (1992, 159). In E.H. Coleridge's 1912 edition of Coleridge's poetry, these lines are quoted as a footnote with the annotation "First Edition: Erased H. 1816: Not in any MS". However, Duncan Wu includes the lines in question in *Romanticism: An Anthology*. This is, I think, a wise revision. The lines in question are relevant to the conception of a Fallen World and are thus appropriate in the context. Believing that these lines have anything to do with the poet's or Christabel's presumed sensuality surely amounts to a misreading. The lines make a clear point, which is easier to understand if we compare Christabel's behaviour to Eve's discompose during her devil-inspired dream. Adam observes her and is surprised to find "unwakened Eve / With tresses discomposed, and glowing cheek, / As through unquiet rest" (V. 9–11). Both passages have been regarded as erotically suggestive; but when viewed from the perspective of the Fallen World, they suggest that the Fall is near. Thus the elimination of the mentioned lines is not a Coleridgean "concealment", as Fruman thinks. Coleridge (or someone else) erased those lines. In this connection it should be noted that as the Fall approaches, Eve's innocence is expressed more and more in sexual terms (Fowler 453). However, "Milton makes it quite explicit that having evil motions and feeling tempted does not mean being fallen" (Fowler 259). No one would, as far as I know, seriously understand Milton's erotically suggestive passages as an indication of his own sexuality.

Christabel acts on an impulse derived from a dream that she had the night before. She leaves the castle in the middle of the night to seek a place to pray. The gentle voice of Satan in *PL* could be compared to Geraldine's, "faint and sweet", repeated twice (72, 77). One indication we have that Christabel has had a satanic dream is the result of that dream, i.e. that she really does find something evil out there in the night, which she brings home. Here again wandering is associated with error.

According to some critics, Milton links Eve to the "Nightwanderers" by presenting her as being tempted. After tasting the forbidden fruit, it has generally been believed that she falls into pagan worship:

> So saying, from the tree her step she turned,
> But first low reverence done, as to the power
> That dwelt within, whose presence had infused
> Into the plant sciential sap, derived
> From nectar, drink of gods.
> (IX. 834–38)[16]

Christabel is a nightwanderer, too, inspired by a dream. She might not be worshipping a tree or the remnants of a tree, but still she prays "beneath" and "at" it.

Another description of wandering has to do with the spirit of the dead mother, who anxiously hovers over the girl's chamber. The poem states that on her death-bed, Christabel's mother had said she would hear the castle-bell strike twelve upon her child's wedding-day. In a postlapsarian world, spiritual

---

[16] Applying a typological reading, she is in fact worshipping the Cross: the Fall is the type here, foreshadowing the Crucifixion. The Tree of Knowledge is juxtaposed with the Cross.

forms were and are considered to be frightening. The quality of the dead mother's spirit could be compared to the spirits referred to by Gabriel in *PL*, in a speech where he makes the following admission:

> (...)if spirit of other sort,
> So minded, have o'erleaped these earthy bounds
> On purpose, hard thou know'st it to exclude
> Spiritual substance with corporeal bar.
> But if within the circuit of these walks,
> In whatsoever shape he lurk, of whom
> Thou tell'st, by morrow dawning I shall know.
> (IV. 582–88)

Judging from Gabriel's speech, he admits to being able to recognize evil "in whatsoever shape", though it is known that the angelic guard was not effectual, and that spiritual or mental realities – "if spirit of other sort" – are hard to exclude. The spirit of the dead mother could be such a spirit passing through some kind of spiritual boundary; she is also, as was pointed out above, called "wandering mother" by Geraldine. The fallen humans, like the fallen angels, from being wanderers in thought soon became wanderers in action.

Geraldine's wanderings, described in the story of her fantastic ride, have overtones of Satan's voyage in *PL*, and both accounts evoke the reader's sympathy.[17] Though Geraldine's "wood-wanderings" are not exactly like Satan's prototype of the dark journey, both protagonists are archetypal exiles in the sense that they are seeking rest and refuge. Both are intent on doing evil, but their physical wanderings may be interpreted as a metaphor of their spiritual "wandering". They are erring and lost, homeless in a psychological sense. The unquiet of evil is a common enough motif and often metaphorically conveyed as a picture of fallen man's lost and homeless state, in which mental wandering materializes in a form of psychological flight. This motif can also be found in Milton's contemporaries, as well as among the Romantics.

---

[17] The wanderings of Satan in *PL* have been compared to cosmic travel in the manner of traditional quest stories, but his voyage is in fact a kind of inverted quest. From his involuntary descent into Hell, his "quest" to re-ascend is not motivated by any constructive impulses. He is destructive, and his only goal is to do evil. His mental deterioration is well explained and has affinities with Geraldine's behaviour.

Names and Characters

It is strange that somehow neither the actual choice of the different names in the poem, nor their connection with characters and functions in it, has attracted interest except from a few critics. One of them is Richard Gerber, whose article "Onomastic Symbolism in Coleridge's Christabel" expresses the opinion that a "detailed onomastic analysis can perhaps make us feel that there may be a more deeply meaningful Christian pattern under the surface of the strange supernatural romance than could otherwise be recognized"(194). As his article is relevant to my own argument, it will be discussed at some length.

Gerber wants to consider the name "Christabel" as signifying "beautiful Christian" or "beautiful maiden belonging to Christ" or, as he writes, "she might even stand for the Christian soul" (188). He has also given some consideration to the name Leoline, which reminds us, as he says, of "Leo", the name of several well-known popes. He arrives at the conclusion that "while Christabel is the representative Christian, her father Leoline can appear as a symbol of the Christian church, represented by the pope, the father who protects the Christian, his child, who lives in his house" (190). He furthermore discusses the name of Sir Roland de Vaux of Tryermaine and points out that the name has connotations of the legendary Christian warrior-hero Roland of the *Chanson de Roland* and even more so with the full name Roland de Vaux which is, as he states, "a close parallel with Roland de Roncevaux, the legendary fighter in the cause of Christianity, waging an almost apocalyptic Holy War against Islam. He is, though, betrayed and dies" (191). Moreover, the name Tryermaine, or Triermain, is also suggestive. The word consists of two easily recognisable elements: trier and main. Gerber concludes: "The first and most important meaning of trier is judge. Trier main, a kind of Miltonic inversion of main trier, means the main judge, which would point to Christ, the universal judge" (191).

Tracing Geraldine's name, Gerber mentions that "Fair Geraldine was the name of a lady to whom the earl of Surrey addressed some of his poems", but as he admits, "this in itself leaves us without a connection with the insidious snake-woman" (193). He brings up Hutchinson's *History of Cumberland*, where Hutchinson identified Surrey's Fair Geraldine with the daughter of Gerald Fitzgerald, Earl of Kildare. Gerber draws the conclusion that "the name Kildare or Killdare with its strong lethal implication was a wonderfully suggestive name for a deadly serpent-woman representing sin in a symbolic Christian poem" (193).

As for the name of the bard in the poem, Bracy, we know it was important to Coleridge since he wanted to christen his second child by that name. Nethercot pointed out that Coleridge came across the name in a three-page account of the town Cotheridge, which is, as Nethercot says, an "echo of Coleridge" (qtd. in Gerber 193).

The suggestions made in Gerber's article are interesting, particularly as he is one of the few critics who realize that the names in themselves contain indications supporting the view that the poem could be placed and viewed in a Christian-religious context.

It is a well-known fact that adopting a name for a fictional character is one of the shortest and most convenient ways of "explaining" the nature of that character. According to Judaeo-Christian tradition, a person's name provides information about his identity, origin and family, as well as frequently indicating the place he comes from, as was implied in the chapter on *AM*. Furthermore, as Robert Lowth pointed out, all the names of the "ancients" were derived from some distinguishing quality, which means that names were not always given at birth (362). It is true that the name Leoline makes us think of the animal "leo" (the lion) and that it is quite a fitting name for a medieval knight. As the character is presented in the poem, though, his knightly behaviour is certainly corrupted. It is also conceivable that he stands, as Gerber says, "as a symbol of the Christian church".

Gerber's reading of the name Roland de Vaux of Tryermaine is very suggestive. As he points out, "a very strong suspense is built up around him and at the end of the fragment everything moves towards a meeting with him" (190). It is also significant that Geraldine refers to Sir Roland de Vaux of Tryermaine as her father. His name does not only evoke the famous Christian hero of the *Chanson de Roland* but also – as Gerber suggests – Christ or God, the universal judge. Geraldine's referring to him as her father can also be viewed from an ironical perspective.

Gerber's interpretation of the name Christabel does not contradict that of generations of readers who have not found any difficulty in looking upon her name as being composed of Christ and Abel, two well-known victims. In the poem, Christabel is portrayed as the victim and sufferer. Another critic, Stuart Peterfreund, who has looked into the names of the characters in the poem and discussed their possible symbolic significance arrives at the conclusion that "Christabel (Christ-Abel) symbolizes the expiatory sacrifice of good to redeem a fallen humanity" (1988, 143). It is doubtful, however, if it is possible to look on Christabel as a symbol of redemption as the poem stands.

It should be pointed out here that the poet's choice of the name Christabel is obviously connected with the Romantics' well-documented interest in the mythical figures of Cain and Abel. Coleridge's *The Wanderings of Cain* and *AM* are well-known examples of it, as the preceding chapter on *AM* showed. Cain is often presented as the outcast and rebel whereas Abel is the victim, though there are times when both are seen as belonging to the latter category. The mark of the wandering Jew was also the mark of Cain. Lowes offers some interesting comments in his chapter XIV, where S. Gessler's *Der Tod des Abels* (1790) is discussed in relation to Klopstock's *Messiah.*[18] In respect of popularity, *The Death of Abel* has been compared with *The Pilgrim's Progress* and *Robinson Crusoe* (*Quarterly Review* in 1814).

Lowes tells us that Scott as a child was allowed to read *Der Tod des Abels* on Sundays. Byron read it when he was eight. In *The Prelude*, Wordsworth names "him who penned, the other day, the Death of Abel"; Coleridge had plans to translate Gessner's poem "Der erste Schiffer", although in a later letter to Southey, of 13 July, 1802, he desisted from the project.

The Death of Abel itself is not the only interesting factor here; another is its connection with Klopstock's *Messiah.* Klopstock (1724-1803), after reading Milton's *Paradise Lost* in the translation of J. J. Bodmer, chose a religious theme for his epic poem *Der Messiah.* Coleridge visited the poet when in Germany. We can read about their meetings in *Biographia Literaria*, Ch. XXII, Letters III. The general impression of these encounters is that they were something of a disappointment, perhaps in part owing to the difficulty in communicating fluently in a common language. However, it is clear that the old German poet was reticent in acknowledging his debt to Milton.[19] Coleridge, responding to information derived from Wordsworth, ends his letter with the following lines: "(...) and as to my opinion (the reason of which

---

[18] *Der Tod des Abels* was translated into English as *The Death of Abel (The Death of Abel, in Five Books, Attempt from the German of Mr. Gessner,* by Mary Collver*)* and achieved enormous popularity. Lowes tells us it was also suggested that Gessner's *Abel* and Klopstock's *Messiah* might be read alternatively before or after Holy Communion (256).

[19] Coleridge writes: "Today [Klopstock] informed me that he had finished his plan before he had read Milton. He was enchanted to see an author who before him had trod the same path. This is a contradiction of what he said before" (*Biographia Literaria* Ch. XXII).

hereafter) you may guess it from what I could not help muttering to myself, when the good pastor this morning told me, that Klopstock was the German Milton – a very *German* Milton indeed!" (Coleridge's italics)

These points concerning the names Cain, Abel and Messiah may seem anecdotal and merely incidental. Even so, they show Coleridge's familiarity with these characters and may provide some indications regarding the name of, and names in, the poem. Coleridge's interest in mythical figures such as Cain and Abel is thus in line with an orientation present in almost all the Romantics, in Germany and in England; one should therefore be very careful not to interpret it as inspired by purely biographical considerations, as Fruman wants to do (1971, 363).

Christabel

It remains to be considered how the name Christabel relates to her character as defined in the poem itself. The physical description of her is more or less confined to her eyes, which are said to be "innocent and blue". But there are other strong indications about her personality in the adjectives used to portray her, which should give us some clue to her function in *CH*. In the first part of the poem, before her encounter with Geraldine, she is three times referred to as "the lovely lady" (23, 38, 47). Why did Coleridge repeatedly use 'lovely' about Christabel, and what implications could the word have for him? Chambers explains Coleridge's choice of the word 'lovely' in this way:

> Coburn tells us that whenever and wherever Coleridge used this word, it held for him highly moral connotations – in fact 'connotations of purity' (Inquiring Spirit, 100). To demonstrate this point, Coburn cites this manuscript note of Coleridge's: Lovely is (...) a word that should never be applied except to objects that excite a *moral* feeling of attachment. (52)

Chambers concludes that for Coleridge a 'lovely' person is a person who is "essentially moral, pure, innocent". These are appropriate connotations of the word as used when describing Christabel, as well as proper attributes for someone who was given a symbolic name composed of Christ and Abel. The epithet 'lovely' is furthermore repeated in the bedroom scene, where Christabel "lay down in her loveliness" (238). Loveliness thus does not carry any erotic or sexual innuendoes in this context. Moreover, the attribute appears again in the opening lines of The Conclusion to Part I: "It was a lovely sight to see / The lady Christabel, when she / Was praying at the old oak tree" (279–81). Even after the night spent with Geraldine she is referred to as "lovely" in the passage: "O Geraldine! since arms of thine / Have been the lovely lady's prison" (303–04).

There are other epithets given to Christabel which serve to reinforce the image of her as representing an exalted moral standard and are appropriate for the composite name she bears, namely "gentle" and "holy" ("gentle limbs" 237, "her gentle vows" 285). Geraldine addresses her as "holy Christabel" and relates Christabel to those "who live in the upper sky". (" 'All they who live in the upper sky, / Do love you, holy Christabel!' ") (227–28). These statements are made by Geraldine, and they could, as we shall see, be true, though she uses them ironically and deviously. Throughout the poem, Christabel is described in favourable terms associated with moral and spiritual beauty; and even after her ordeal she is referred to as "the (sweet) maid".

Geraldine

Most criticism on *CH* has focused on the two female characters in the poem. Several critics also maintain that understanding the poem is a matter of understanding the function of Geraldine. Her affinities with witch lore, lamias and kindred legends have been pointed out. There are certainly many "snakes in the grass" in literature, and the tradition of literary serpents is ancient and extensive.

The name Geraldine was of course not chosen at random. Therefore it is somewhat surprising that neither the choice of it nor the link between name and character has attracted more interest. One exception was Gerber, as already noted. Another critic, Stuart Peterfreund, argues that an anagrammatic approach should be applied to the name Geraldine. He considers that her symbolic name, i.e. "Dire Angel", "points to Geraldine's origins in, and significance in terms of Book VI of PL" (143) (Peterfreund's abbreviation). This leads him to equate Geraldine with Satan, drawing parallels with *PL* for an understanding of *CH*. In support of an anagrammatic interpretation of the name Geraldine, it is relevant to mention Kathleen Coburn's observations concerning Coleridge's various systems of concealment in his notebooks, which "began with transliterations into Greek characters" (*Notes* II, App. C,

412–15). She gives some examples: "Southey's name appears in cryptogram: 'Austral'"(*Notes* I. 172), "'Rota' stands for Dorothy Wordsworth "(*Notes* I. 892). Other examples are Coleridge's turning the poet Klopstock into 'Club-stick' and his own pseudonym when joining the dragoons, which was 'Comberback'. His anagram 'Asra' for Sara is well known, as is the appellation 'Spy Nose' for Spinoza. In Geraldine's case, the concealment is anagrammatic: her anagrammatic name"Dire Angel" is symbolic and agrees well with her satanic qualities as revealed in the poem. Her character not only carries connotations suggestive of Satan in *PL*, but also of other evil literary creatures. Geraldine is a description and incarnation of evil, and her name reinforces those functions.

While Christabel's physical characteristics are not described, Geraldine's are depicted in some detail, and so is her development generally throughout the poem. There are enough clues to determine her character as definitely evil. I will examine the attributes given to her, and study her reference and relation to evil seen in a Fallen World context, with specific references to *PL*.

One conventional literary device by means of which seventeenth-century writers indicated that a character was evil or satanic was by showing his/her ability to act in a false or deceitful way, or to be able to change his/her appearance. These characteristics are all present in the personification of Satan in *PL*: "Artificer of fraud (...) the first / That practised falsehood under saintly show" (IV. 121-22). When discussing Satan's habit of metamorphosis, Broadbent remarks that "all fluctuations of shape, changes of nature are presented as evil, symptom of the Fall itself" (106). To act in a deceitful way thus not only implies being able to change one's appearance, i.e. size, sex, stature, etc., but also false pretension, half-lies, fraud and trickery. The fallen angels' ability to metamorphose is clearly stated in *PL*: "All intellect, all sense, and as they please, / They limb themselves, and colour, shape or size / Assume, as likes them best, condense or rare" (VI. 351–53).

For evil to be able to establish the first contact with good and win its complicity, it needs some convincing and seductive appearance alluring enough to capture its victim with its fascination. Thus the external beauty of the serpent was also designed "To lure [Eve's] eye" (IX. 518).[20] It also very cunningly makes use of elements of surprise which put the victim off her guard: In Eve's

---

[20] As Fowler remarks: "No doubt Milton was aware of the tradition that Eve was charmed by the serpent's beauty" (469).

dream Satan appears by the side of the Tree of Knowledge as "One shaped and winged like one of those from heaven" (V.55). In the final temptation scene the element of surprise is even stronger; Eve is "[n]ot unamazed" when asking the serpent how it came by its voice: "What may this mean? Language of man pronounced / By tongue of brute, and human sense expressed?" (IX. 553–54). However, to strengthen its bond and alliance with good, evil needs some persuasive and seductive story to tell, often appealing to the innocent victim's pity and charity. Fruman poses some pertinent questions on Geraldine's role in the poem:

> What is her function? In fact, precisely what does she do? We do not know what crime has been committed, though we are led to believe it was a singularly horrible one. The reason the implications of these problems are not confronted is that it is always assumed that Geraldine is acting purposefully, and that we don't know what her motives are only because the poem is unfinished. (1971, 355)

Geraldine as the embodiment of evil of course operates purposely according to a cleverly and psychologically devised plan. Her motive is pure hatred, and her aim is to corrupt.

Evil's first move in order to invade and ruin is well described in the poem. In a night four times described as "chilly"and "chill" (14, 15, 20, 43), Christabel appears wearing a cloak: "She folded her arms beneath her cloak", (55) whereas Geraldine appears "unsandal'd" and dressed in a sleeveless silk robe:

> (...) a damsel bright,
> Drest in a silken robe of white,
> That shadowy in the moonlight shone:
> The neck that made that white rob wan,
> Her stately neck, and arms were bare;
> Her blue-veined feet unsandal'd were,
> And wildly glittered here and there
> The gems entangled in her hair.
> (58–65)

Geraldine's appearance is 'romantic' to say the least, and it dazzles her victim. In connection with the above presentation of Geraldine, the speaker of the poem exclaims: "I guess, 'twas frightful there to see / A lady so richly clad as she – / Beautiful exceedingly!" (66–68) His remark reinforces her beauty, but at the same time there is a hint that the mere sight of her should be alarming and a cause for vigilance and fear. Gems – Geraldine is plentifully supplied with them – are traditionally considered as a metaphor for the light of Heaven.[21] It is not without some sense of fear that Christabel exclaims at the sight of this lady: "Mary mother, save me now!"(69) Geraldine manipulatively answers in a voice "faint and sweet", immediately appealing to Christabel's sense of charity by saying: "Have pity on my sore distress"(73). The innocent victim answers: "Stretch forth thy hand, and have no fear!" (75) Geraldine claims to be exhausted and in need of protection, and one of her psychological tricks is to persuade her victim of their common social background by declaring that she is of noble birth. It serves in her intent to create a bond with her victim, just as Satan understands that to be able to carry out his evil deed he has to, as he says himself, seek "league with you (…) / And mutual amity so strait, so close, / That I with you must dwell, or you with me" (IV. 375–77). Geraldine calls herself "a maid forlorn" (82) and a "wretched maid" (103) in order to appeal to Christabel's sense of charity. Nowhere else is she mentioned as a "maid". It is a term reserved only for Christabel. The victim becomes the protector, and it is clearly expressed in the poem that Christabel takes Geraldine into the castle "in love and charity". As Paglia points out, Geraldine "assumes the frailest feminine persona. Five warriors have kidnapped her from her father's house and abandoned her: 'Me, even me, a maid forlorn.' The irony of Geraldine's tale of rape is that she is herself a rapist"(333).

Geraldine's story has hardly been commented upon by critics. It is a satanic story, i.e. full of half-lies and improvisation; but as with all the satanic stories and arguments in *PL,* there seems at a first hearing to be a germ of truth in it, which is difficult entirely to dismiss. However, when carefully analysed, Satan's arguments turn out to be twisted and incongruous. Geraldine's story of the nightly "ride" has overtones of Satan's escape before the threats of Gabriel in *PL*: "By night he fled, and at midnight returned / From compassing the earth, cautious of day" (IX. 58–59), and "[t]he space of seven continued

---

[21] The gems in her hair in a Fallen World context might even be an indication of her having been in Eden: "Thou hast been in Eden the garden of God, every precious stone was thy covering, the sardius, topaz, and the diamond, the beryl, the onyx, and the jasper, the sapphire, the emerald and the carbuncle, and gold. (…) Thou wast perfect in thy ways from the day that thou was created, till iniquity was found in thee.' (Ezekiel 28.13, 15).

nights he rode / With darkness, thrice the equinoctial line / He circled, four times crossed the car of Night" (IX. 63–65). Gabriel tells Uriel of his persecution of Satan but unfortunately, as he explains, he "under shade [i.e. the tree] / Lost sight of him." Finally Satan "by stealth" found his way to a place where "Rose up a fountain by the tree of life", and "involved in rising mist, then sought / Where to lie hid" (IX. 73, 75–76). The tree by which Satan hides is the Tree of Life. Geraldine emerges behind the broad-breasted oak tree in the middle of the night in a landscape where there is no mist but where "The thin grey cloud is spread on high, / It covers but not hides the sky" (16–17). According to Geraldine, after the nightly "ride" one of the five warriors[22] placed her under the oak, swearing that they would soon return. Her story of the nightly ride, during which they even "crossed the shade of night" (88), contains the following lines:

> As sure as Heaven shall rescue me,
> I have no thought what men they be;
> Nor do I know how long it is
> (For I have lain entranced I wis)
> Since one, the tallest of the five,
> Took me from the palfrey's back,
> A weary woman, scarce alive.
> (89–95)

Her reference to Heaven as the agent of her rescue may be taken to be ironic. Geraldine's claim to have "no thought", and to be ignorant of how long she has been "entranced", is perhaps the most valid part of her story: She is like the rebel angels in *PL* who are as if emerging from drug-induced stupor; they remember nothing of the intervening period between the war and their release from chains: "[Satan] stood and called / His legions, angel forms, who lay entranced / Thick as autumnal leaves" (I. 300–02). Later on the fallen angels "Disband, and wandering, each his several way / Pursues, as inclination or sad choice / Leads him perplexed "(II. 523–25). One of the few scholars who discuss Geraldine's story is Peterfreund. Equating

---

[22] It is possible that the mentioning of "five" warriors (81) is important, since the number five stands for the pentangle, the symbol of truth as well as the symbol of man after the Fall. It is also a marriage symbol; in addition it might symbolize Jesus' five wounds.

Geraldine with Satan, he finds the original of her account in *PL* VI, where "the Son, commanding the Chariot of Judgement, drives the fallen angels out of Heaven and into Chaos" (145). As for her claim to be of noble lineage, she would then be "of the most noble lineage of all: as an angel she is begotten of the Father" (146). Her words "[a]s sure as Heaven shall rescue me, / I have no thought what men they be" (89–90) could then – as Peterfreund points out – be seen as "a monstrous irony. Heaven will not rescue Geraldine; it has already consigned her to oblivion" (146). With such an interpretation, Gerber's idea of reading "Tryermain" as the chief judge would make excellent sense.

Christabel describes Geraldine as "the bright dame" (106). With such an address, we understand that Christabel not only finds Geraldine impressive; a clue to Geraldine's identity can be perceived, too, suggesting that Geraldine is in fact older than Christabel herself and not at all a "maid forlorn" or "wretched maid", *which are attributes that Geraldine gives to herself.* Geraldine is referred to as "The lady strange" (71) but also simply as "The lady" (129, 133, 138). Her story is a mixture of horror and fantasy, full of irrational elements, but it works on Christabel and it has the desired effect. Geraldine establishes a bond with her, and the first obstacle to evil is removed: Christabel invites Geraldine "to share her bed". (Apparently both Eve and Christabel are left dramatically to the seductive powers of evil.)[23]

The next barrier to cross for Geraldine is the threshold of the castle. All crossings or transgressions of boundaries are conventionally associated with evil or with the devil. Evil spirits cannot enter a Christian building without human assistance; they have to be helped, and by someone who does it voluntarily. "The little door" in the middle of the gate is described as "ironed within and without", which means, according to tradition, that it has been consecrated.[24] This is how Geraldine's passing of the threshold is described:

> The lady sank, belike through pain,
> And Christabel with might and main

---

[23] Here one may agree agree with Paglia, who acknowledges that "once Geraldine has won her first victory, she has won everything. She has made her first penetration of Christabel's psyche and now manipulates her thoughts. It is Christabel who introduces the idea of 'stealth' "(333).

[24] Compare the custom of fastening a horseshoe over the threshold. Paglia mentions the old Scandinavian custom of burying "an axe (...) beneath the threshold to guard a house against lightning – and to prevent a witch from entering" (334).

Lifted her up, a weary weight,
Over the threshold of the gate:
Then the lady rose again,
And moved, as she were not in pain.
(129–34)

As many critics have pointed out, Christabel thus actively helps evil over the threshold by removing impediments to its entering the castle. The burden of evil is metaphorically and ironically expressed as "a weary weight" (131). Evil is traditionally thought to suffer pain when encountering consecrated objects or places.

This idea also emerges in *PL*, which explains that the fallen angels became vulnerable to pain when their natures were impaired by sin ("Save what sin hath impaired") (VI. 691). The tradition of evil's suffering in the presence of light is epitomized in Satan's expression: "O sun, to tell thee how I hate thy beams" (IV. 37).[25] Geraldine's reaction to the brightness of Christabel's lamp is relevant to this response, as is pointed out below.

After Geraldine's faintness caused by Christabel's lamp, the latter once more helps Geraldine to regain her composure, this time by offering her the "cordial wine", "of virtuous powers", which her mother had made of wild flowers.[26] Christabel is, like Eve, "on hospitable thoughts intent" (V. 332), offering her guest to drink. Eve "crushes, inoffensive must" (V.345) to entertain her angel guest, "Native of heaven" (V.361), before the Fall.[27] At the mention of the wine, Christabel's mother seems to be present as some kind of guardian spirit. The idea of an angelic, spiritual guard occurs in *PL* as well: "Millions of spiritual creatures walk the earth / Unseen, both when we wake, and when we sleep" (IV. 677–78). At the naming of the dead mother, Geraldine's voice which previously was "sweet and faint" undergoes a change, and with "altered voice" she orders: "Off, wandering mother! Peak and pine!" (205) This sounds more like an evil magic formula than anything else. She stares

---

[25] "Every one that doeth evil hateth the light" (John 3. 20).

[26] Eve in *PL* is portrayed as "gatherer and guardian of flowers".

[27] This procedure refers to the unfermented juice of the grape. Intoxicating wine was connected with the rebellion against God. After the Fall Eve is "heightened as with wine" (IX. 793). The wine in *CH* is called "cordial" and "virtuous", which are favourable words, and apparently it helps evil to recover.

with "unsettled eye"(208) and cries with "hollow voice"(210). The spiritual guard proves ineffectual here, as does the angelic guard in *PL*, though it leaves Geraldine with a "moist cold brow" (218), faintly stating " 'tis over now!"

At this point Geraldine has crossed the last barrier, and ironically it is Christabel who helps her recover by offering her the wine again. She stands up, "a lofty lady", and she is "most beautiful to see, / Like a lady of a far countrée" (224–25). Her beauty is emphasized, but the hint of foreignness conveys a renewed warning that there is something ambiguous, to say the least, in her identity. It was believed that the fallen angels' names were blotted out in Heaven:

> Though of their names in heavenly records now
> Be no memorial blotted out and razed
> By their rebellion, from the books of life.
> Nor had they yet among the sons of Eve
> Got them new names, till wandering o'er the earth[.]
> (I.361–65)

Satan is addressed by Chaos in the following manner: "I know thee, stranger, who thou art" (II. 990), which means that Chaos recognizes Satan's identity but does not know his name. As early as line 71 in *CH*, Geraldine is given the epithet "stranger", "the lady strange". However, the ability to move from being a "dire angel" – which implies being an outcast from heaven, deprived of her God-given name – to inventing a new name, making use of her condition as a fallen angel for the construction of the anagrammatic name "Geraldine", entails a very cunning irony as well as defiance in the face of her destiny.

From here on Geraldine takes command of the situation.[28] She will have her way ("Thou'st had thy will!", 306), and nothing can hinder her now. She

---

[28] I wonder whether Geraldine's drinking of the wine might have some connection with the common belief in the unsatiable thirst of the devils, which is also described in *PL*. One of the fallen angels' punishments was to suffer from "scalding thirst and hunger fierce" (X. 556). In this connection it is interesting to note the legendary bloodthirstiness of the vampires described in Romantic literature and in Gothic novels (Southey's Oneiza, the heroine of *Thalaba the Destroyer*, is one example). Jean Marigny, in his impressive work *Le Vampire dans la littérature Anglo-Saxonne*, notes that this thirst is mostly "suggérée par une allusion". As such an allusion to "cette soif immonde" he mentions "La Belle Dame sans Merci", "où Keats, après avoir évoqué les spectres qui apparaissent en rêve au chevalier 'pale kings, and princes too / Pale warriors, deathpale,' (6) donne a leur sourire grimaçant une signification sinistre: 'I saw their starved lips in the gloom / With horrid warning gaped wide. (7)'"(383).

is gaining in stature, which metaphorically means that her evil characteristics are growing, and she is finally depicted as "the lady *tall*"(393) (my italics).

Thus, Geraldine addresses Christabel in the following manner:

> And thus the lofty [29] lady spake-
> 'All they who live in the upper sky,
> Do love you, holy Christabel!
> And you love them, and for their sake
> And for the good which me befel,
> Even I in my degree will try,
> Fair maiden, to requite you well.
> But now unrobe yourself; for I,
> Must pray, ere yet in bed I lie.'
> (226–34)

In connection with the lines above, it has been argued that Geraldine seems to be an agent working under the direction of some force, evil or beneficent. Fruman, for example, is of the opinion that "the poem itself provides substantial hints that Geraldine may not be entirely evil" and comments on the above lines:

> Of course, all this may be merely diabolical cunning in Geraldine, but it seems unlikely. Certainly no poem could have been reputably published in the nineteenth century in which Satanic forces have powers superior to benevolent ones, and Coleridge is the least likely of poets to have written such a work. (1971, 357)

What might have induced critics to believe that Geraldine is not entirely evil are the lines: "And for the good which me befel, / Even I in my degree will try, / Fair maiden, to requite you well" (230–33). There are, however, strong indications that these lines are truly menacing when read in context. Geraldine is acting on her own behalf. Her behaviour exhibits an ironic counterpart to Jesus' self-sacrifice, as does Satan's double-edged self-sacrifice when "for the general safety he despised / His own: for neither do the spirits damned / Lose all their virtue", offering as he says to his peers "Deliverance for us all: this enterprise / None shall partake with me" (II.481–83, 465–66).

---

[29] "Lofty" characteristically means "tall" in *PL*.

116

With ironic arrogance, Geraldine implies a relation to those "who live in the upper sky" (227) which refers, of course, to the heavenly powers, i.e. to God. Like the devils in *PL*, she avoids mentioning God directly. The fallen angels prefer paraphrases for God such as "Our supreme foe" (II.210), "heaven's lord supreme" (II. 236), "heaven's all-ruling sire" (II.264), "the king of heaven" (II.316) and "heaven's high arbitrator" (II.359). This alludes to the devils' attempts "to assert dualistic equality with their creator", as Broadbent explains (130). The manner of avoiding a direct mention of or appeal to God (or Jesus and the Virgin) is hinted at in the passage where Christabel, after she and Geraldine have crossed the court, "devoutly cried / To the lady by her side, / Praise we the Virgin all divine / Who hath rescued thee from thy distress!" (137–40) To this Geraldine answers: "Alas, alas! (...) / I cannot speak for weariness" (141–142). In a copy of the poem from 1816 (now at Princeton, CoS63), in Coleridge's handwriting, nine prose glosses are entered in the margins in the same style as the glossing in *AM*. Next to lines 141–42, the poet noted: "The strange lady makes an excuse, not to praise the Holy Virgin." Geraldine's pretension that she is on intimate terms with God, or the heavenly powers, intensifies her satanic pride. Her presumptuous intimation that she is connected with those "who live in the upper sky" alludes to a passage in the Bible, where Jesus speaks of the power of Satan to deceive man into believing that he is divine (Mark 13.5–6, 21ç23).

Moreover, the devious irony in Geraldine's speech in the above lines is fully understood when it is compared to the "tyrant's plea" in *PL*. The following issue emerges: Satan is spying on Adam and Eve and "with necessity, / The tyrant's plea, excused his devilish deeds" (IV. 393–94). He soliloquizes thus:

> And should I at your harmless innocence
> Melt, as I do, yet public reason just,
> Honour and empire with revenge enlarged,
> By conquering this new world, compels me now
> To do what else though damned I should abhor.
> (IV. 388–92)

In his tyrant's plea, Satan is excusing his evil actions by resorting to values such as "public reason" and "honour and empire", but also to necessity. These principles, as he says, force him to do something that even an infernal agent would recoil from. The manipulative character of the plea is further strengthened by his bringing concepts such as "pity" into play. Fowler remarks that "Satan's pity is by no means to his credit" (217). The idea of Satan's use of "pity" is illustrated in the following passage:

> Happy, but for so happy ill secured
> Long to continue, and this high seat your heaven
> Ill fenced for heaven to keep out such a foe
> As now is entered; yet no purposed foe
> To you whom I could pity thus forlorn
> Though I unpitied: league with you I seek,
> And mutual amity so strait, so close,
> That I with you must dwell, or you with me
> Henceforth[.]
> (IV. 370–78)

It is not only Satan's lack of pity for others that shines through in his rhetorical speech, but his self-pity. His evil purpose is brought home by two lines which are paramount for the nature of the bonds that evil intends to establish: "That I with you must dwell, or you with me / Henceforth"(377–78); they were commented upon earlier in this study. These lines imply, as Fowler succinctly points out: "I with you (i.e. temptation and sin, inner hell): you with me (damnation, the eternal hell)" (217). Evil exacts a very intimate relation indeed, which is the case in *CH* as well.

Thus Geraldine not only excuses her actions by resorting to implied connections to those "in the upper sky", but justifies herself by stating that "for their sake, / And for the good which me befel", she will try to deal appropriately with her victim. As we have seen, she arrogantly appeals to Christabel's relation to "those in the upper sky". This could be interpreted as embodying some kind of pity for her victim. However, her declaration that she will in her "degree" requite Christabel well suggests her knowledge of doing evil. As we know from *PL*, Satan's pity is not to be believed in, and nor should Geraldine's pity be trusted. When regarded from a Fallen World perspective, the quoted lines hence reveal that she is in point of fact aware of doing evil; the lines in question are menacing rather than pitying.

Geraldine orders Christabel to undress; says that she must pray before she goes to bed; bows beneath the lamp, slowly rolling her eyes around (a strange kind of behaviour when praying) and drawing in her breath, which suggests a hissing sound; she then undresses and in full view reveals:

> Behold! her bosom and half her side -
> A sight to dream of, not to tell!
> O shield her! shield sweet Christabel!
> (252–54)

In Part II this vision reappears. A fearful recollection of the night spent with Geraldine falls as a vision on Christabel when she is standing in front of her father:

> Upon the soul of Christabel,
> The vision of fear, the touch and pain!
> She shrunk and shuddered, and saw again-
> (Ah, woe is me! Was it for thee,
> Thou gentle maid! such sights to see?)
> (452–56)

Again the speaker reacts very emotionally as if overcome by grief, transmitting a feeling of sorrow and frustration at the ongoing tragic and highly turbulent drama which he is involved in as a spectator. The reader is also affected. Wilson Knight considers that "[t]he poem expresses fear of some nameless obscenity" (84) and that "[Coleridge's] use of *fear* is (...) the secret of his uncanny power, this being the most forceful medium for riveting poetic attention "(83).

The lines can be compared to Adam's exclamation at the vision of Death in *PL*:

> But have I now seen death? Is this the way
> I must return to native dust? O sight
> Of terror, foul and ugly to behold,
> Horrid to think, how horrible to feel!
> (XI. 462–65)

The important thing to notice in both Adam's and the *CH* speaker's exclamation at the terrrible vision is that they make a proper response to tragedy, i.e. react with terror and fear. The second response to it is "compassion" and "pity", or "sorrow" and "shame", which are the words used by the speaker in *CH*. The person who is "free from fear" (repeated twice, 135, 143) is Geraldine. "Fear" as well as "touch" are words which are "fallen", as is the expression "vision of fear". The same applies to pain, which is connected with sin. This is suggested in Geraldine's difficulties in passing the threshold, which were commented on above.

An explanation of the vision comes in the ensuing lines:

> Again she saw that bosom old,
> Again she felt that bosom cold,
> And drew in her breath with a hissing sound[.]
> (457–59)

A witch's bosom was conventionally described as "old" and "cold", and these words are in line with Geraldine's evil character. Paglia identifies Geraldine's bosom as the possible mark of a witch: "A withered bosom, misplaced nipples, multiple breasts: the witch's body is a perversion or parody of the maternal. It is fitting, therefore, that Geraldine's sole opponent is Christabel's benevolent mother" (336). What is more significant and disquieting, though, is the fact that Christabel draws in her breath with a hissing sound at the mere remembrance of the sight and the touch of this bosom, since hissing is a sign of evil in its guise of serpent. A hissing sound is also hinted at in the lines which describe Geraldine when, shortly before undressing, she "[draws] in her breath aloud, / Like one that shuddered" (247–48). Later on, when the two women stand in front of Sir Leoline and Geraldine turns to Christabel and looks "askance" at her, the speaker exclaims: "Jesu, Maria, shield her well!" (581–82). The *OED* emphasizes that the word 'askance' has been put to varied uses, but that writers have characteristically employed it to indicate "disdain, envy, jealousy, and suspicion". It is significant that Milton uses 'askance' in the passage where Satan, tormented and full of hatred, looks at Adam and Eve kissing: "aside the devil turned / For envy, yet with jealous leer malign / Eyed them askance" (IV. 502–04). At this moment Satan starts losing some of his lustre; this is where he is called "devil" for the first time. The word 'askance' is thus a word with satanic connotations of ill-will and jealousy. At this point in the story, the speaker in *CH* is aware of fear and evil and reacts emotionally. Geraldine's eyes assume the appearance of a serpent's:

> A snake's small eye blinks dull and shy;
> And the lady's eyes they shrunk in her head,
> Each shrunk up to a serpent's eye,
> And with somewhat of malice, and more of dread,
> At Christabel she looked askance!-
> One moment – and the sight was fled!
> (583–88)

This momentary sight makes Christabel fall into a dizzy trance, so that she stumbles and shudders aloud "with a hissing sound" (591). What stays in her mind is "no sight but one!" Though she is, as the speaker points out, a "maid, devoid of guile and sin",

> So deeply had she drunken in
> That look, those shrunken serpent eyes,
> That all her features were resigned
> To this sole image in her mind:
> And passively did imitate
> That look of dull and treacherous hate!
> (601–06)

The above lines cause Fruman to italicize: "*Christabel is becoming like Geraldine*" (1971, 407). He goes on to give them a biographical explanation: "Is not what is being expressed here Coleridge's fear of being overmastered by evil impulses and becoming the demon he feared and hated?" (407). Fruman continues: "When, in later years, Coleridge gave it out that Christabel was wholly an innocent, suffering from the guilty of this world, he was projecting an inner wish that his own sufferings had been visited upon him, from outside, for some providential end"(407). These statements seem unfair both to the poet and to the poem. There is *no proof whatsoever* of Coleridge's projecting any inner wish, equating his own sufferings with Christabel's. Christabel must be understood as wholly innocent. It is as important to understand that, as it is to understand the complete evil of Geraldine. There is no good reason for disbelieving Coleridge's own explanation.

Christabel sleeps "[w]ith open eyes (ah woe is me!) /(...) and [dreams] fearfully"(292–93), expressions which illustrate evil's corrupt and contagious power. Christabel undergoes a humiliating alienation, expressed in the hissing sound she makes after having "drunken in" the look of evil. The sound which she utters against her will, and her passive imitation of a satanic look, stand in sharp contrast to Satan's change into a serpent by God. Satan voluntarily disguises himself as a serpent in his determination to deceive man, and is then ironically turned into one.

The idea that satanic corruption, even when only experienced as visual exposure to it, remains forever in the mind is furthermore exemplified in the experience of the bard Bracy, who gets up in the middle of the night "[w]arned by a vision in [his] rest!"(530). What he sees amounts to a nightmare: it is "a bright green snake" coiled around the wings and neck of a dove (549–50). The dove he recognizes as Sir Leoline's daughter, "That gentle bird, whom thou dost love, / And call'st by thy own daughter's name" (532–33). This is to say that having seen evil at work is a sight which will never recede, or, as the bard expresses it: "This dream it would not pass away – / It seems to live upon my eye!" (558–59)

Hesitation – Images of Recoil, Stricken and Doleful Looks, Pride and Scorn

At this point, it might seem superfluous to give more space to exposing the thorough evil in Geraldine's character. However, since I depart from the common belief that her hesitation and stricken look could be regarded as a sign of her being partly good, I need to show that these attitudes underline rather than mitigate her satanic personality.

As was pointed out above, these elements in Geraldine's behaviour have been regarded as implying that she is not entirely evil, as an indication that she is acting as an agent for someone else, or even as a sign that her behaviour is compulsive. In his attempt to show that "Coleridge's fears, conflicts and repressed desires break through his normally vigilant censor", Fruman quotes line 259 as an example ("And eyes the maid and seeks delay"), a line which was not published until 1828. In Fruman's view, what the relevant passage tries to show "is that Geraldine was *not* an evil agent, that she was acting under some kind of compulsion" (162) (Fruman's italics). More surprisingly, to strengthen his argument he brings up what he calls "the little-known set of seven [there are nine] marginal glosses to the poem", which Coleridge entered in the margins of the Ramsgate copy of 1816 now at Princeton (CoS 63) (see Stillinger 89). As an example, Fruman mentions the fifth gloss: "'As soon as the [w]icked Bosom, with the mysterious sign of Evil stamped thereby, [touches] Christabel, she is deprived of the power of disclosing what had occurred'" (1992, 162–63).

The gloss by no means lessens Geraldine's evil character; on the contrary, it reinforces it. I have already argued that Geraldine is acting on her own account. Her apparent hesitation and her stricken and doleful look do not moderate her evil characteristics; they actually emphasize her evil intention when they are understood in their Fallen World context and with *PL* as an intertext. The attribute "doleful" is also appropriate for Geraldine's look; according to *OED*, the word semantically implies both "full of or attended with dole or grief, sorrowful, suffering and sad". The following lines exhibit the very essence of evil:

> Yet Geraldine nor speaks nor stirs;
> Ah! What a stricken look was hers!
> Deep from within she seems half-way
> To lift some weight with sick assay,
> And eyes the maid and seeks delay;
> Then suddenly, as one defied,
> Collects herself in scorn and pride,
> And lay down by the Maiden's side! -
> And in her arms the maid she took,
>   Ah wel-a-day!
> And with low voice and doleful look
> These words did say:
> 'In the touch of this bosom there worketh a spell,
> Which is lord of thy utterance, Christabel!
> Thou knowest to-night, and wilt know to-morrow,
> This mark of my shame, this seal of my sorrow[.]
> (255–70)

Since I wish to refute the idea that Geraldine's hesitation suggests that she is not completely wicked, a long quotation from Fruman is necessary, as it constitutes a useful summary of this notion:

> Surely it is difficult in the face of this to conceive of Geraldine as a purely malevolent spirit – all the more terrible because of her beauty.

Why would Coleridge add this passage – after a hiatus of twenty years – to the other hints, if not to clarify that Geraldine commits her loathsome act – whatever it is – against inner resistance. She must be herself either the victim of malevolent forces, or at least the half-unwilling agent of forces ultimately tending toward good. Yet if this is so, how to explain the complete absence in both of Gillman's accounts – and we must remember that Coleridge lived under his roof for eighteen years – of any indication that Geraldine was not intended to be evil? On the contrary, Gillman regularly refers to her as such. Does it not appear that the poet himself was undecided?

Thus, at several key points in Coleridge's poems, we find deep and inexplicable confusions, a world in which unmotivated or mysterious crimes are committed, in which the characters of the protagonists scarcely exist .(71, 358)

First of all, one might question the appropriateness of accusing the poet if there are key points in his poems which seem to convey "deep and inexplicable confusion" for the reader, or, worse still, for the critic. This amounts to dismissing the poem before giving it a fair reading; surely one would at least expect an attempt to analyse the apparent confusion. Second, why not consider Coleridge's insistence that Geraldine is evil? Certainly, evil is apparently beautiful, as here represented by Geraldine; but on closer examination we are able to see the flaws in her beauty, as has been shown. Evil does not become less harmful just because we have difficulty in imagining it as beautiful. It is admittedly "terrible" that Geraldine is a handsome woman, but it does not lessen her harmful qualities. Geraldine commits a "loathsome" act, but her resistance has nothing to do with her being some "victim of malevolent forces."

The idea of evil's recoiling and hesitating in front of beauty was a literary convention during the seventeenth century. It was also developed in connection with the villains of the Jacobean drama. Likewise, Milton used it in his characterization of Satan. Evil's scornful pride and stricken look were also literary conventions. They go back to the traditional view that a sinner is a sufferer, which is, as Schaar points out, "a well-known classical and Christian thought" (1982). An examination of satanic behaviour in *PL* will cast some light on the lines from *CH* quoted above.

In Book IV, Satan's "many passions, envy and despair" are disclosed, as is his hesitation. He, however, "confirms himself in evil". Before his final decision to opt for evil, he looks towards heaven and the full-blazing sun with a "grieved look" (IV. 28). His sadness is also due to the fact that he is conscious of being a fallen angel. Satan's pride and scorn are stressed several times in *PL*. One example is when he tries to reach Eve's "organs of her fancy, and with them forge / Illusions as he list[s], phantasms and dreams" (IV. 802–03). He is found out by the angels Ithuriel and Zephon who accost him, but he answers them "filled with scorn" (IV. 827). In his encounter with Abdiel, he looks at the latter with "scornful eye askance"(VI. 149). His behaviour could be compared to Geraldine's looking at Christabel with serpent eyes: "And with somewhat of malice, and more of dread, / At Christabel she looked askance! "(586–87) (The word 'askance' is furthermore repeated: "And looked askance at Christabel!"(581), "that look askance" (608).)

The best example of Satan's hesitation is, however, when he sees Eve on her way to the Fall:

> (...) her heavenly form
> Angelic, but more soft, and feminine,
> Her graceful innocence, her every air
> Of gesture or least action overawed
> His malice, and with rapine sweet bereaved
> His fierceness of the fierce intent it brought:
> That space the evil one abstracted stood
> From his own evil, and for the time remained
> Stupidly good, of enmity disarmed,
> Of guile, of hate, of envy, of revenge[.]
> (IX. 457–66)

But soon "Fierce hate he recollects, and all his thoughts / Of mischief, gratulating, thus excites" (IX. 471–72); and finally: "Hate stronger, under show of love well feigned, / The way which to her ruin now I tend" (492–93).

Satan in front of his peers is described in the following manner:

> (...) he his wonted pride
> Soon recollecting, with high words, that bore
> Semblance of worth, not substance, gently raised

Their fainting courage, and dispelled their fears.
(I. 527–30)

It will be obvious from all this that what is being described in the characters of Satan and Geraldine, and moreover with great psychological acuteness, is their mental activity. Satan knows "many passions"; he suffers from "inner hell"; he is full of hate, envy, revenge and despair; he feels "abashed" and "abstracted" at the sight of beauty; he pines, and is reminded of his loss. It is in the knowledge of the traditional satanic character that we should read the lines on Geraldine's hesitation and recoil: they certainly do not mean that Geraldine regrets doing evil. By merely looking at evil, Christabel passively imitates "That look of dull and treacherous hate!" (606). In "dizzy trance" she stumbles, and "[shudders] aloud, with a hissing sound" (590–91). One of the most striking qualitites of the hissing in *PL* is that it is contagious. What makes it so appalling in Coleridge's poem is the idea that it was a kind of punishment for the fallen angels as well. At Christabel's hissing, Geraldine turns round "And like a thing, that sought relief, / Full of wonder and full of grief, / She rolled her large bright eyes divine / Wildly on Sir Leoline" (593–96). Her grief or pity is not for her victim, but for herself. A further indication of evil is that her eyes, though called "divine", roll "wildly".

Anatomical Images

Preceding pages have argued that Geraldine's character is unconditionally evil, and an examination of her physiognomy will give us additional clues to her evil personality. The discussion will look at anatomical images in *CH* and their relation to *PL* as well as to the motif of the Fallen World.

The following lines describe Geraldine undressing:

> (...) she unbound
> The cincture from beneath her breast:
> Her silken robe, and inner vest,
> Dropt to her feet, and full in view,
> Behold! her bosom, and half her side –
> A sight to dream of, not to tell!
> O shield her! shield sweet Christabel!
> (248–54)

The last line (254) was added in the principal text beginning with the edition of 1828. It was a substitution for "And she is to sleep by Christabel". Again, an exclamation from the speaker expresses his anguish at the danger Christabel is in. What Christabel actually sees when Geraldine undresses is not directly stated, but Coleridge added in pencil in one of the annotated copies of 1816 (CoS62): "It was dark and rough as the Sea Wolf's hide"(see Stillinger 89). This indicates her evil character, but the annotation never went into print.

It is true that the actual condition of Geraldine's "bosom and half her side" is never explicitly described, and indeed one may well ask why it should be. Still, there are some lines which could guide us in trying to determine the nature of her body. There is apparently something about her "bosom and half (...) side" which makes the speaker react very strongly. The following morning the vision of this bosom falls upon Christabel's soul:

> The vision of fear, the touch and pain!
> She shrunk and shuddered, and saw again-
> (Ah, woe is me! Was it for thee,
> Thou gentle maid! such sights to see?)
> (453–56)[30]

The nature of Geraldine's bosom is brought out again in repetitions: "Again she saw that bosom old, / Again she felt that bosom cold"(457–58). Geraldine remarks upon her own body with these words: "This mark of my shame, this seal of my sorrow" (270). Lines 257–58 are relevant, too ("Deep from within she seems half-way / To lift some weight with sick assay"). These lines convey a disturbing sense of something disagreeable and perverse, the more so in view of the sexual and religious connotations of the passage. This has been noted before, and could be summarized in Wilson Knight's words that "[s]ome sort of sexual desecration, some expressly physical horror, is revealed by Geraldine's undressing"(83).

What can be deduced from Geraldine's anatomy is that her bosom and half her side is something so horrifying that it defies actual description; the only designations used to characterize it are "old", "cold"(457–58) and implicitly

---

[30] To lines 451–56 Coleridge wrote as a gloss, in Co S63, the following: "Christabel then recollects the whole, and knows that it was not a Dream; but yet cannot disclose the fact, that the strange Lady is a supernatural Being with the stamp of the Evil One on her" (see Stillinger 90).

"hollow" (257–58). The mere sight of her bosom produces fear and pain. Geraldine herself refers to these characteristics as marks of shame and sorrow. Furthermore, she acts both as a lover and as a mother:

> And lo! the worker of these harms
> That holds the maiden in her arms,
> Seems to slumber still and mild,
> As a mother with her child.
> (298–01).[31]

Applying the above-mentioned characteristics to the context of the Fallen World, it is conceivable that the physical traits in the character of Geraldine have something to do with the ways in which anatomical images were used and understood in the religious poetry in the seventeenth century. Favourable anatomical images, particularly associated with the womb and pregnancy, have strong relations to concepts such as "Mother Earth" and to Nature. However, in connection with Fall poetry, unfavourable anatomical images are connected with unnatural sexuality, often expressed in metaphorical images of vacuity. This has to be understood as a parody of God's creative force in the void, a corrupt nature being conceived as a demonic counterpart.

The metaphoric use of deformity in a character is conventional and a well-established device for depicting evil. Thus the traditional anatomy of evil was often rendered by the corrupted or demonic counterparts of anatomical images related to womb, bowels, entrails, or ribs.[32] These images have connections with earth and nature. It was also a convention to point out some abnormality or deformity to disclose certain qualities on the part of the characters. This corruption of the natural has to be understood as both real and metaphysical. The corruption of the natural in Hell is elaborated in *PL* II, but also in the monstrous fecundity of Sin, revealed in the hourly-born hell-hounds. As Fowler points out, after the Fall "Images of unnatural sexuality begin to be mingled with the images of vacuity"(169).

---

[31] Paglia discusses whether there might be a phallic subtext to the demonic intercourse, mentioning the ambiguity of the body of Spenser's Duessa: "'Her nether parts misshapen, monstrous, / Were hid in water, that I could not see, / But they did seeme more foule and hideous, / Than womans shape man would beleeve to be'" (I.ii.41) (337)

[32] Fowler refers to Broadbent, who "suggests that the traditional physiognomy of the fiend is in Milton's hell displaced on the landscape. And it is a dead or corrupt body imaged as scurf, belching, ransacked womb, bowels, entrails, and ribs"(82).

In *CH*, there is a hint that Geraldine is hollow: "*Deep from within* she seems *halfway* / To lift some weight with sick assay" (257–58) (r italics). Apart from their ambiguity and perversity, these lines suggest a hollow body. The conventional imagery of evil as hollow or vacuous was assumed to be, paradoxically, a picture of a devilishly aggressive interior. Vacuity implies that the hollow person is insincere, false. Hollowness in Renaissance poetry is almost always an image of evil (one thinks particularly of Spenser's Archimago).

Geraldine has traits of Milton's Sin, who speaks of herself as "[l]ikest to thee [Satan] in shape and countenance bright, / Then shining heavenly fair, a goddess armed / Out of thy head I sprung" (II.756–58). In the same manner as Geraldine, Sin gives a favourable account of herself; but this is how Milton describes her:

> (...) Before the gates there sat
> On either side a formidable shape;
> The one seemed woman to the waist, and fair,
> But ended foul in many a scaly fold
> Voluminous and vast, a serpent armed
> With mortal sting: about her middle round
> A cry of hell hounds never ceasing barked
> With wide Cerberian mouths full loud, and rung
> A hideous peal: yet, when they list, would creep,
> If aught disturbed their noise, into her womb,
> And kennel there, yet there still barked and howled,
> Within unseen.
> (II. 648–59)

Later, Sin explains to Satan that he "[Became] enamoured, and such joy thou took'st / With me in secret, that my womb conceived / A growing burden" (II. 765–67). This "burden" is Death. Sin tells Satan how her "burden"

> Tore through my entrails, that with fear and pain
> Distorted, all my nether shape thus grew
> Transformed: but he my inbred enemy
> Forth issued, brandishing his fatal dart

Made to destroy[.]
(II. 783–87)

So Death is born.
  Death then rapes his mother Sin and of

> (…) that rape begot
> These yelling monsters that with ceaseless cry
> Surround me, as thou sawest, hourly conceived
> And hourly born, with sorrow infinite
> To me, for when they list into the womb
> That bred them they return, and howl and gnaw
> My bowels, their repast; then bursting forth
> Afresh with conscious terrors vex me round,
> That rest or intermission none I find.
> (II. 794–02)

Such incestuous relationships are characteristically associated with the Fallen World. Comparing the above passages from *PL* with *CH*, one could conclude that what Geraldine would unload with sick assay might be Death; but another possibility is Sin, as her mark of shame and sorrow. There will be reason to return to this below, when the bedroom stanzas are examined in a typological context.

Clearly, then, Geraldine's anatomy shows that she is devilish and false – another powerful indication that she is indeed completely evil.

A Typological-Metaphorical Approach to Christabel – Liturgy

The origins of typology are found in the way in which the New Testament writers interpreted the Old Testament prophecies. Their main purpose was to show that the life and work of Jesus were pre-ordained fulfilments of earlier prophesies in the Old Testament. Typology as a method of exegesis was elaborated by succeeding generations of exegetes. Stephen Prickett is of the opinion that this method afforded a "'key', a theory or rather set of literary critical theories by which both sacred and profane texts must (...) be read" at a very early stage (1991, 6). He also considers that "[t]hese theories were to shape the subsequent development of European literature and criticism (6). One explanation of why this method became so popular is that "[s]ince the Bible was the model for all secular literature, such ways of reading naturally also became the way in which *all* books were to be read"(7) (Prickett's italics).

In 1957 G.W.H. Lampe, a biblical exegete, explained:

> As late as a century ago the reader took a large measure of allegory and typology in his stride, as it were, when he turned to his Bible. The headings of the pages of the Authorized Version told him plainly that in the Song of Songs, Christ was addressing the Church. (9)

Reading the Bible typologically was not an approach that the reader of the nineteenth century had to work out for himself, since "it was traditional and standard"(10). Interpreting the Bible along these lines, the reader found himself in the position of the spectator of a drama who already knows how the play will end, since he knows the plot. Such a reader was at home in the world of Old Testament imagery:

> He was accustomed to hear from the pulpit and in school the traditional typological and allegorical expositions of Scripture [and] the simpler interpretations of Old Testament narratives which had gradually come to be commonplace in preaching, teaching and liturgical expression, and which rested on the principle that the Bible is a unity. (12)

Typology as a method of writing also occurred in secular literature. Milton is of course particularly "biblical", but the "point applies in varying measure to almost all the major writers in English" (Alter and Kermode 3). Prickett points out:

> We cannot hope to understand what is going on in Dante or even Chaucer without some grasp of how they themselves relate to the then current ideas of what constituted a book – derived in turn from the Bible. Spenser, Shakespeare and Milton cannot be understood in their contexts without some appreciation of the new Protestant emphasis on reading as a route to salvation. (1991, 8,9)

The typological method is not something particular to the Protestant church, though it flourished during the Reformation. The symbolism and metaphors of this method were also important components in the work of the so-called Metaphysical poets, for Donne, Herbert, Vaughan, Marvell and Traherne as well as for Crashaw.[33] Several of the conceits of these poets can only be understood when one realizes their attitude to the Bible. They not only regarded it as a literary source, but they were aware of, and had a working knowledge of, its typological potential.

According to Lewalski, important critics such as M.H. Abrams, Joseph A. Wittreich and Northrop Frye, to mention only a few, define the "biblical prophetic mood relevant to the major poetry of Spenser, Milton and a number of Romantics"(4). Lewalski herself is, as she points out, "parallel but at the same time distinct from [the mentioned critics]". She specifies her difference in this way:

> Despite the impact of biblical language upon the eighteenth century sublime, and of the true principles of Hebrew versification upon the Romantic poets' perception and use of the Bible as poetic model ... [T]he articulation and practice of a fully-developed theory of biblical aesthetics is not preromantic or Romantic but a Renaissance/seventeenth-century phenomenon. (4)

Her statement is relevant to this study. As was pointed out above, there was a close connection between the Renaissance and the seventeenth century on the one hand and the Romantic age on the other. This is particularly true of the relationship between Coleridge and the poets of the seventeenth century.

It is obvious, as Lewalski writes, that

> though the terminology used to define this concept of typology is not consistent, the new Protestant emphasis is clear: it makes for a different sense of the Bible as a unified poetic text, and for a much closer fusion of sign and thing signified, type and antitype.(17)

---

[33] Crashaw is included among these Protestant Metaphysical poets for several reasons. One is that he also uses the Bible as a source or general model for his poetry. It is pointed out by Young that "Protestant and Catholic poets of the seventeenth century still shared, for all their difference, a common Christian culture centered on the person of Jesus" (31). There is, furthermore, Coleridge's appraisal of Crashaw to consider. He was probably the most insightful reader of Crashaw among the Romantics.

This refers to the seventeenth century, but it is evident that the typological reading of texts continued well into the nineteenth century. Prickett mentions novels by Fielding, Jane Austen and George Eliot which are bound up with this kind of reading, from which he gives examples (1991, 9). The popular biblical commentary-exegesis around 1800 was firmly typological. Coleridge's time produced large numbers of preaching manuals where the guiding principle was a typological reading of the Bible.

Typology can be variously defined. As was mentioned above, it was originally a method of biblical exegesis which was later used for secular literature as well. The concept was also employed as a designation for a certain method of writing. Auerbach sees typology as a relation between two historical persons or events, "the first of which signifies not only itself but also the second, while the second encompasses and fulfills the first" (29). As the present study uses *PL* as a foil or intertext, one specific example could serve to illustrate this manifest kind of typology: In typological exegesis Eve was the type of the Virgin Mary. In *PL* the angel Raphael salutes Eve in this way: "Hail (...) the holy salutation used / Long after to blest Marie, second Eve. / Hail mother of mankind"(V. 385–88). This refers to and foreshadows Eve's antitype the Virgin Mary, who at the Annunciation was addressed by the angel Gabriel in these words: "Hail, thou that art highly favoured, the Lord is with thee: blessed art thou among women"(Luke 1.28).

This method could also be viewed as an attempt to understand or make sense of man's existence by relating historical or biblical characters/things/events to later and present-day characters/things/events. That way, typology may be employed as a kind of guiding principle to show that what had happened earlier in history could be seen as foreshadowing present-day occurrences, the whole resulting in a coherent pattern of events. With such a reading it could be shown not only that present-day events could be truly understood, but also that earlier ones could be seen in their true significance. Another important aspect of this kind of reading is the understanding of historical/biblical characters as not only "individuals but moral types, general representatives of the ethical view of the Bible"(Wallerstein 40).

This way of understanding a text can only function in a closed system of thinking, within a specific historical context and with a belief in some kind of symmetry on the part of historical events. It is hence connected with the Christian view of history and its linear aspect of time, "where the progress of events follows a meaningful pattern"(Evans 99). It is only within a historical context of this kind that a personality can emerge and be understood. Frye speaks about typology as a "specialized form of the repeatability of myth" (1982, 84). This view of history is also reflected in *PL* and forms part of the Fallen World conception. Linear and diachronic, it describes the history of fallen man's journey through time. At the basis of this view lies the whole Christian scheme of history: the Creation, the Fall, the Incarnation (or the Nativity), the Crucifixion, the Second Coming and the Final Judgement. The Incarnation marks the direct entrance of a living God into the historical process with some kind of plan for mankind. Consequently, the Christian view of history is connected with the idea of some "higher truth" which is fulfilled according to a plan present in the mind of God, but manifested through a span of time in history. As a result of this belief, typology is often connected with a providential view of history.

Typology is furthermore linked to the idea of prophecy. According to Evans,

> [i]t is, simply, an aspect of prophecy. A type or a figure, like a prophecy, looks forward to a future fulfilment, the only difference being that, whereas prophecy is explicit and verbal, typology is implicit and historical. Both can exist only in a universe in which the progress of events follows a discernible and meaningful pattern, in which prophecies come true and types are fulfilled. (99)

A certain terminology is needed for the understanding of the typological method. Frye supplies a definition of it: "Typology is a figure of speech that moves in time: the type exists in the past and the antitype in the present, or the type exists in the present, the antitype in the future" (80).[34] Events, characters and things can be recognized and moved backwards and forwards in time, described in terms of type and antitype. Types and antitypes can also be used in juxtaposition, for example the Nativity with the Crucifixion and the Fall with the Crucifixion. Rosamund Tuve points out that the "juxtaposition of the events of the Nativity and Epiphany with those of the Passion, of the Word made manifest with the Word rejected, is traditional and ubiquitous"(65). This has to do with the idea that the Fall is the type of the Crucifix-

---

[34] Some established and well-known examples of types and antitypes are these: Christ is the antitype of Adam and Abel, but also of other Old Testament types, such as Moses, Noah, Samson, or David who trace their antitype in the Incarnate Christ.

ion, or with another terminology which carries prophetic connotations, that the Fall foreshadows the Crucifixion. In this way Eden and Calvary are type and antitype, but can at the same time also be seen in juxtaposition. Another example from *PL* will serve as an example of this. After tasting the forbidden fruit, Eve turned from the tree:

> But first low reverence done, as to the power
> That dwelt within, whose presence had infused
> Into the plant sciential sap, derived
> From nectar, drink of gods.
> (IX. 835–38)

Here Eve is worshipping the Cross. The Fall is the type, foreshadowing the Crucifixion. The tree of knowledge is hence juxtaposed with the Cross.[35]

Moreover, it is possible to identify and spiritually connect one type with several antitypes. The Book of Revelation, for example, in itself can be interpreted as a mosaic of allusions to the Old Testament, thus advancing antitypes in a kind of temporal dialogue. Calvary is therefore not only an antitype of Eden; it also relates to other places associated with evil. This has been pointed out by Frye, who writes that "[t]he word 'spiritually' (...) means a good many things in the New Testament, but one thing that it must always centrally mean is 'metaphorically' "(56). He quotes Rev. 11.8 as an example of this: "And their dead bodies shall lie in the street of the great city, which *spiritually* is called Sodom and Egypt, where also our Lord was crucified "(56) (my italics). Calvary is thus metaphorically connected with other places of wickedness. In connection with the above lines from Rev., Shaffer writes: "All great cities are places of corruption, and may be called by their names; and in all places of corruption was, and is, the Lord crucified. This is unstated typology of immense extent" (101).

It is believed that Jerusalem was sacked a short time before Revelation was written and that it is therefore spiritually and metaphorically the antitype of Sodom. It could also be seen as an antitype of the Red Sea, where the Egyptian army was drowned. Reading metaphorically, we have to understand that place-names have a "mobility [which] is uncannily combined with exact loca-

---

[35] "She who thought it beneath her dignity to bow to Adam or to God, now worships a vegetable. She has at last become primitive in the 'popular' sense." Lewis, *The Allegory of Love* Oxford 1951 (qtd. by Fowler 122).

tion, timelessness with precise and known history" (Frye 1990, 101). The same system operates when a character/event/thing is mentioned, which can also have its own metaphoric "spiritual" translation. Traditionally, as Frye explains, the sinister images of Antichrist and the Great Whore in Revelation were identified with Babylon, but also with the Rome of the author's own day. Dante identified it with the Papal court, which had been dragged away to captivity in Avignon by a giant identical with the French monarch (Philip of France). During the Reformation, the Roman Church was identified with the Whore and the Pope with Antichrist, but the symbols were also read "as messages about moral conflict within each person and in the Church in general" (McGinn 528).

What follows from the above is that typology was used as a method of interpretation where contemporary actualities could be viewed as antitypes of events which had already happened, or else earlier events in history were used to foreshadow present-day events. Auerbach explains it in this way:

> Figura [type] is something real and historical which announces something else that is also real and historical. Real historical figures are to be interpreted spiritually but the interpretation points to a carnal, hence historical fulfilment – for truth has become history in flesh. (53)

This way of presenting a kind of topicality "whereby readings of biblical history could be seen to incorporate significance for contemporary England, and the history of the new elect nation of latterday Israelites" (Zim 86) was of fundamental significance during the Reformation. It implied analogies between the heroes of ancient Israel (or other historical or mythical persons) and the rulers of Protestant England. Milton's *History of Britain* (1670) was written with the idea of an elect or chosen people in mind. God's providence is the pervading idea in history-writing during the seventeenth century.

The typological method was not only made use of by biblical exegetes, especially in Milton's time, but also by poets in organizing their writings, particularly on religious subjects. The Metaphysical poets have already been mentioned. The method flourished during the Reformation and the seventeenth century. This could be explained by a wish on the part of Protestant exegetes to show that the Reformation was a biblical event in itself and that the historical events which led to it had been foreshadowed in the Bible. In this way, the method was given political propaganda status and was thus used for a religious and/or political purpose. One example will supply a more specific idea of how this system was employed:

> In 1559 the English Calvinists who translated the Psalms for the Geneva Bible dedicated their works to Elizabeth I partly in the expectation that she would acknowledge a correspondence between her own life before she became Queen and the 'perils and persecutions' King David 'systeyned before he came to the royall dignitie'. Such a parallel was supposed to induce Elizabeth to follow David's example in other respects. The praise of Elizabeth as the redeemer of England from 'poperie – the shadowe of death' – became a feature of sermons and poems commemorating her accession day. (Zim 87)

Elizabeth is thus presented as the antitype of David, who was in his turn a type of Christ. Parallels were drawn in detail: "just as 'David was the least and last of his father's house, so was Elizabeth' of the Tudors; just as he was 'condemned of his brethren' so was she of 'her sister'"(87).

The rise in literacy promoted by the Protestants was prompted by the idea that everyone should be able to read God's word, the Bible. Knowledge and interpretation of the Bible were further strengthened by weekly sermons. It follows very naturally from this that a writer could

> exploit correspondences between his new work and a biblical sub-text in order to invite his readers to look for hidden senses. At the same time, it enabled the writer to evade responsibility for any particular underlying sense thus construed by the reader as interpreter of his text. The habits of mind fostered by typology were an expedient hedge against censorship. (Zim 88)

Moreover, these stories were considered to be "true", since they were biblical. They could be used as a vehicle for criticism of the abuse of power. A well-known example is Dryden's *Absalom and Achitophel* (1681). This poem derived its inspiration from a typological interpretation of scriptural themes. Dryden draws a parallel between the contemporary constitutional crisis and the plot against king David by Absalom and Achitophel. The idea behind such a method has been described as follows:

[A]ncient history could shed light on modern times [and this] was based on the assumption that history could repeat itself, in so far as similar situations would bring about identical effects. ... and lessons could be learnt from their analogy with contemporary events. (Deconinck-Brossard 146)

It is also apparent that contemporary readers, as Zim informs us,

[were invited] to see national and personal histories foreshadowed in biblical histories, [and therefore] came to expect serious literature in English to carry several layers of intended meaning. Habits of indirect reading – 'catching the sense of two removes' (the phrase is George Herbert's)[36] were both reinforced by contemporary biblical hermeneutics and condemned when abused or misapplied. Biblical truth was not simple, naked truth, except by contrast with the inflated rhetoric which, many poets claimed, abused men's wits, either by hiding the absence of any moral substance, or by veiling something noxious and likely to deprave. (89,90)

A personal application of the typological method could thus be resorted to in order to evade censorship. The metaphors and the symbolism were sometimes far-fetched even for contemporary readers, as Zim points out.

It is strange that there has been no study of Coleridge's knowledge of typology, nor of a possible application of it in his poetry. According to Frye, this may be explained by Coleridge's reticence about his own method:

Coleridge's brilliant insights into Biblical typology make it clear that he would have made things much easier for his students, and more productive for his influence, if he had provided an interconnected statement of his views on that subject. (1982, xix)

I have not been able to find any particular discussion on typology in Coleridge's writings. It is, however, natural to assume his acquaintance with it, considering not only his extensive readings of seventeenth-century writers

---

[36] "Must all be veiled, while he that reades, divines, / Catching the sense at two removes?" ("Jordan [I] " 9–10).

who made use of it, but also his profound knowledge of the Bible, as well as the vast philosophical-religious-theological erudition which emerges in his writings.

Metaphors

The essence of typology is metaphorical, and it is only natural that every poet should have his personal approach to typological symbolism and that he might, as Lewalski writes, "extend [it] beyond recognition"(14). Poets approach the Bible as a complex literary work, and its full meaning is only revealed by way of understanding its "pervasive symbolic mode of typology" (1982, 117). Lewalski brings up different biblical metaphors with typological symbolism as examples. These metaphors were developed over centuries and often have a conventional shared meaning. They can be recognized exactly for what they are, "just" metaphors, or – as Frye puts it – "rhetorical expressions of pious emotion" (167). However, the historical dimension of conservative typology is sometimes lost in a more extended and elaborated typological metaphor.

Lewalski has studied five seventeenth-century poets, starting with Donne and ending with the American poet Edward Taylor. A few of the metaphors she examines will be recapitulated here, as they are not only central to any study of these metaphysical poets but also to any work dealing with typological metaphors. Such a work focused on Coleridge has particular reason to refer to them, as he was such a careful and dedicated reader of seventeenth-century poetry and so intimately acquainted with its metaphorical dimensions.

One example is George Herbert's *The Temple,* especially the collection of lyrics called "The Church", which presents the process of sanctification under the metaphor of building the Temple in the heart. Another is Henry Vaughan's focus upon the process of sanctification through the motif of the wandering pilgrim or exile, which is a pervasive metaphor for the Christian life. The rising and setting of the sun is a type of the death and resurrection of Christ. Christ died as evening star, but he was resurrected as morning star. Another central metaphor was the Christian soul as the Bride engaged in a love-relationship with Christ the Bridegroom; its terms are drawn from the Song of Songs, which was also typologically interpreted as an expression of Christ's love for his Bride the Church. The role of the Song of Songs in Christian imagery is of peculiar significance. Another important source of typological imagery is, of course, Revelation.

In addition, it should be pointed out that anybody who wishes to comprehend these metaphors must be acquainted with the fact that in the Bible there often exists an ironic negation or counterpart of a given metaphor or of a situation, which is sometimes expressed as a demonic parody. Frye comments on this relationship in the following terms:

> [E]ach apocalyptic or idealized image in the Bible has a demonic counterpart and (…) there are two varieties of demonic imagery: the parody-demonic, associated with the temporary prosperity of heathen kingdoms, and the manifest demonic, the wasteland of drought that lies in wait for them. (1982, 145)

Some examples from *PL* may illustrate this idea of a demonic counterpart. For instance, Satan is described as the "great Sultan". For Milton's contemporaries, "the phrase would have reminded them of tyranny rather than of splendour" (Rajan 95). Another satanic counterpart is the description, also referred to in the chapter on *Kubla Khan,* of how the fallen angels build Pandaemonium. Here, as Fowler remarks, "we are probably meant to see the rising of Pandaemonium as a grotesque travesty of the rising of earth out of chaos at the creation" (84, 85). Pandaemonium was the building of an edifice in Hell. It was "a fabric huge / [which] Rose like an exhalation, with the sound / Of dulcet symphonies and voices sweet, / Built like a temple"(I. 710–13). The fact that it rises like an exhalation "suggests the insubstantial, elusive, mystifying, the edifice [forming] a façade for the ugly discomforts of Hell", according to Broadbent (101). Several scholars also point out that the palace in Hell rises like the machinery of a masque: it is artificial, temporary, illusory.

It should be pointed out that such demonic imagery is apocalyptic and that these inverted metaphors further stress the qualities of the Fallen World, constituting images of extreme alienation. Such demonic imagery could also be called a transmutation of conventions, or be regarded as some kind of metaphoric replica of apocalyptic or idealized biblical images but with satanic distortions, a kind of perverted metaphor. As Frye puts it, they "turn the traditional form of the metaphorical structure inside out"(1982, 167).

An awareness of typological metaphors with their demonic and/or satanic distortions may actually have been present in what we call "Romantic irony", which was defined by M.H. Abrams as

> a mode of dramatic or narrative writing in which the author builds up artistic illusion, only to break it down by revealing that he, as artist, is the arbitrary creator and manipulator of his characters and their actions. (1984, 92)

Piper outlines a variety of approaches to Coleridge's imagery. He stresses that "those critics who set out to interpret the symbols of Coleridge's major poetry as simply figures of speech [immediately face] a serious problem of method"(1981, 175–76). He is furthermore of the opinion that Coleridge did not provide a system which made his metaphors clear, but that much of the fascination of his images lies in their very difference from any traditional system of symbols in English poetry (175–76). He quotes various schemes provided by different critics, but, as he says, "the schemes themselves are all orphans. Not one has been generally adopted and, to vary the figure, the free coinage of explanations has debased the currency"(177).

The contention put forward in this study is that the imagery in *CH* is based on metaphors which are conventionally Christian, abound in English literature and are particularly frequent in those works of seventeenth-century poets which deal with religious themes.

One of the major problems when interpreting metaphors lies in the fact that we can never claim with certainty that there is a 'scheme' behind them. In any metaphorical interpretation of a polysemous text, even when a 'true' or literal meaning is adopted for a metaphor or for a whole poem, it will always be a "a choice among a number of metaphorical possibilities, and those other possibilities will still be there"(Frye 1982, 59). Much of the fascination of great poetry lies in the possibility of multiple interpretations. Poets, in general, do not provide a system for the reading of their poetry. However, as the ensuing discussion attempts to show, Coleridge's images and metaphors belong within the traditional system of symbols in English poetry. Coleridge had a wealth of fully developed metaphors at hand, derived particularly from traditional biblical imagery elaborated and amplified over the centuries.

Coleridge criticism, particularly of *CH,* has confronted difficulties of interpretation, but a typological-metaphorical reading might assist in understanding it. The poem associates disparate expressions of feeling, such as the ones articulated in the Conclusion to Part II, in a way which strikes the reader as odd. It mixes apparent paradoxes of innocence and evil with secular and religious allusions which strike even a modern reader as unsettling, even obscene. This is perhaps one reason why some critics have preferred to rationalize the obscene parts of the poem, turning the evil Geraldine into some kind of beneficial agent necessary for the sexual awakening of Christabel. These circumstances would also to some extent explain the biographical interpretations of the poem.

Finally, it has to be stressed that the demonic counterpart of a metaphor is always connected with disorder and chaos, as the overall characteristic of these metaphors is their relation to the corruption of nature, to alienation, to "non"-Nature, which shows that they belong to a Fallen World. These metaphors are in themselves apocalyptic. They may seem exaggerated to a modern reader, but in the very exaggeration lies the idea – not to exaggerate the "object" itself, but to stress what it represents metaphorically or spiritually. They are to be seen as a demonstration of how evil looks and works in a Fallen World. We could call these peculiarly parodic expressions of alienation an anatomy of evil.

The Nuptial Theme

An IDEA, in the *highest* sense of the word, cannot
be conveyed but by a *symbol*, and, except in geometry,
all symbols of necessity involve an apparent contradiction.
(*Biographia Literaria* I ch. 9, 156)

The nuptial theme occurs in several of Coleridge's poems. It can be found in *The Ancient Mariner*, where it has been seen as suggesting both marriage and death. Another poem from about the same time, "The Three Graves", includes wedding scenes whose importance has been stressed by Fruman. He rightly points out that in *CH*, "[l]inks between demonic crime and marriage reverberate (...) there are reiterated interconnections between death bells and marriage bells" (1971, 409). Unfortunately, though, Fruman does not develop the theme beyond trying to relate it to Coleridge's personal circumstances. By way of an example, he quotes the lines where Christabel explains how her mother died at her birth:

I have heard the grey-haired friar tell
How on her death-bed she did say,
That she should hear the castle-bell
Strike twelve upon my wedding-day.
(198–201)

There is certainly a relation between death and marriage in *CH*, but hardly in the biographical sense advocated by Fruman.[37] The nuptial theme and its appertaining metaphors are essential to an understanding of the poem, and to dismiss them as being a projection of Coleridge's own anxieties and personal experience is to avoid serious engagement with them.

The following discussion aims at demonstrating that the nuptial metaphors are central to the poem by establishing their biblical intertext, and also that several passages and metaphors prove to be commonplace in a Christian context and thus are not necessarily strange or even 'romantic'. I will particularly refer to The Song of Songs (referred to below as Song) and Revelation (Rev.), since both books have been core texts in the elaboration of the Christian Bride/Bridegroom symbolism. The Bible also contains other passages featuring nuptials; they will be referred to when they possess a direct relevance to this perspective. Parallels with some seventeenth-century religious poets will be brought up, notably Donne and Crashaw, in order to illustrate the argument. There is a metaphoric unity in *CH* in which the underlying motif is the Bride and the Bridegroom. As I hope to have established, the poem depicts a Fallen World; hence Coleridge mainly uses biblical metaphors in their parodic/demonic counterparts. The typological interpretation of the poem will also show that Coleridge makes use of biblical themes, often juxtaposing one event/person with another.

The texts of Song and Rev. are well known, but to facilitate the comprehension of this reading of *CH* a short general explanation of what the nuptial theme and the motif of the Bride/Bridegroom stand for in a Christian tradition is provided at this point.

Nuptial imagery is frequent in the Bible. One example is the parable in Matt. 25.1–13, which tells us of the ten bridesmaids who are to meet the

---

[37] Fruman finds "a link between *Osorio* and *Christabel* perceived in the resistance of both Maria and Christabel to parental pressure towards unwanted marriages, a theme which has obvious personal meaning for the unhappily married Coleridge" (410). There is no such theme as "parental pressure towards unwanted marriages" in *Christabel.*

bridegroom and accompany him to the wedding. Tradition holds the bridegroom to be Christ, and the Virgins are usually seen as representing the Church or congregation, or the Christian soul. Another parallel is the Bride/Bridegroom symbolism in Song. Rev. has also been commented upon in terms of Christian Bride/Bridegroom symbolism; one might say that it presents a kind of demonic counterpart to the biblical imagery of the Bride/Bridegroom. The context in Rev. is the eschatological struggle between good and evil constructed around antagonistic characters: God, Christ, and the Bride on one side, and Satan, Antichrist, and the Harlot on the other. There is no possible redemption without the extermination of Satan, Antichrist and the Harlot. The woman of ch. 12 and the Bride in 21 have been interpreted as the Church, but a Marian conception has also been advocated. The heavenly Jerusalem can also be identified as the Bride of Christ (Rev. 21.2–9), and in the concluding words of the book, which are also the end of the New Testament, the "Spirit and the Bride say, Come" (22.17), as a type of the evangelist's prayer, "Even so, come, Lord Jesus". These words were often compared to the love-invitation of Song. St Paul uses nuptial imagery several times. In 2 Cor. 11. 2–3, he addresses the congregation in Corinth as the Bride of Christ, "for I have espoused you to one husband, that I may present you as a chaste virgin to Christ", contrasting it, as he says, to Eve, who was beguiled by the subtlety of the serpent.

Very early in Christian tradition the whole life of Christ was constructed in terms of nuptial metaphors. These metaphors were used in the liturgy and in the sacraments, particularly those of the Eucharist and baptism, and then especially in the context of the Paschal liturgy of the Easter Vigil which is given nuptial overtones in Christian texts. The Eucharist is regarded as the eating of the body of the Bridegroom and the drinking of his blood. This was explained metaphorically as a marriage union or a wedding banquet, which was juxtaposed with the Last Supper. The image of the Bride was later also applied to the Virgin Mary. Thus the Mother of God is paradoxically turned into the Bride of Christ. She is also thought of as the Bride in Song. In this way the Bride could be the Church in general or the congregation, or the Virgin Mary, but also an individual faithful soul. However, the bride metaphor and the whole complex of nuptial symbolism also became attached to certain female saints and later to holy women, or to every individual devout soul. In the apocalyptic banquet in Rev., Christ is figured as the Lamb and his Bride can be understood as the Church or the heavenly Jerusalem. This marriage can only take place after the annihilation of the Bride's demonic parody, the scarlet Whore of Babylon, who symbolizes all kinds of tyrannies, profane or spiritual.

The classics in the literature of nuptial spirituality are, of course, the writings of the sixteenth-century Spanish mystics, notably San Juan de la Cruz (St John of the Cross) and Santa Teresa de Jesús. In English literature the Bride/Bridegroom metaphor and the nuptial theme occur in various contexts, both in religious-devotional literature and in love poems such as the Renaissance epithalamia, where biblical imagery was used to praise the maiden by comparing her to the heavenly bride. There were, however, parodies of the theme.

We know that Coleridge was acquainted with the two Spanish mystics mentioned in the preceding paragraph. That familiarity was not only derived from Crashaw – Coleridge claimed that ll. 43–68 of Crashaw's "A Hymne to Sainte Teresa" "were ever present to [his] mind whilst writing the second part of Christabel: if indeed by some subtle process of mind they did not suggest the first thought of the whole poem". In a lecture in 1819, Coleridge also commented on the life and mysticism of Saint Teresa, quoting from "The Flaming Heart". Lorraine and John Roberts have offered the following appraisal of Coleridge's importance to Crashaw criticism:

> Coleridge's comments on individual poems marked a new direction in Crashavian criticism, because he singled out for special attention not the secular poems of the translations, which, up to this point, had received most of the comment, but those that have mysticism as their subject – 'Ode on a Prayer Book', 'A Hymn to Sainte Teresa,' 'The Flaming Heart,' and the Epiphany hymn. (8)

Coleridge's knowledge of the classic mystics and his indebtedness to Crashaw have never been studied in detail. One thing Crashaw and Coleridge have in common is the misfortune of having given rise to cliché-ridden interpretations of their poetry, which have sometimes even led critics to wonder about the sanity of their (the poets') psychological dispositions. This kind of misconception is obviously damaging,[38] telling us more about the critic than

---

[38] Fortunately, the excellent volume *New Perspectives on the Life and Art of Richard Crashaw*, ed. by John R. Roberts (1990), has punctured several of the misguided notions concerning this poet.

about the poet. Much energy has been devoted to pointing out the differences between Crashaw and the Anglican seventeenth-century English religious writers, instead of seeing their similarities.[39] Similarly, emphasis has been laid on the differences between the Spanish mystics on the one hand and the Protestant religious writers from the seventeenth century on the other; but they all wrote within a Christian devotional tradition. Their writings are Christo-centric and the imagery above all biblical. What they have in common, as I see it, is their search for a direct relation with God. They differ in their styles; but in their works emotion, devotion and piety set the tone. The English religious writers from the seventeenth century have been labelled "metaphysical" poets. Louis Martz, in *The Poetry of Meditation*, suggests the term "meditative" as a more accurate description of the poetry of Crashaw, Donne, Herbert, Vaughan and others. The following review of their links with Coleridge accentuates the devotional aspect of their writings.

All the above-mentioned poets use Bride/Bridegroom imagery. In Crashaw the nuptial theme is often connected with female saints or religious women. In "The Hymn in the Assumption", he makes the conventional identification of Mary with the Bride of Song. In "A Hymne to Sainte Teresa", he acclaims her (Teresa) as a spouse of Christ, whereas "The Flaming Heart" portrays her as Christ's enraptured bride. In other poems Crashaw advises devout women to take Christ as their spiritual husband.

Other seventeenth-century poets also employ significant nuptial imagery. Donne, for example, refers to the Church/Bride metaphor in "Annunciation and Passion". He remarks that as God has joined creation and judgement ("Or as creation he hath made, as God, / With the last judgement, but one period", 37–38), death and conception belong together ("Death and conception in mankinde is one" (34); hence the Church, which is seen as "His imitating Spouse" (39), occasionally celebrates Annunciation and Passion simultaneously in its liturgy.[40] This has, of course, to do with the typological way of seeing different events in juxtaposition, and in Donne's poem that dimension is further reflected in the liturgy. In "The Second

---

[39] This was pointed out as early as 1921 by T.S. Eliot (*TLS*, 1031, October 20, 1921, 669–70), in a review of Herbert Grierson's *The Metaphysical Poets*.

[40] "Th'Abridgement of Christs story, which makes one (…) Of the'Angels *Ave'*, and *Consummatum est*" (20, 22).

Anniversary", he speaks of the deceased as she who "was here/Betroth'd to God, and now is married there" (461–62). The individual soul as the spouse of God is also implicit in the erotic paradoxes of Holy Sonnet XIV, "Batter my Heart".[41]

Once again, it should be underlined that when a typological reading is applied to a text, two or more events or passages can be read in juxtaposition or interchangeably. Hence a text has a referential power, but is still limited to a certain pattern. Christian history as perceived in a typological reading includes the understanding of a divine plan for mankind, with the significant events on the road to salvation being the Creation, the Fall, the Nativity (the Incarnation), the Crucifixion, the Second Coming and the Last Judgement. This pattern of history is, moreover, celebrated in Christian liturgy, particularly in the central Christian mysteries which are commemorative rituals. We could say that liturgy serves as a typological, symbolic ritual where past, present and future time, places, events and characters are presented and united in juxtaposition. We could even state that the liturgy itself is a typological ritual. Song is read in the liturgy of Holy Week to commemorate the Passion. In the Easter liturgy, the Passion is also juxtaposed with the Fall, since the Fall gave rise to the Passion.

In view of all this, it seems advisable to incorporate the liturgical overtones of *CH* into the typological reading, proceeding from the contention that reverberating throughout *CH*, liturgically speaking, is the Easter Vigil which is celebrated on the night of Holy Saturday. That night is the climax of the Christian year. It commemorates a kind of "unitive celebration, not re-enacting any single historic episode, or aspect of the story of Jesus' passion, death and resurrection, but presenting it whole as God's work of saving his people" (Irvine 1). Though the celebration of the Easter Vigil is not uniform in every detail, it includes four main components, the sequence of which may vary. For example, the Vigil proper may precede the Service of Light, and the selection of Old Testament readings is not always the same; but the story of the Fall is always included, since the main purpose of the Vigil is to show God's redeeming work in Christ, that is resurrection, redemption and joy in the

---

[41] Many other examples could be given to illustrate the importance of the nuptial theme in English literature; only a few more examples from the metaphysical-meditative-devotional poets will be given: Herbert calls the Church Christ's Spouse in *The Church Militant* (9–13). Vaughan frequently employs nuptial metaphors in "*Silex Scintillans*" e.g. in "The Search" (9–13), "Faith" (6), "The Dawning" (2), "The World" (59–60), "The Constellation" (57), "The Knot" (2), and "L'envoy" (3).

Risen Lord. The Vigil starts in gloom but ends in joy. Evil and Death are thought to be defeated.[42]

I believe that it is only by means of a typological reading incorporating the liturgical component that we will be able to understand "what [the poem] says and then what it talks about properly", to use Paul Ricoeur's phrase (1976, 87–88). In establishing the identity of metaphors and liturgic components, I will make comparisons with the Bible and, as mentioned, with other religious literature, particularly from the seventeenth century, which Coleridge knew so well.

The chapter ends with a discussion of the speaker in the poem.

* * *

En una noche obscura,
con ansias, en amores inflamada,
¡oh dichosa ventura!
salí sin ser notada,
estando ya mi casa sosegada.
(1–5)[43]

This is the first stanza of Juan de la Cruz' "Songs of the soul in rapture at having arrived at the height of perfection, which is the union with God by the road of spiritual negation". Some readers might object to this Spanish mystic being made to serve as a starting-point for this part of the study, but his poem is a prototype of the unperverted use of the nuptial metaphor and thus illus-

---

[42] It is interesting to note that Paglia has also observed a kind of "abstract formality" in Geraldine's and Christabel's slow passage through gate, court, hall and chamber. There is "religious solemnity" in their procession which "moves through the castle as if through a church, nave to chancel to altar, the bed of seduction" (335).

[43] CANCIONES DE EL ALMA QUE SE GOZA DE HABER LLEGADO AL ALTO ESTADO DE LA PERFECCION, QUE ES LA UNION CON DIOS, POR EL CAMINO DE LA NEGACION ESPIRITUAL DE EL MISMO AUTOR, *San Juan de la Cruz, Poesías completas*, ed. Cristobal Cuevas, Editorial Bruguera, S.A., 1981. English translation: "Upon a gloomy night, / With all my cares to loving ardours flushed, / (O venture of delight!) / With nobody in sight / I went abroad when all my house was hushed". Roy Campbell, The Penguin Classics 1960.

trative for the present purpose. The lines can be identified with the soul's longing for Christ's coming, forming part of the song between the Soul and its heavenly Bridegroom. The poem deliberately re-enacts and uses the nuptial imagery of Song, describing the amorous relation between God, seen as the masculine part which finally takes command over the situation, and the soul which finally responds passively and receptively. It starts with the nocturnal egress of the soul in search of her beloved . The literary style is emotive and erotic, and though it stylistically resembles the text in Song, it is also inspired by profane literature. This is explained by Cuevas:

> In San Juan de la Cruz profane texts were given a new religious meaning by means of presenting them in different contexts. This implied that profane literature could be a fountain of inspiration. There was a long Christian tradition, initiated at the very beginning of Christianity, to incorporate and assimilate the sacred text with profane works. (LI) (my translation)

We can discern this fusion of religious and profane components in *CH*, which is a poem with a religious dimension, but presented in the context of a Gothic atmosphere and heightened by the spirit of the ballad. This blend of genres is typical of Romanticism.

Christabel steals out of the castle in the middle of the night to pray anxiously for the welfare of her lover, who is said to be far away. This incident recalls Song: "I sleep, but my heart waketh: it is the voice of my beloved that knocketh" (5.2). The reader might recall the previously quoted lines: "Dreams made [Christabel] moan and leap, / As on her bed she lay in sleep". As Stillinger stated, these lines might have been cancelled since they could be read as "too overtly sexual". Indeed they can; but viewed in a Christian tradition they fit into the pattern of Christian poetry, where the name of Christ (Isaiah 5.1) as the "well-beloved" was sometimes used with sexual connotations which are quite physically explicit. This feature, particularly often "found in Counter-Reformation texts" (Healy 52), might appear exaggerated to a modern reader. With regard to the "overtly sexual" connotations in the lines quoted above, Fray Luis de Leon's explanation seems pertinent. He writes: "All things, guided by a secret motion loving their own good, also love Him and *pant* with their desire and *moan* for his coming" (qtd. in Young 47) (my italics). This description could be relevant to the understanding of sexual connotations in the love relation where Christ is regarded as the "well-beloved" (amado). In *CH* the theme of love is already introduced in the mention of Christabel's distant "lover". The anxiety, the desire, the moaning and leaping, are certainly in the tradition of the idea of the Bride's longing for her "well-beloved", Christ. That is, words such as "moan", "leap" and "pant" have sexual connotations and are conventional in religious poetry where love is the key-word.

The first stanza of the poem describes a nocturnal atmosphere, as does Song. Christabel's midnight prayer in the woods also carries connotations of the waking night in the Garden of Gethsemane. This nocturnal prayer is emphasized, recurring in the Conclusion to Part I, where Christabel is seen kneeling to make her "gentle vows". In the Gospel story, the lack of vigilance in the Garden of Gethsemane is epitomized in the sleeping disciples (Matt. 26.40). The dormant atmosphere in *CH* is apparent and the owls, omens of death, waken the cock, which crows drowsily. In the Passion the cock, an animal of vigilance, also stands for the betrayal of Christ by Peter.

A collocation of nocturnal atmosphere (also present in the temptation of Eve in *PL*) and nuptial theme occurs in the parable of The Wise and Foolish Virgins. The general tone of the opening stanzas in *CH* is one of chilly expectancy and anticipation. We sense the lack of vigilance, in persons and in animals. A further indication of the absence of watchfulness is the fact that there is no wind, which is one of the most powerful images for the Spirit of God or the Holy Spirit (Landry 142). The Edenic breeze functions here in its demonic counterpart; there is no wind, silence reigns. Christabel is totally exposed. It is said to be the "month before the month of May", that is April, which is normally the time when Pascha or Easter is celebrated. All the above-mentioned circumstances stress the ominous aspects of Christabel's situation.

The night of the Easter Vigil was commemorated by the earliest Christians at the time of the full moon. The Vigil is, of course, a time of watching. The entrance into the temple or church in silence, which is the custom even today, creates a sense of expectation and the church is in semi-darkness as dusk falls. The reality of Calvary is spiritually present and symbolized by the darkness in the churches. Man is, so to speak, still in the "shadow of death". The vigil is considered to be a time proper for reflection and prayer. It is, I believe, with this in mind that we should read the first stanzas of *CH* with their silence, expectation and anticipation, with the semi-darkness (where there is a "thin gray cloud" and a moon which is full but "yet she looks both small and dull"), and with the anxious girl who goes out to pray in the night by the oak tree, which is a symbol of the Cross.

In Song, Spring is celebrated in paradisiacal words connected with fertility and new life, words that identify the coming of Spring with the Incarnation or public manifestation of Christ. In Song "the garden is the longest episode as well as the central image in the poem" (Landry 317). The garden image in Song is epitomized in the following verse: "For, lo, the winter is past, the rain is over and gone; The flowers appear on the earth; the time of the singing of birds is come, and the voice of the turtle is heard in our land" (2.11–12). In *CH*, on the contrary, sterility and a negation of paradisiacal characteristics predominate, epitomized in the huge oak tree. As for the rest of vegetation, the forest is bare. It is apparently a wasteland and can thus be regarded as a demonic counterpart of Eden, representing Calvary and at the same time the places of evil in a biblical typology. Frye explains: "In the Bible the waste land appears in its concrete universal form in the tree of death, the tree of the forbidden knowledge in Genesis, the barren fig-tree of the Gospels, and the Cross" (1990, 149).

The tree in *CH* is bare except for

> The one red leaf, the last of its clan,
> That dances as often as dance it can,
> Hanging so light, and hanging so high,
> On the topmost twig that looks up at the sky.
> (49–52)

The intertext of the leafless oaktree is the traditional legend according to which the Tree of Knowledge grew without leaves after the Fall. For a fuller illustration of this interpretation, and for a further discussion of the tree in *CH*, I will make use of a central literary text which brings up this story: Dante's *Divine Comedy*, "Purgatorio" Canto XXXII, which deals with "Earthly Paradise – Through the Forest: The Tree of Adam and the Tree of Christ: Wednesday Morning".[44] It narrates how the Beatrician pageant turns northward, Dante and Statius passing through the "lofty forest" which is bare be-

---

[44] In Dorothy L. Sayers's translation, Penguin Classics ed. 1988.

cause of Eve's "fault that to the snake gave ear"(31–32). They arrive at the Tree of Knowledge, which is described as follows: "a tree whose boughs were shred / Bare of all flowers and leaves on every hand" (38–39). In her commentary, Sayers supplies a short but very useful exposition of this legend. The Tree of Knowledge in its bare state is also an image of Adam in his fallen condition. According to tradition, the Cross of Christ was made from the wood of the Forbidden Tree. In a typological reading, as we have seen, this tree foreshadows the Cross. Dante here follows both an allegorical and typological interpretation of the Fall and the redemption by the Cross.[45]

With this background, the "one little leaf" in *CH*, which is said to be "the last of its clan", could be seen as the only survivor of the once rich foliage of Paradise. Coleridge, like Milton, seldom mentions the colour of anything, but when he does, that colour has a symbolic meaning. The colour red in *AM* is used in this way: "The charmèd water burnt away / A still and awful red" (270–71). Clearly, the colour red has negative connotations in that context. As for the use of 'red' in *CH*, the implication may be a positive one. The red colour is traditionally a symbol of love. The leaf is described as defiant in a gloomy world where it "dances as often as dance it can". It is also significant that its existence seems somewhat precarious: "Hanging so light; and hanging so high / On the topmost twig that looks up at the sky". It is possible that the red leaf is a counterpart to the famous apple in the Garden of Eden. *PL* explains and stresses that the "alluring fruit" hung high up, and Fowler comments that "if the fruit was so difficult of access there was no chance of its being plucked without a firm decision" (473). The passage in *PL* runs as follows:

> About the mossy trunk I [Satan] wound me soon,
> For high from ground the branches would require
> Thy utmost reach or Adam's: round the tree
> All other beasts that saw, with like desire
> Longing and envying stood, but could not reach.
> (IX. 589–93)

Reading *CH* as a Fall story, it would not be difficult to identify this oak as the Tree of Knowledge. In a typological reading the tree stands for the Cross as

---

[45] "We thinke that *Paradise* and *Calvarie*, / *Christs* Crosse, and *Adams* tree, stood in one place" (John Donne, "Hymne to God my God, in my sicknesse"(21–22).

well. If this identification of the oak tree is accepted, the next question is what the red leaf stands for. It could represent the forbidden fruit and thus typologically the Incarnation. We would then have the Tree of Knowledge, the Cross, the forbidden fruit and a picture of the Incarnation in its suffering dimension. This tree carries connotations both of the Fall and the Crucifixion. Geraldine as a "Dire Angel" is violating a sacred place.

Christabel kneels at this tree, and from behind it she helps Geraldine to rise: "Stretch forth thy hand and have no fear" (75). As Geraldine is aided over the threshold, bride-fashion, she is described as a "weary weight". This passage resembles the following lines from Song: "Who is this that cometh up from the wilderness, leaning upon her beloved? I raised thee up under the apple tree: there thy mother brought thee forth: there she brought thee forth that bare thee"(8.5). Geraldine is then a demonic counterpart of this "burden" in Song and in the context a symbol of the "burden of evil", which Christabel with all her might drags into the castle, following Christ who, metaphysically speaking, took the burden of evil on himself. The full irony of the following lines are then understood in their whole significance:

> So free from danger, free from fear,
> They crossed the court: right glad they were.
> And Christabel devoutly cried
> To the lady by her side,
> Praise we the Virgin all divine
> Who hath rescued thee from thy distress!
> (135–40)
>
> ....
>
> So free from danger, free from fear,
> They crossed the court: right glad they were.
> (143–44)

These lines have a serious undertone. For a Christian, the Easter Vigil is the waiting for the Risen Christ and thus connected with praise and joy; here that circumstance is ironically echoed and twice repeated in the expression "right glad they were" (136,144), as well as by Christabel's "devout cry": "Praise we the Virgin all divine"(139). Perceiving the grim irony of these lines, we realize what is being rescued from its distress here is evil, which is set "free from danger, free from fear".

The Lamp Metaphor – The Service of Light

Christabel and Geraldine pass the hall of the castle, and their passing is described in the following terms:

> The brands were flat, the brands were dying,
> Amid their own white ashes lying;
> But when the lady passed, there came
> A tongue of light, a fit of flame;
> And Christabel saw the lady's eye,
> And nothing else saw she thereby,
> Save the boss of the shield of Sir Leoline tall,
> Which hung in a murky old niche in the wall.
> (156–63)

This scene could also be seen as embodying a reference to the Easter Vigil service. Originally, all lamps and lights in the church were extinguished on Good Friday, as a symbolic representation of the significance of Jesus' death on Calvary, when "there was darkness over the whole land" (Mark 15. 33). It was the custom to maintain a "dying fire" in churches and in monasteries at the doorway or in the hall, in order to make the lighting of the Easter candle a safe procedure. The making of a new fire on Holy Saturday by striking a flint or the like also gave scope for allegorical interpretation, "[t]he spark flying from the flint could represent Christ rising from the stone tomb" (Irvine 6). What was being stressed was the fact that it was a matter of a new fire relighting a "dying fire". In *CH*, however, the *new* fire is recast in its demonic counterpart; "the brands were flat, the brands were dying", and at Geraldine's passing "a fit of flame" revives the "dying fire". The lack of faith and vigilance discussed above is further stressed by this incident. A shield, which traditionally symbolizes faith and vigilance, is here relegated to a hidden and dark place, to a "murky old niche in the wall".

The entrance, in silence and gloom, into the church building at the Vigil also created a sense of expectation. Christabel's and Geraldine's entering the castle in an atmosphere of hush and shadowiness is expressed in the following manner:

> And jealous of the listening air
> They steal their way from stair to stair,

Now in glimmer, and now in gloom,
And now they pass the Baron's room,
As still as death, with stifled breath!
(167–71)

This silent darkness as the two women go up the stairs in a sleeping house resembles the second stanza of the above-mentioned poem by St John of the Cross:

A oscuras, y segura,
Por la secreta escala disfrazada,
¡O dichosa ventura!
A oscuras, y en celada,
Estando ya mi casa sosegada.[46]

The moon does not enter into Christabel's chamber, which is described as "carved so curiously, / Carved with figures strange and sweet, / All made out of the carver's brain, / For a lady's chamber meet" (178–81). Once in her bedroom, Christabel trims the lamp:

The lamp with twofold silver chain
Is fastened to an angel's feet.

The silver lamp burns dead and dim;
But Christabel the lamp will trim.
She trimmed the lamp, and made it bright,
And left it swinging to and fro,
While Geraldine, in wretched plight,
Sank down upon the floor below.
(182–89)

Particularly during the Easter Vigil the lighting of the lamps is of great significance, since the act symbolizes the allegorical return of life from darkness to light, hell having been cheated of its prey: death and evil are defeated. In the

---

[46] "In safety, in disguise, / In darkness up the secret stair I crept, (O happy enterprise!)/ Concealed from other eyes / When all my house at length in silence slept."(Roy Campbell, The Penguin Classics 1960)

liturgy this increase of light is often celebrated with candles and praise. Light has manifold symbolic meanings, but in the celebration of the Easter Vigil it signifies the *lumen Christi*. It is in this context that we should understand Geraldine's "wretched plight" when she is exposed to the light of the lamp. Apart from the general idea that evil shuns light, Geraldine's situation must truly be "wretched" if we read the light as *lumen Christi*. The lamp metaphor, connected with the nuptial theme evoking the parable of the Wise and Foolish Virgins, was employed by English writers from the seventeenth century as well. The girl adressed in Milton's ninth sonnet is hailed as one of the parable's virgins, who fills her "odorous Lamp with deeds of light", in order to be prepared:

> (...) when the Bridegroom with his feastful friends
> Passes to bliss at the mid hour of night.
> (10, 11–13)

In "The second Anniversary", Donne uses the lamp metaphor as a metaphoric conceit, making the blood of the martyrs of the Christian Church "Oyle to th'Apostles Lamps, dew to their seed" (352). In similar fashion, Marvell compares the Cistercian nuns to the wise virgins, who trim their "chasted Lamps" hourly, "Lest the great bridegroom find them dim" ("Upon Appleton House", XIV. 107–08). Henry Vaughan opens his poem "The Dawning", on the Second Coming and the Last Judgement, by evoking the parable's nocturnal atmosphere.

Thus, the use of typology and of metaphors linked with liturgic elements was not a novelty in English literature; again, Coleridge shows his allegiance to tradition and to writers from the seventeenth century.

The Wine Metaphor – The Baptismal Liturgy – The Offering of the Eucharist and Easter Communion

A brief summary of lines 190–238 may help the reader to grasp the situation. Geraldine sinks down upon the floor "in wretched plight" on being exposed to the lamp-light. She is then offered wine which Christabel calls "cordial", a beverage with "virtuous powers", and is restored. Christabel's mother is directly referred to as having said on her death-bed that she would hear the castle-bell strike twelve upon Christabel's wedding-day. Christabel then herself invokes her mother, "O mother dear! that thou wert here!" Upon this Geraldine, with all her sadistic irony, comments: "I would, she were!" At this point, it seems that Christabel's mother is spiritually present, something which induces Geraldine to command in an altered voice: "'Off, wandering mother! Peak and pine!'" (the term "wandering mother" recalling Eve in *PL*). She stares with "unsettled eye", and with "hollow voice" s e cries: " 'Off, woman, off! this hour is mine – / Though thou her guardian spirit be, / Off, woman, off! 'tis given to me'" (211–213).[47] Geraldine again drinks of the wine. Both females kneel, Geraldine wipes "her moist cold brow" and says faintly: "'tis over now!" She drinks again from the wine and stands up a "lofty lady". From here on, she assumes command of the situation. She tells Christabel to undress, since she herself must pray before she goes to bed. Christabel obeys, saying: "So let it be!" (235)

The wine-offering in *CH* echoes Song: "I would lead thee, and bring thee into my mother's house, who would instruct me: I would cause thee to drink of spiced wine of the juice of my pomegranate"(8.2) It is even more important, though, to understand the wine offering's connection with the ceremony of the Easter Vigil, as the perception of such a link yields a special religious meaning. Thus, the night of the Easter Vigil comprises a ceremony of Christian initiation; Christians "participate in the Paschal mystery of Christ's death and resurrection through baptism "(Irvine 9). At that moment questions are asked, such as: "Do you turn to Christ? Do you repent of your sins? Do you renounce evil?" It was argued above that Geraldine offers a sort of 'tyrant's plea' justifying her evil deeds. It is possible to understand Geraldine's 'plea' as an answer to such questions. The questions would furthermore represent her last chance to repent and desist from her evil purpose.

In the Eucharist, of course, the wine represents Christ's blood. In *CH*, wine is given to evil which, on drinking it, recovers to be able to fulfil its evil intentions. The Eucharist at the Easter Vigil is of special significance, as it symbolically celebrates the encounter with the Risen God.

Since the poem displays a Fallen World, the Fall and Calvary will, as already mentioned, always be re-enacted as some sort of confirmation of that world. Christabel's mother is spiritually present in the bedroom stanzas. However, earlier in the poem, another mother is referred to, presumably the Virgin Mary: Christabel, at the sight of Geraldine behind the oak tree, exclaims:

---

[47] "Hour" here is, of course, to be understood as "moment", "opportunity".

"Mary mother save me now!" (69) These two occasions when a mother figure is invoked form an oblique reference to the Virgin Mary's role in the Passion. Her presence at the Cross is not uncontroversial. The only biblical account of it is in John 19. 25–27. In literature and in painting, she is seen as either fainting or standing. In "Santa Maria Dolorum", Crashaw portrays Mary as passive: "Here must she stand / Charg'd to look on" (IV. 6–7). Mary's passivity is emphasized in Crashaw's description of her as grieving to the point of death:

> (...) and with a stedfast ey
> See her life dy:
> Leauing her only so much Breath
> As serues to keep aliue her death
> (*Sacred Poems*, IV.7–10)

A "steadfast" eye is a symbol of the faithful Christian, whereas Geraldine's "unsettled" eye is a satanic counterpart of this symbol. Christabel's mother is forced to be passive, like Mary at the Cross. Although Christabel's mother is said to be dead, she seems to be present in some way, able to draw "so much Breath / As serues to keep aliue her death", to borrow the Crashavian expression. What further strengthens her Marian character is that she is mentioned by Geraldine as Christabel's "guardian spirit", which is semantically similar to the term "'tutelary deity', a deity who (…) often possesses characteristics of the Christian mother Mary" (Revard 92).

Christabel finally says: "So let it be!" These are words of passive acceptance, appropriate in view of her Christ-like qualities: "O my Father, if it be possible, let this cup pass from me: nevertheless not as I will, but as thou wilt" (Matt. 26.39). Her attributes, such as the "gentle[ness]" and "loveliness" which were discussed earlier, agree with such a dimension, too. Her Messianic character is further stressed in the Conclusion to Part I, when she prays among the "jaggèd shadows / Of mossy leafless boughs" (282–83) and makes her gentle vows. Christabel – although her breast sometimes heaves – is said to have a face "resigned to bliss or bale" (288). She shows her anxiety and emotion, as well as her passivity, in the same manner as Jesus in his nocturnal prayer in the garden of Gethsemane.

Hence, the spiritual marriage feast between Christ and his Bride appears in its sinister demonic counterpart in *CH*. The wine metaphor, when understood as a demonic Eucharist, reinforces the nuptial theme, since the presence of wine in a nuptial context symbolizes the union of the Bridegroom with his Bride. According to a typological interpretation, the Eucharist was foreshadowed by the Last Supper and can thus be read in juxtaposition with it.[48] But the wine of the Last Supper, as we know, was also a foreboding of the approaching betrayal scene.

The Wedding

Before venturing into a discussion of the marriage theme proper in *CH*, some recapitulation is required in order to make the exposition of the ensuing bedroom stanzas more comprehensible.

In the course of the poem, as has been argued above, there are recurrent evocations of the Fall and of Calvary. Adopting a typological approach to the text, we are able to read these events in juxtaposition. The metaphors of the poem are substantially consistent with those used by other poets writing in a Christian tradition. This fact, viewed in conjunction with the liturgical components of the Easter Vigil which are linked to the nuptial theme in the poem, still leaves us with a sense of dislocation, particularly when we consider the difficulty in determining the function and the core personalities of the two main characters, Christabel and Geraldine.

The precise significance of a metaphor in *CH* cannot be appreciated separately; it has to be understood as related, interconnected and subordinated to the themes of the Fallen World. As modern readers of a two-hundred-year-old poem, we realize that *a single* metaphor represents "something", but we might have difficulty in appreciating its interconnections, which finally develop into a larger pattern or into some unity of structure. This is because we are not familiar with the inherent conventions present in the metaphors, nor with the associations between them. Frye expresses more or less the same idea: "Poetic images do not state or point to anything, but, *by pointing to each other*, they suggest or evoke the mood which informs the poem" (81, ed. 1997) (my italics). It is true that all images – in a wide sense, comprising symbols, metaphors, and associative clusters – can have complex alternatives, but in the case of Coleridge they are consistent with a Christian tradition.

---

[48] The water-and-wine metaphor was also used by other Romantic poets but in its ironic counterpart. In *Don Juan*, Byron compares the consequence of love and marriage to the turning of wine into vinegar (III.5.5)

At this point, Lowth's remarks on what he calls the Mystical Allegory in Hebrew poetry are relevant:

> In the sacred rites of the Hebrews, things, places, times, offices, and such like, sustain (…) a very double character, the one proper or literal, the other allegorical; and in their writings these subjects are sometimes treated of in such a manner as to relate either to the one sense or the other singly, or to both united. (114)

Here Lowth discusses typology and its inherent metaphors, stressing their double character as well as their possible juxtapositions or conflations. With regard to this kind of mystical allegory, or – as we would call it – metaphor, he supplies the following further explanation:

> The exterior or ostensible image is not a shadow colouring of the interior sense, but is in itself a reality: and although it sustains another character, it does not wholly lay aside its own. …
> But the mode or form of this figure (…) is when the two images, equally conspicuous, run as it were parallel through the whole poem, mutually illustrating and correspondent to each other. (116–17)

Similarly, a reading of *CH* which takes account of its unity requires the bedroom stanzas to be read within the context of the liturgy of the Easter Vigil concurrently with the biblical nuptial theme. As Coleridge's lines embody a demonic parody of the spiritual marriage between the heavenly Bridegroom and his Bride, we have to be aware of reversals both in the actions and in the characters of the two females. We can discern different characters in "parallel", as Lowth puts it, or juxtapositioned, as was mentioned above. A considerable portion of this analysis has been devoted to showing that Geraldine is *completely* evil, and that Christabel is to be regarded as good and innocent. When we realize that several biblical events are evoked, reversed, juxtaposed or conflated in the poem, then the two female characters might be better understood.

There are three main disquieting aspects to consider here. They have been considered as indecorous and given rise to manifold interpretations, some of which I touched upon in my introduction to this chapter. First, there is the disconcerting feeling that Geraldine is acting both as a lover and a mother; second, there is the question of the nature of her bosom and half her side, which she calls "her mark of sin and shame", and finally the sadistic as well as erotic overtones of the bedroom stanzas.

As a lover Geraldine acts in her satanic capacity, as a "Dire Angel", and as such also as the serpent of Eden, as the Beast of Revelation, as the Antichrist, and as the Whore of Babylon: all these capacities are demonic counterparts of Christ, the heavenly Bridegroom. Her mark of sin and shame, the sign of evil, can be read as a demonic counterpart of Jesus' wounds, a fact which is ironically echoed in Sir Leoline's oath when he swears by the wounds in Jesus' side. This is a case of tragic irony, since he misunderstands the situation and puts himself on the side of evil. Defending Geraldine from those who have "wronged the dame", he will "dislodge their reptile souls / From the bodies and forms of men!"(436, 442–43)

Intimacy with evil is described in sadistic and erotic terms, epitomized in the expression "The vision of fear, the touch and pain!" (453). Such overtones are not seldom used in religious poetry. Discussing Crashaw, Praz argues that he was not "in some way peculiar for having combined physical torture with sensual love in religious poems, noting that the Council of Trent had encouraged such fulsome and explicit depictions of martyrdom" (qtd. in Roberts 19). It is thus possible to see Christabel as a victim, or as a martyr anticipating the Final Judgement. Of course, describing a "spiritual wedding" in a sensual and physically explicit way amounts to drawing attention away from the literal meaning; what we think of as hyperboles are used to represent a spiritual reality. This is traditionally done in religious poetry; it is not something peculiar to Coleridge. As was mentioned in my theoretical explanation, it is in the very exaggeration – i.e. in demonic imagery – that the idea lies not to exaggerate the 'object' itself, but to stress what it metaphorically or spiritually represents.

The representation of Geraldine as a mother with a child has never been understood or explained satisfactorily. In religious poetry, the phenomenon of gender reversal is used by Crashaw among others as a means of "achieving the desired mystical union" (Cunnar 119). It is a kind of interplay between male and female characteristics.[49] Geraldine's two aspects as a lover and a mother are distinct but at the same time indivisible and conflated. The word

---

[49] Earlier in this study, evil's capacity of metamorphosing was explained.

"mother" needs not only be a direct reference to the Virgin; it had a broader meaning in a religious context: "My mother and my brethren are these which hear the word of God, and do it" (Luke 8.21). The Christ-as-mother motif was not the exclusive province of female writers, such as Catherine of Siena, Margery Kempe and Juliana of Norwich. It was expressed by males as well, including such well-known medieval authors as Saint Thomas of Aquinas and Saint Bonaventure (Healy 50). We could also argue with Paglia that "Geraldine is the mother of lies. The serpent in the garden is a suave forked tongue, eating and entering the sanctified body of innocence" (344). However, the purpose of this particular kind of gender reversal was to stress Christ's favourable maternal aspects, such as nurturing. One extreme example of this is a Crashaw epigram which reads as follows:

> Suppose he had been Tabled at thy Teates,
>   Thy hunger feeles not what he eates:
> Hee'l have his Teat e're long (a bloody one)
>   The Mother then must suck the Son.
> (*Steps to the Temple*)

Whatever our reaction when reading this epigram, which refers to Luke 11. 27, it clearly draws attention to the eucharistic quality of the nourishment offered by Christ. The idea of Christ as food is also present in the metaphorical picture of Christ as grapes or wine, or of Christ as being "pressed" for mankind in Isaiah 63.3 – a text which Herbert uses as a point of departure in "The Agony":

> Who knows not Love, let him assay
> And taste that juice, which on the crosse a pike
> Did set again abroach; then let him say
>   If ever he did taste the like.
> Love is that liquour sweet and most divine,
> Which my God feels as blood; but I, as wine.
> (13–18)

The relation between a mother figure and nourishment can also be found in Song, where the mother is "a prominent figure, with whom both lovers identify" (Landry 313). As Landry also points out, "mother love is the archetype of love and in Songs the lovers reenact this primordial relationship"(313). In Song the lover imagines himself as an infant at the breast, and in 8.1 the Beloved imagines him as a fellow suckling ("O that thou wert as my brother, that sucked the breasts of my mother!").

Moreover, in religious literature the Virgin Mary is often depicted as the healthful womb. Womb and bosom are – as was pointed out above – associated with fertility, but if we read Geraldine's "bosom and half her side" as a demonic counterpart of Mary's womb, we have the image of sterility and perversion, characteristics appertaining to a demonic character. Geraldine 'as mother' would then be a demonic counterpart of Mary, a kind of Whore of Babylon.

Evil's sexual relations are conventionally depicted as incestuous and perverse as well as sterile; this is often shown in metaphors of unnatural sexuality, mingled with images of vacuity (Fowler 169). This kind of sexual activity was also metaphorically understood as a corruption of the Church or of secular authorities.

There are two central episodes in Christian history, apart from the Incarnation, one being the Crucifixion and the other the encounter with the Resurrected Christ, particularly highlighted in the Eucharist during the Easter Vigil. Christ has risen, death is defeated. These moments are hinted at in the line "A star hath set, a star hath risen"(302), which is an allusion to the belief – already referred to above – that Christ died as an evening star but was resurrected as a morning star.[50] But the line could also be regarded as a demonic counterpart of such a belief, since Satan's fall from Heaven was represented as an evening star, while looked upon as the morning star, Lucifer, he mimics the brightness of Christ. Fowler explains that there was "a long-established symbolism whereby the morning star represented both Satan and Christ" (301). A seeming planetary disorder is also suggested in the eclipse of the sun during the Crucifixion of Christ (Matt. 27.45, Mark 15.33, Luke 23.44–45). Crashaw calls it the "elaborate love-eclipse" in "Hymn in the Glorious Epiphanie"("In the Glorious EPIPHANIE of ovr Lord God, A Hymn, Svng as by the Three Kings", *Sacred Poems*, 153). Since we are dealing with a Fallen World and with demonic counterparts of non-perverted metaphors, the fol-

---

[50] Rosamund Tuve has commented on this tradition in the following manner: " The emphasis upon Christ as the morning Star, the Sun, the light occurring uncountable times in hymns, is too frequent in the liturgy of the Passion season for me to notice its occurrences. I will mention only the long Holy Saturday apostrophes to Christ as 'That morning Star' " (1952, 66).

lowing lines make reference not only to the Crucifixion but also to the Fall of Lucifer, and as such, they could be interpreted as a kind of demonic counterpart of the Crucifixion:

> A star hath set, a star hath risen,
> O Geraldine! since arms of thine
> Have been the lovely lady's prison.
> O Geraldine! One hour was thine -
> Thou'st had thy will! By tairn and rill,
> The night-birds all that hour were still.
> But now they are jubilant anew,
> From cliff and tower, tu – whoo! tu – whoo!
> Tu – whoo! tu – whoo! from wood and fell!
> (302–10)

Nature is often described as holding its breath during the Fall, being still like the night-birds in *CH*. The description of these birds as jubilant carries heavily ironic connotations. If we consider the context, we cannot avoid catching the sinister tone of their song : "tu – whoo! tu- whoo!"

As was stated above, the Easter Vigil commemorates Christ's resurrection, his victory over death and sin. Its termination is often celebrated in churches with bell ringing and with music of joy, the *Gloria in excelsis* and organ fanfares. George Herbert's poem "Easter", for example, expresses the great surge of joy in the Gospels of Easter after the long darkness of Holy Week: "Awake, lute, and struggle for thy part / With all thy art (...) Consort both heart and lute, and twist a song / Pleasant and long" (7–8, 13–14). The demonic counterpart of this joy operates in *CH*. We are back in a world of death, reminded of it by the order of the Baron: "Each matin bell, the Baron saith, / Knells us back to a world of death" (332–33). The celebration of death is added to by the mocking tone of the devil's "merry peal" which rings loudly in the silent morning, making Geraldine shake off her dread and rise lightly from the bed. The bells in *CH* are death-bells, which ring in a joyless atmosphere. Leoline, the father figure, misunderstands the situation completely; he chooses evil and betrays good. Therefore, the music and joy of the Easter morning are sounded here in the honour of evil. Sir Leoline orders the bard:

Go thou, with music sweet and loud,
And take two steeds with trappings proud,
And take the youth whom thou lov'st best
To bear thy harp, and learn thy song,
And clothe you both in solemn vest[.]
(485–89)

These lines understood and interpreted in their contextual circumstances are an invitation to take part in a procession and a celebration of death and evil rather than of joy. Christabel is betrayed by her father who turns "from his own sweet maid". Hence death and evil prevail in the poem. The Fallen World is unredeemed.

The Speaker

Finally, an attempt to comprehend *CH* calls for the function of the speaker in the poem to be examined – an aspect which has been overlooked so far.[51] The narrative situation could be defined in accordance with the speaker's relationship both to the narrative and to an audience. The speaker is personally involved; it is in the same mood and voice that he both sees and speaks. He acts like a mediator or a kind of witness on the scene.

A speaker acting as a witness with a direct address to an audience is a characteristic of classical rhetoric, a feature which was also common among seventeenth-century religious poets, notably Richard Crashaw and George Herbert.[52] The function of such a device is to direct attention in a particular direction. It is a fiction to imagine that the speaker and the audience are "in it together". Crashaw uses frequent questions, exclamations, and commands which "enhance the dramatic colloquies that the poet has with God, his soul, the saints, and others", as Lorraine Roberts points out (69). The purpose of these designs is, as she demonstrates, to "affect the emotions not only of the persona but also of the reader, who is brought close to an event from the past through the dramatic witness and mediator, a person like himself" (71).

---

[51] I have only been able to find an article from 1964, by Lawrence D. Berkhoben, who realizes that "[l]ike a stage director, the narrator calls the reader's attention only to particulars of setting which contribute to a mood of mystery and strangeness" (401).

[52] For my discussion of this aspect I am indebted to Bernt Olsson's chapter on rhetoric in *Spegels Guds Werk och Hwila*, pp. 332–92.

Donne's and Herbert's speakers differ in style from Crashaw's, but confidence in God's love is still inherent and present in their poetry. What makes *CH* such a disquieting poem is partly that this confidence is wanting, partly the speaker's ultimate inability to believe in an ordered and good world. The only character who retains a measure of confidence, in spite of being assaulted by evil, is Christabel herself. However, there might – as Paglia suggests – even be an irony in the lines "But this she knows, in joys and woes, / That saints will aid if men will call: / For the blue sky bends over all!" (329–31).

The speaker in Christabel resembles Crashaw's persona who is "similar to that of a witness, inside or outside, of a Counter-Reformation baroque painting" (Lorraine Roberts, 71). These painters used techniques which were aimed at involving the viewer emotionally in the motif of the painting, to "break down the barrier between the work of art and the real world" (72), thus presenting the subject as coexisting in time and space with the observer. In doing so, the artist invited the spectator of his painting, in the same way as the speaker of a poem his audience, to take in and to come closer to an event from another place and time. Another technique employed in order to involve the audience was to incorporate a witness from the painter's own time into the historical period that was being depicted. The purpose of such a juxtaposition was also to make biblical or supernatural stories more comprehensible to contemporaries, or to emphasize "the human aspects of such subjects as Christ's birth and death and Mary's role as a mother" (Roberts 74). Thus the painter uses his artistic technique to dramatize, to draw attention to certain aspects of his work, to move, and to unite past and present, in the same manner as the poet with his pen, by placing a speaker-witness on the scene or as a mediator on the event. Thereby he hopes to achieve, to borrow Roberts's phrase, "the immediacy of the present" for something which happened long ago. This technique is in fact typological in nature.

Three chief rhetorical figures are used in *CH*: exclamation, the rhetorical question and aposiopesis. This last device could go some way towards explaining the end of the poem. As we shall see, the speaker's exclamations and questions point to key scenes in the drama of *CH*.

By employing rhetorical figures, also used by seventeenth-century religious poets, Coleridge actually establishes some kind of hermeneutic dialogism, or what was referred to in the general introduction of this work as the establishing of "a kind of historical community."

Exclamation and the Rhetorical Question

While the exclamation cannot always be separated from the rhetorical question, one of the purposes of both is to create pathos and compassion. In *CH* they are used at climactic points in the narration. It should thus be noted in what circumstances they occur. Coleridge uses a variation of the rhetorical question, in such a way that the speaker replies to his own question. One example of this occurs in the lines: "Is the night chilly and dark? / The night is chilly, but not dark"(14–15). The chilliness is insisted upon, as well as the lack of wind:

> Is it the wind that moaneth bleak?
> There is not wind enough in the air
> To move away the ringlet curl
> From the lovely lady's cheek-
> There is not wind enough to twirl
> The one red leaf, the last of its clan[.]
> (44–49)

However, as the drama proceeds, the speaker himself does not provide satisfactory answers and explanations when making this kind of question. His inability to give straight answers to his own questions can be perceived in lines 149–53, where he is ostensibly unable to explain the behaviour of the mastiff bitch: "*Perhaps* it is the owlet's scritch: / For what can ail the mastiff bitch?" (152–53) (my italics). The speaker, in fact, becomes more and more unsure in answering or explaining his own rhetorical questions. Geraldine's reaction at the encounter with the spirit of Christabel's dead mother is commented on by the bewildered narrator in the following manner:

> Alas! what ails poor Geraldine?
> Why stares she with unsettled eye?
> Can she the bodiless dead espy?
> And why with hollow voice cries she,
> 'Off, woman, off! this hour is mine-
> Though thou her guardian spirit be,
> Off woman, off! 'tis given to me.'
> (207–13)

Rhetorical questions like these, which indicate the helplessness of the speaker, are a device intended to stir emotion and augment tension in the audience.

The speaker signals a kind of unconscious awareness of danger before the discovery of Geraldine behind the broad oak tree, an anxiety hinted at in his exclamation: "Jesu, Maria, shield her well!"(53–54). However, he is not quite certain of how to react to Geraldine at first: "I *guess,* 'twas frightful there to see / A lady as richly clad as she – / beautiful exceedingly!" (66–68) (my italics). The speaker does not make the proper response to tragedy until lines 252–54, where he influences the audience in a certain direction by calling out: "Behold! her bosom and half her side / A sight to dream of, not to tell! / O shield her! shield sweet Christabel!" The speaker is aware of evil at work, he is deeply moved and wants to convey his emotion to the audience; and with his exclamation of wonder and pain, he focuses attention on the dire drama.

At the sight of Geraldine's bosom, the speaker's naiveté is lost, and all his emotion is concentrated on what follows, that is Geraldine (literally) sleeping with Christabel: "And lay down by the Maiden's side! – And in her arms the maid she took, / Ah wel-a-day!" (262–64)

It is important to note that the speaker reacts very emotionally, with exclamations of sorrow, to key scenes in the poem. The first one is the sight of Geraldine's bosom, as was mentioned above; a second passage can be found in lines 292–01, which clearly tell us about the involvement of the speaker ("ah woe is me!"). At the sight of Christabel and Geraldine asleep, when Geraldine "[s]eems to slumber still and mild / As a mother with her child", (300–01) the speaker expresses sorrow. He is unable to explain exactly what he sees: "O sorrow and shame! Can this be she, / The Lady, who knelt at the old oak tree?"(296–97) The speaker's inability to explain his experience accentuates the importance of his observation.

There is, furthermore, the conclusion to Part I, which includes the speaker's own feelings of sorrow ("Ah woe is me!") as well as the exclamation "O sorrow and shame!" This is, again, a device for drawing attention to the fact that something is wrong. The speaker is not innocent any more. A similar expression of sorrow, indignation and pain occurs in lines 452–456, when "[t]he vision of fear, the touch and pain!" falls "[u]pon the soul of Christabel (Ah, woe is me! Was it for thee, / Thou gentle maid! such sights to see?") Here the exclamation of sorrow, indignation, and pain is followed by the rhetorical question which expresses the speaker's own helplessness, with an emotional understatement echoing the lines in the Conclusion to Part I ("O sorrow and shame should this be true!"). The speaker seems unable to accept or even fully grasp the injustice of the situation.

Moreover, the speaker intercedes for Christabel when Geraldine looks askance at her, at which point Christabel stumbles in a dizzy trance and passively imitates "That look of dull and treacherous hate!" (605–06). The speaker is now well aware of evil at work and tries to intervene, and again he draws attention to the appalling situation, in the cluster of rhetorical questions and exclamations in lines 621–35. A cluster of this kind can be used to accentuate the importance of a situation. It is almost as if the speaker is overcome with frustration: these features in lines 621–35 are connected with lines 636–41:

> Within the Baron's heart and brain
> If thoughts, like these, had any share,
> They only swelled his rage and pain,
> And did but work confusion there.
> His heart was cleft with pain and rage,
> His cheeks they quivered, his eyes were wild[.]

The father figure certainly reacts with confusion, which could be the result of a bad conscience at work once he has been reminded of a rupture with a friend in his youth. The speaker is almost defeated. In the conclusion to Part II, as some kind of summarizing of his dismay, he finally exclaims: "And what, if in a world of sin / (O sorrow and shame should this be true!)"

There are three times when the helpless speaker passionately exclaims: "Jesu, Maria, shield her well!" (alternatively "shield her! shield sweet Christabel!" (254)). The first occasion is shortly before Christabel is about to discover Geraldine; the second instance is at the sight of her bosom and half her side; and the third time is when Geraldine looks at Christabel with a serpent's eye. These occasions all involve sight/eye imagery. All these incidents are critical moments for Christabel. The sight/eye images might be understood as implying that the mere sight of evil is enough for contagion and corruption. Thus, from being an innocent witness, the speaker of the drama becomes more and more involved. In the end, that is in the Conclusion to Part II, he finally falls into despair, being forced to acknowledge his lost innocence. The following apparently paradoxically statements seem to suggest such a loss: "love's excess" "must needs express" its thoughts and feelings "with words of unmeant bitterness". He realizes that an alienated person who "in a world of sin", that is in a Fallen World, can be so separated from his emotional life that he cannot deal with it, is still less able to express proper feelings of love.

Aposiopesis

Two passages in *CH* are particularly problematic, and both are highly emotional. One is the "non-description" of Geraldine's "bosom and half her side", which is followed by the line, "A sight to dream of, not to tell!" The other is in fact the very ending of the poem, that is the Conclusion to Part II, which has for two hundred years left readers to ponder the end of the story, thus accepting the poem as unfinished. A great many guesses or suggestions have been presented, and Coleridge's own discussions around the poem have been examined. What is generally agreed upon is his inability to give the poem an ending or a conclusion which would satisfy the reader. There is still such a thing as a literary convention which arouses expectations in the reader regarding what is acceptable as an ending for a literary work. But could not this "non-ending" in fact be the clue to the poem's "real" ending? Oblique access to a subject can also be due to some obscurity which, as Lowth pointed out,

> is not entirely (...) without its uses: it whets the understanding, excites an appetite for knowledge, keeps alive the attention, and exercises the genius by the labour of the investigation. The human mind, moreover, is ambitious of having a share in the discovery of truth. (268)

The ambition to discover the "truth" of *CH* has certainly invited many interpretations. Following the definitions of classical rhetoric, the figura called aposiopesis could briefly be described as "becoming silent". It is considered to be "a rhetorical figura in which speech is broken off abruptly, often with a sentence unfinished" (Cuddon 55). Generally speaking, there are two kinds of situations when this device is used. One is aimed at creating pathos. It can also be used to express the poet's feeling of inability to continue his story, and at the same time a fear that he might interpret a deep secret incorrectly; that is, in respecting the subject's dignity as well as the feelings of the audience, he uses aposiopesis. By drawing on an extended comprehension of aposiopesis, a possible ending of the poem could be conceived. The poem reaches its zenith in the bedroom stanzas, and when this climax has been reached aposiopesis is consciously resorted to in order to let the audience's imagination go on (often in a story where the end is already known or could be guessed at): where the poet stops, that is, the audience starts. A typical example of aposiopesis is the line where the speaker makes us aware of Geraldine's bosom and half her side. His comment "A sight to dream of, not to tell!" (253) implies that evil's obscenity goes beyond the understanding of both the poet and the audience, both in its heinousness and its offensiveness. Hence it can only be hinted at, not explained. This could be compared to Milton's device of depicting evil (death) as an entity "that shape had none". Evil in itself lacks wholeness: it is shapeless, yet limitless; it lacks core, a characteristic often described in images of vacuity. The description of it can only be pursued in metaphorical terms, which are paradoxical in themselves. The idea of an extended aposiopesis could then be applied to conclusion to Part II, where the speaker has reached the limits of his comprehension of evil and fears to venture further.

Concluding Remarks

The preceding discussion of *CH* has used *PL* as an intertext in order to illustrate and give greater depth to the Fallen World motif, particularly as it involves the characterization and understanding of evil.

Appreciating cross-references and/or juxtapositions from Scripture requires a sense of the typological unity of the Bible. A typological-metaphorical approach to the poem enhances a reader's awareness of the paradoxes inherent in the mainly religiously inspired metaphors in the poem, imagery which was also used by seventeenth-century poets. The liturgical elements in the poem draw attention to its ritualistic overtones; however, by their demonic reversal they show that the drama of *CH* takes place in a Fallen World where evil, sin and death prevail. There is no redemption or love. It could also be argued that Coleridge uses the whole of Christian tradition, its themes and imagery, as a contrivance in order to stress the human experience or situation in the world generally as an exploration of man's ontological status. It is a dark vision of the human predicament, presenting man's denial of and resignation to evil: "And what if, in a world of sin / (O sorrow and shame should this be true!)"

A typological reading of this poem represents evil, embodied in the character of Geraldine, as the demonic counterpart of the heavenly Bridegroom who rapes the Bride, the Christian soul, which metaphorically also represents the congregation, the Church, and all Christians. The heavenly love-knight is turned into the satanic counterpart, corrupting and violating the Bride.

As was discussed at the beginning of this chapter, authors have traditionally made use of typology in the sense that they have concealed their own time behind historical/mythical events and characters in order to avoid censorship and repression by authorities. Drawing out the potentials and consequences of a typological interpretation, *CH* could consequently be a description of the historical present of Coleridge's own time. The repression by authorities, both secular and spiritual, as well as the general decay of the church of Coleridge's own time were referred to at an earlier point in this study. Together with disillusionment at the outcome of the French Revolution and the apparent betrayal of its ideas and ideals, this led Coleridge, particularly in *Religious Musings* and *The Destiny of Nations*, to denounce the corruption and the abuses of authorities as well as the social and economic system of his own day. Events from the poet's own time are not difficult to trace in these poems. The political and social injustices of the "fallen" contemporary world are displayed as possessing apocalyptic properties. Society's fallen condition is depicted as a state of dryness without vernal sap, disbranched from the tree of knowledge (*Religious Musings* 264–66). In the same poem Coleridge denounces the "Fiends of Superstition", castigating "The erring Priest" who "hath stained with brother's blood [the] grisly idols"(135–37). The doings of these "erring Priests" do not only stand as a reference to heathen or barbarian worship of images; they also form a general representation of both religious and profane idolatry. He attacks the war on the continent, referred to in the poem as the "plain that steameth to the sun / Peopled with Death" (*Religious Musings* 139–40), clarified in a footnote as "the plains of Flanders". Moreover, the actuality of the slave trade is condemned in the following manner in the poem: "where more hideous Trade / Loud-laughing packs his bales of human anguish"(140–41), stated in a footnote "on the coasts of Africa". Contemporary political events alluded to in the poem are often further commented on in a footnote. Coleridge is mainly concerned with the abuses of various authorities, for which he employs such designations as "the thirsty brood of War"(170) and the "Moloch Priest"(185). The passage describing the "Evil Ones' " psychological characteristics in *Religious Musings* depicts traits typical of the personalities of the fallen angels in *PL*, as the following lines suggest: "listening Treachery lurks / With pious fraud to snare a brother's life" (164–65) and "O blasphemy! to mingle fiendish deeds / With blessedness!" (191–92). In these two poems Coleridge takes into account the actuality of the Fallen World and all its evils, such as war, murder, death, superstition and abuse of authority. He presents corruption as not only real, but metaphysical and moral.

The mystical and demoniac components of *CH* have been pointed out by critics, who have emphasized the way in which it constitutes a break with Coleridge's earlier poetry. One might, however, question whether there is actually such an abrupt rupture with those radical ideas, and that deep social and moral concern with contemporary politics, that were displayed in earlier poems. *CH* depicts an abstract fallen world. When typologically interpreted, the poem takes on an added significance beyond the mystical and demoniac. An actual, contemporary fallen world emerges, and a denouncement of the abuses of authorities, both religious and secular ones, then comes to the surface. Like other poems mentioned here, *CH* is apocalyptic. The corruption of the Church was often associated with the coming of Antichrist and with the end of the world. Such a conjunction symbolizes betrayal of or disappointment in an ideal. In this case it is natural to think of the aftermath of the French Revolution. At the time when *CH* was written, it had led to terror, followed by the cynical corruption of the Directory in France, as well as to repression and abuse of authority in England. *CH* could then be seen as embodying a political position and a protest, and as such it would not offer any "proper" solution or ending.

Kubla Khan

Perhaps, Kublai thought, the empire is nothing but a zodiac of the mind's phantoms.

"On the day when I know all the emblems," he asked Marco, "shall I be able to

possess my empire, at last?"

And the Venetian answered: "Sire, do not believe it. On that day you will be an emblem among emblems".

Calvino (22, 23)

Up to now the grim view of the Fall has been expounded. Penance for life features in *The Ancient Mariner.* The chapter on that poem studied inner hell with its despair, where a vexed conscience makes hell a condition rather than a place. In *Christabel,* evil and corruption are victorious in a Fallen World. A typological reading of that poem also suggests the abuses and moral decay of contemporary authorities, along with the motif of the betrayal of an ideal. In both poems the Fallen World is left unredeemed. These two poems stand as embodiments of the harsh realities of a Fallen World, as they are considered both on a literal and a moral level.

As was mentioned in the general introduction, the idea of a Fortunate Fall is as old as the traditional grim view of the Fall. Generally speaking, the idea of a Fall in itself presupposes a standard from which one has been separated downwards. The conventional idea of a Fall lies on an ontological as well as on an epistemological level. After the Fall man was separated from unity and perfection, and his perception, understanding and knowledge became fragmentary. But man's awareness of a loss of unity makes him yearn for and dream of prelapsarian perfection. In this search for the impossible, fallen man will always move along the edge of creation/chaos. Hence fallen man's perception, understanding and creativity must be contingent on subjectivity and on cultural relativism. In a Fallen World, where both reconciliation and redemption seem uncertain, and where the core does not hold either in subject or object, it would be tempting for fallen man to lapse into solipsism. But fallen man builds, creates, writes. In doing all this, he uses the materials of what is already given, and out of fragments and pieces he strives to grasp unity and coherence. This is the essence of the Fortunate Fall: in spite of, or thanks to, the Fall, man creates. In this resides man's greatness; made out of his own fragility and out of fragments, his creations, while never perfect, can be splendid in part. In his creativity, he can thus occasionally attain a prelapsarian standard. The Fortunate Fall with its yearning for a prelapsarian state is apparent in all the Romantics. In his longing for prelapsarian unity, however, fallen man might resort to fundamentalism as a means of relieving him from anxiety, longing and moral responsibility. This would in the end lead him to a demonic (or perverted) prelapsarian status where the dialogue, the questioning, the creative powers will cease, or in one word: stagnation.

In this study, the Preface to *Kubla Khan* (from now on *KK*) is regarded as an integral part of the poem. It is possible to argue that the mode of presenting the poem with a preface, the statement that it is "A Vision in a Dream", "A Fragment", could – together with the shifting narrative levels – be a consciously worked-out irony which teases the reader into various directions. The poem's peculiar enchantment would in part explain how it has acted on readers' preconceptions, conditioning the ensuing understanding of it and making contact with the mythical subconscious which forms part of our Western cultural heritage. This statement calls for some explanation: I regard *KK* as a poem about the poem, which implies that it is not allusive to anything but itself. Its exclusiveness and self-referential quality are also manifested in the use of words which appear curiously conventional in a conception of the 'poetic', such as 'river', 'garden,' 'hill', 'tree', 'forest', 'fountain', 'rock', and 'sea', as well as in the different place-names which seem to have released hidden resources from the depths of its readers' subconscious. We are apt to fail to maintain a distance from the poem, which is a necessary strategy in the interpretative act according to Ricoeur, as discussed previously in the chapter on *AM*. However, even the strategy of interpretation is coloured by the reader's own situation, as was pointed out above with reference to *AM*. The poem also works on readers through its use of words not found in earlier literature, particularly in connection with the "pleasure-dome" ("the shadow of the dome of pleasure", "a sunny pleasure-dome with caves of ice"). This dome is, as we shall see, one of the key images of the poem.

KK can furthermore be understood as a Romantic manifesto. In this interpretation of it, the reader will be supported by comments from Coleridge's own writings, which could help us in our understanding not only of the poem itself but also of ideas connected with Romantic literary theory. All poetry consists in the building-up of an illusion. The ensuing interpretation of *KK* raises such epistemological issues as knowledge and reason, mental capabilities which are very fragile in fallen man. The problem of communication will be addressed, as well as the Romantic idea of creativity, the relation between the poet and his work, and the gap between poem and reader. *KK* is regarded as an epitome of the consequences of a Fortunate Fall: it features the interplay of reality and illusion, and it illustrates the redemptive powers of poetry in the struggle between Chaos and creativity.

Coleridge referred to *Christabel* on a great many occasions during his life. He often quoted or referred to his own work in correspondence and notebooks. However, I have not been able to find any reference to or quotation from *KK* except the following one: "I wrote Kubla Khan in Brimstone Farm between Porlock and Ilfracombe – near Culbone" (*Table Talk* 26 September 1830, 205). The history of the poem from its composition, traditionally dated November 1797, to its publication in May 1816 is unknown, except that Coleridge occasionally recited it to a restricted circle of friends and acquaintances. As John S. Hill points out, its history "is almost a complete enigma" (69).[53] Rosemary Ashton, commenting on the "many mysteries" surrounding the poem, writes: "Unusually, no references to it survive in Coleridge's letters; nor do Coleridge's friends and correspondents discuss it in their surviving papers" (111).

Earlier Criticism

While the critical corpus on *Christabel* is not as large as one might have expected in view of its central position in English literature, *KK* has generated a very large amount of criticism, expressing a wide variety of views. As J. S. Hill says, "no poem of comparable length in English or any other language has

[53] John S. Hill's *A Coleridge Companion: an introduction to the major poems and Biographia Literaria* (1983) presents a survey of different approaches to Coleridge's poetry, which makes it a useful book for the Coleridge scholar.

been the subject of so much critical commentary" (61). However, as he writes:

> Despite this deluge [of criticism] (...) there is no critical unanimity and very little agreement on a number of important issues connected with the poem: its date of composition, its 'meaning', its sources in Coleridge's reading and observation of nature, its structural integrity (i.e. fragment *versus* complete poem), and its relationship to the Preface by which Coleridge introduced it on its first publication in 1816. (61)

This "deluge" of commentaries could be seen as a dialogue between different times and persons on the one hand and the poem on the other. Having tried to grasp the enormous amount of criticism on *KK*, I have formed the impression that most critics have been in search of a structure or a tradition on which to build hypotheses. As late as 1990, Graham Davidson writes:

> Some critics have asserted that *Kubla Khan* is a poem of veritable (sic) no meaning; and when a work has been loaded with such a weight and such a variety of meaning, the freighted critic, finding a port in the opinions of such respected men as J.L. Lowes, for whom 'the linked and interweaving images' form a 'pageant as aimless as it is magnificent' (...) or T.S. Eliot who thinks that the imagery is unused, is tempted to unship his cargo. (90)

This state of affairs is not surprising; but the danger is, as Davidson hints, that where strong critics lead, many will follow. There is, in fact, a kind of tradition of critical assessments. Some characteristics of these evaluations of the poem will be briefly outlined.

Contemporaneous readings, as well as Victorian ones, were mainly based on subjective value judgements. The poem was praised, if at all, for its suggestiveness and musicality as well as for the visualness of its imagery. Apart from responses expressing a sense of cultural relativism, there have been, as I see it, five major approaches to the poem in the twentieth century. It has been considered in terms of: 1) its status as a poem about the poetic process; 2) its usefulness as an exemplification of aspects of Coleridge's prose-writing; 3) its relevance to Freudian-psychoanalytical-biographical lines of thought; 4) its relation to biblical imagery and/or the mythological school of the Bible;

5) the ways in which it lends itself to the tracing and discussion of sources, references and allusions; this last approach, fascinating as it is, leads into a jungle of positions.

These different approaches will be touched upon in my interpretation of the poem, and they are seen as dissimilar but not mutually exclusive strategies. Their variety testifies to the richness of the poem. My point of departure is the first of these approaches, which reads the poem as a description of the poetic process, and I will deal with it at some length. It has usually proceeded from the last few lines of the poem, which have been read as an evocation of the inspired poet:

> Beware! Beware!
> His flashing eyes, his floating hair!
> Weave a circle round him thrice,
> And close your eyes with holy dread,
> For he on honey-dew hath fed,
> And drunk the milk of Paradise.
> (49–54)

Interpreters who have read along these lines have usually linked the conclusion of *KK* with the Orphic cults of Ancient Greece, perceiving it as an analogy to Plato's description of the lyric poets who, seized with Bacchic ecstasy, draw milk and honey from the rivers (*Ion* 534 a). As an example of this kind of interpretation, the following quotation from Hill will serve: "Even apparent verbal echoes may easily be paralleled: the Platonic and Coleridgean conjunction of milk and honey, for example, turns up again in familiar analogues in Exodus 3:8 and in Ovid's *Metamorphoses* (I. 111–12)" (92).

However, Exodus 3.8 is not a parallel to the idea of the inspired poet, nor is the Ovidian passage an analogue to *KK*. The metaphor of "milk and honey" is a common one in biblical and religious tradition, where it has nothing to do with the inspired poet but a great deal with paradise lost and regained, traditionally seen as the New Jerusalem or Israel in the Bible, "a land flowing with milk and honey" (Exodus 3.8). A reference to Plato's *Ion* is appropriate, however, since "[i]n the *Ion* the connection is made between the poet and the divine, and the poem is understood as a gift from beyond the poet himself. Literally possessed by the divine, the poet embodies a mystery which must remain within the encircled sanctuary" (Jasper 1985, 45). However, as Hill points out: "Despite the popularity of the view that 'Kubla Khan' is a poem about poetry, (...) there is no consensus about just *what* is being said about the poetic process" (97) (Hills italics). The issue of the poetic process will be addressed in the ensuing discussion.

The Preface

The Crewe manuscript – an autograph manuscript of *KK*, disclosed in 1934 and now in the British Museum – provides a much shorter account of the birth of the poem. There is no reference to the person from Porlock in it. The poem itself differs slightly from the version given in the 1816 edition.[54] This manuscript has led scholars to ask questions such as: How much of the account given in the 1816 Preface should we believe, and what relation does it bear to the poem? It has been argued by some critics (Elisabeth Schneider and Fruman among others) that the Preface served as a shield against criticism, and "[o]ne school of thought maintains that it is untrustworthy and should be dismissed as a fabrication intended only to apologize for the publication of a fragment" (Hill 82). Schneider argues that

> As a whole (...) the preface of 1816 sounds a good deal like the self–justifying memory of Coleridge on other occasions – [and in this particular case] a marvellous origin and the man from Porlock could bear the blame and serve as a natural shield against criticism, while Lord Byron's admiration and the description of the fragment as a 'psychological curiosity' might justify its publication. (qtd. in Hill 82)

Fruman, who fails to grasp the Romantic idea of the poet in relation to his work and audience, dismisses the Preface as a "*claim made for Kubla Khan* [which] *was but one of a long series made by Coleridge concerning spontaneous composition*" (71, 335) (Fruman's italics)[55]. As late as 1996, Ashton considers the subtitles and Preface to the poem in the following manner: "As a protec-

---

[54] Fruman is of the opinion that "the Crewe manuscript should have thrown a bombshell into Coleridge studies" (71, 337).

[55] Fruman resentfully avers that "Coleridge was 'romancing' when he said that 'the words here preserved' [1816 Preface] were the words he had written in the farmhouse 'without any sensation or consciousness of effort', since many changes were made *after* he wrote the document now known as the Crewe MS. And may not this text be a reworked draft of many early attempts?" (343) (Fruman's italics).

tion against the scorn of critics, he subtitled 'Kubla Khan' 'A Fragment'–
which, unlike 'Christabel', it may not have been – and appended to it a self-
justificatory and self-deprecating preface" (112). These two statements are
mere conjectures, of course; but as Hill points out, "With the exception of
[Walter Jackson] Bate (...) all the critics who read the Preface as an elaborate
fiction also assume that 'Kubla Khan' is not a finished piece but a fragment of
a longer work" (82).

As Kathleen Wheeler maintains, "[i]n few of the well-known studies of
'Kubla Khan' is the preface discussed as of literary significance, nor is its aesthetic relation to the poem considered" (168). Wheeler's study of the Preface
to *KK* is a valuable contribution to an understanding of its relation to the
poem. In her "Concluding Remarks" to *KK*, she makes a particularly significant statement. It is hence quoted at some length:

> Thus, just as the apparent irreverence of the speakers in lines 49-54 is
> changed to worship, so the criticisms and belittling comments of the
> preface are changed into descriptions of what art should be. The perso-
> na is dropped when we read the preface as written by Coleridge the
> genius, who had confidence in his poetry and had the ability to devise
> every conceivable mode of helping the reader to see its richness, in-
> cluding the risk of making himself a 'laughing-stock' in order to make
> available to the reader the tool of irony and indirectness if metaphor
> and symbol proved too difficult in the first stages. To sacrifice his right
> of authorship to the muse and the poem's claim to meaning by origi-
> nating it in a dream, in order that the reader may be stimulated to a
> kind of authorship by interpreting the dream, is a gesture of incalcula-
> ble generosity. (38)

With regard to the function of the Preface, Wheeler argues that it serves "as a
link between the reader and the poem" (40). However, as she admits, this also
implies that "as such its relation to the verse is as problematic as is the relation
of art to reality or of spectator to art" (40). She concludes that

> since [the Preface] engages the reader aesthetically and not discursively,
> it is proper to consider it as an integral part of the text, not merely as an
> external prose commentary, though of course it seems to be only that
> to the unimaginative, reductive reader parodied in the persona. (40)

In this connection, one is reminded of one of Coleridge's favourite maxims: "Until you understand a writer's ignorance, presume yourself ignorant of his understanding" (*Biographia Literaria* I, 12, 232).

Another group of critics who consider *KK* as, on the whole, a poem about poetry and the poetic process maintain that the Preface, whether or not its statements are actually true, could be seen as a kind of prose counterpart to the poem. Unfortunately, though, this idea was never developed. E. S. Shaffer regards matters from another angle:

> The claim Coleridge made in his Preface to 'Kubla' to a form of spontaneous composition is not an excuse for a fragment, but a presentation of his credentials for writing apocalyptic, for assuming the prophetic role. In however small a degree, he could claim to have shared the experience of the great prophets, of Ezekiel, and of the great apocalyptic, John. These experiences were in one form or another so persistent with Coleridge, and figure so largely in his theory of the imagination, that his account of the writing of 'Kubla' should not be dismissed as a figment. ... The Prefatory 'Vision in a Dream' becomes a kind of authentication of the poet's right to present the prophetic lays of a 'John'. (89, 90)

This is one feasible way of considering the Preface, but the possibility still exists that the wrong questions are being asked by those who challenge it. Explanations of a text in words and phrases which bear some semantic resemblance to, or evoke connotations of, concepts such as 'meaning' and 'intention' are not popular in literary criticism. Even so, I would venture to quote a passage from Coleridge with reference to these conceptions: "The first question we should put to ourselves, when we have to read a passage that perplexes us in a work of authority, is; What does the Writer *mean* by all this? And the second question should be, What does he intend by all this" (*Aids to Reflection* 266) (Coleridge's italics). The serious issue here, I believe, is to ask questions in a spirit of open-mindedness and even humility, such as: What difference does it make whether the Preface is factual or not ? Why did Coleridge write such an elaborate Preface in the first place? Why did he stress the fragmentariness of his vision; why is it presented as a vision in a dream? What relation does the Preface bear to the poem, if any at all? These questions are more relevant than speculations as to whether the circumstances described in the

Preface actually happened as stated, or whether it was in any sense fabricated as an apology to avert possible criticism. The answers to such questions will always lead to guesses only. The final Preface and poetic text in the 1816 edition differ in some ways from the Crewe manuscript, and there is nothing strange at all about altering a manuscript. These changes, and additions to them, show us that Coleridge went to some trouble over them, which could imply that he considered them important.

The fragment

As was stated earlier, one of the main consequences of the Fall – a consequence also expounded in *PL* – was the transition from unity to division. This implied that man's perception of the universe turned fragmentary, too. This fragmentariness or lack of wholeness affected other human activities and accomplishments as well, such as knowledge, language, human will and reason. The fragmentariness can also be understood as fallen man's experience of the division between his external and internal perspectives or frames of reference:"[f]or the fallen Adam the world appears hopelessly fragmented, and the fragmentation in the structure of Book 10 arrays this new reality as well as Adam's fallen psyche" (Swaim 56).

The words 'fragmentation', 'fragment' and 'fragmentariness' can be found in Milton criticism as well. We are very quick in our judgement sometimes, above all when there is something which does not fit in with our preconceptions of how things 'should' be. Milton has been accused of writing 'fragmentarily', and particularly the last Books of *PL* (11 and 12) have been labelled as " 'careless', 'fragmented', 'curiously bad' (C.S. Lewis); 'deterioration in the quality of writing' (Louis Martz); an 'integument of half-formed and jumbled images' (John Peter)" (qtd. in Swaim 192). The above quotations imply a lack of recognition of Milton's style. It is inseparable from the action of the epic's theme, that is,

> [d]escription is realistic rather than transcendent; the world addressed is fractionated rather than unified ... The small separate poetic events occur as fragments around the core of the historical sequence with its supporting categories of decay, pride, and mechanics. (Swaim 195)

Swaim brings up an explanatory example which pictures this lack of wholeness in the Fallen World: Milton calls God "Presence divine"(VIII. 314) before the Fall, but in the postlapsarian garden there is only a "track divine" (XI. 354) (160). It is thus understood that what we perceive are the fragments of an original whole.

The first thing we notice on turning to *KK* is that the Preface announces that the poem is a fragment. The fragmentary as a piece of art is almost a Romantic subgenre. McFarland comments on the Romantic fragmentariness in the following way: "In addition to (...) fragmentariness within nominal wholes, Romanticism is especially fecund in explicit fragmentation and incompleteness"(1981, 23). In the same book, he also considers Shelley's fragmentariness. Shelley himself summarizes the Romantic position on the fragment in his commentary, as follows: "A single sentence may be considered as a whole though it be found in a series of unassimilated portions; a single word even may be a spark of inextinguishable thought" (485–86). Man's fragmentary perception receives special emphasis in Romantic attitudes; it is thus not in any way peculiar to Coleridge, nor has it anything to do with apologizing for unfinished work. In a Fallen World, the fragment is the norm. Shelley's pointing out that "a single word even may be a spark of inextinguishable thought" indicates that the fragment may afford a glimpse of the wholeness beyond/behind.

There is certainly an interesting parallel between fallen man's failure to perceive and have knowledge of the world as it really is, that is in its wholeness, and post-Kantian epistemology which implies that our perceptions of the real thing are illusory, though we are driven by what we call 'reason' to attempt the unachievable. The idea of fragmentariness becomes more complicated if we stop to consider that even the world itself, in its postlapsarian state, is fragmentary. The aim of fallen man's endeavour is unattainable. This, I believe, can be seen as part of the Romantic yearning, expressed in the fragment. Coleridge illustrates this very well in a poem called *Reason,* quoted in its entirety below. (It was published in 1830, but its date of composition is uncertain):

['Finally, what is Reason? You have often asked me: and this is my answer':-]

WHENE'ER the mist, that stands 'twixt God and thee,
Defecates to a pure transparency,

That intercepts no light and adds no stain -
There Reason is, and then begins her reign!

But alas!
—'tu stesso, ti fai grosso
Col falso immaginar, si che non vedi
Cio che vedresti, se l'avessi scosso.'
Dante, *Paradiso,* Canto i.[56]

In this poem reason is explained in metaphorical terms, and to make his point
Coleridge uses Dante, whose lines are very appropriate here since they also
deal with adherence to the idea of fallen man's condition. Thus, we are all
blinded, "[dulled]", by our "false imagination". It would only be possible to
know, to "see" wholly and truly, if we could leave behind what "[dulls]" our
"wit". This means that our visions depend on the perception of the viewer;
that is, we operate within the constricted framework of our own context, and
the wholeness of the thing perceived is never attainable, even when we resort
to "reason". In the Fallen World our ability to see and perceive and to make a
whole of our perceptions is dimmed and shadow-like, because of our imper-
fectibility as fallen men. As Lewalski points out, "[f]or the Protestant, the Fall
meant the depravity of all his natural faculties – the blinding of the intellect
and the bondage of the will"(15).

The idea of fallen man's mental blindness, as a consequence of the Fall, is
expressed as "mist" or "film" in *PL*. In the beginning of Book III, Milton
invokes the "holy Light" for his assignment:

> So much the rather thou celestial Light
> Shine inward, and the mind through all her powers
> Irradiate, there plant eyes, all mist from thence
> Purge and disperse, that I may see and tell
> Of things invisible to mortal sight.
> (III. 51–55)

and

> (...) but to nobler sights

---

[56] " 'Thou dullest thine own wit / With false imagination, nor perceivest / That which thou wouldst
perceive, being rid of it' ". (*Paradiso* I, 88–90) (Dorothy Sayers's translation 55).

Michael from Adam's eyes the film removed
Which that false fruit that promised clearer sight
Had bred; then purged with euphrasy and rue
The visual nerve, for he had much to see[.]
(XI. 411–15)

Awareness of the dichotomous relationship, or postlapsarian division, between the real thing and how it is perceived was a matter often brought up by Coleridge. In *Biographia Literaria* Coleridge discusses different philosophical systems (Descartes, Spinoza, Leibniz) and is of the opinion that "[n]either of these systems on any possible theory of association, supplies or supersedes a theory of perception, or explains the formation of the associable"(I. 8, 129). The problem between the perceived and the perceiver lies, as he points out, both on an ontological and on an epistemological level: "How the *esse* assumed as originally distinct from the *scire*, can ever unite itself with it; how *being* can transform itself into a *knowing*" (132–33). In this same context he criticizes what he calls materialism, stating that "[m]atter has no *Inward*. We remove one surface, but to meet with another (...) in any given perception there is a something which has been communicated to it by an impact or an impression ab extra" (133) (Coleridge's italics).[57]

In this *Biographia Literaria* passage, Coleridge exposes the idea that our perceptions are always dependent on contextual circumstances and on the personality of the perceiver, addressing the divide beween what is perceived and the perceiver. This gap was something which the Romantics were well aware of.

In the same context, the inherent epistemological dichotomy is further illustrated by Coleridge's bringing in a sentence by Schelling: "It would be easy to explain a thought from the image of the retina, and that from the geometry of light, if this very light did not present the very same difficulty."(137)[58] It is clear that the gap is not only between the perception and the perceived, but

---

[57] Note 3 by the editors (James Engell and W. Jackson Bate) in *Biographia Literaria:* "This sentence connects basic questions and terms Coleridge both formulated himself and picked up not only in Schelling but also in Tetens, Maass, Berkeley, Fichte, and Kant. Cf. TT 15 May 1833"(133).

[58] Note 6 by the editors (James Engell and W. Jackson Bate) in *Biographia Literaria:* "Cf Schelling *Ideen* 440 (SW II 307–8) but esp. *Abhandlungen: Phil. Schrift* 254 n (SW I 389n): 'Wir sehen nur dadurch, dass das Licht unsre Augen rührt, u.s.w. – Aber was ist denn das Licht selbst? Wiederum ein Objekt!'"(137–38)

that there is no wholeness in the very "thing" in itself, "das Ding an sich" to use a Kantian expression. That is to say, *the Fallen World* is not only perceived as fragments but *is in itself fragmentary.*

When the impossibility of wholeness and perfection in a fallen world has been acknowledged, the temptation to fall into a kind of solipsism arises, because one may ask what kind of knowledge is possible in such a world. How does reason operate? Milton addressed the problem of knowledge in a fallen world, which he called the "sore burden of mind", in terms of "how and in what manner [we] shall dispense and employ those summes of knowledge and illumination, which God hath sent [us] into this world to trade with" (*The Reason of Church Government* 3.1. 229, qtd. in Swaim 17). As a Puritan, Milton was bound to stress the importance of knowledge. In *Of Education* he wrote:

> The end then of learning is to repair the ruins of our first parents by regaining to know God aright, and out of that knowledge to love him, to imitate him, to be like him, as we may the nearest by possessing our souls of true virtue, which being united to the heavenly grace of faith makes up the highest perfection. (qtd. in Swaim 17)

From this quotation it can be understood that Milton's idea of learning was to reconstruct the fragments from the Fall. He does, however, stress the religious aspects of the consequences of the Fall; that is, he speaks of knowledge of God and heavenly grace, which will according to him lead up to "highest perfection". This sounds optimistic at a first reading, but what emerges in *PL* is that postlapsarian growth and knowledge will proceed, as Swaim notes, "by leaps and lapses in a world that is fragmented and for a psyche that must create its own spiritual coherence amid insistent uncertainties and with sensory and rational equipment that is known to have been faulty in the past" (15). The postlapsarian world is divided and confusing, but it is also a world where man has to make use of his knowledge and reason, make judgements, make decisions and above all use his will.

PL hence adumbrates the idea of fallen man's progressive comprehension of the world through education; but it is also true, as Swaim points out, that "[t]he energies that allow the fallen to bridge the gap between the separate units of experience are on the one hand faith and on the other imagination" (73). This sounds very much like Kierkegaard's "leap of faith", or a belief, though fragile, in God's grace. It is doubtful whether we can find these "bridging" components in Romantic epistemology. (See also the discussion on *The Ancient Mariner* above.)

For Coleridge, even man's reason is conditioned by *ab extra* circumstances "[b]ecause Man is something besides Reason; because his Reason never acts by itself, but must clothe itself in the substance of individual Understanding and specific Inclination, in order to become a reality and an object of consciousness and experience"(*The Friend* Essay IV 201). Even reason is thus conditioned and restricted, also by the fact – as Coleridge points out – that "though *the reason itself* is the same in all men, yet the means of exercising it, and the materials (i.e. the facts and ideas) on which it is exercised, being possessed in very different degrees by different persons, the *practical Result* is, of course, equally different"(*The Friend* I , 159) (Coleridge's italics).

How, then, does Coleridge solve the problem of the fragmentariness of our perceptions as well as the flaws in our reason? How do we attain any kind of knowledge or "truth"? In a chapter with the eloquent title "On the communication of Truth", he writes:

> Observe, how graciously Nature instructs her human children. She cannot give us the knowledge derived from sight without occasioning us at first to mistake images of reflection for substances. But the very consequences of the delusion lead inevitably to its detection; and *out of the ashes of the error rises a new flower of knowledge.* We not only see, but are enabled to discover by what means we see. So too we are under the necessity, in given circumstances, of mistaking a square for a round object: but ere the mistake can have any practical consequences, it is not only removed, but in its removal gives us the *symbol of a new fact –* that of distance. (*The Friend* I Essay VI 47) (my italics)

This means that out of our failure to capture the 'real thing', some notion of knowledge and a new awareness still come into being. This new awareness is then linked to Coleridge's idea of the primary and secondary imagination, of which more later. The Preface of *KK* conveys the idea that the divine pure vision, originally perceived as a wholeness, given and received without any sensation or effort, was interrupted by the *ab extra*, symbolized in the person from Porlock. As Coleridge writes, "he was unfortunately *called out* by a person on business from Porlock, and *detained* by him above an hour"(26–27) (my italics).[59] As a result of the interruption caused by this person, "all the charm [was] broken" (35–36); "with the exception of some eight or ten scattered lines and images, all the rest had passed away"(31–32). But then we read the lines of the little poem in the Preface which tells us that "soon the fragments dim of lovely forms / Come trembling back, unite, and now once more / The pool becomes a mirror"(42–44). The uniform primal vision is thus transformed, transmuted: "Out of the ashes of the error rises a new flower", to paraphrase Coleridge's own phrase.

The process of the creative act is described as a glorious phenomenon. This is stressed by Coleridge himself in the Preface, which informs us that "[a]s a contrast to this vision [*KK*], I have annexed a fragment of a very different character, describing with equal fidelity the dream of pain and disease" (49–51). Coleridge refers to "Pains of Sleep" in the same edition.[60] However, he describes not only the glory of the primary vision in creation, which – as he points out – was "*given* to him"(47) (my italics), but also its fragility when in contact with the real world: the divinely inspired vision received without effort is threatened and partly destroyed by the unfortunate man from Porlock. This interrupter can easily be metaphorized as an agent of a Fall who destroys the God-given immediate vision, the effortless creativity, which exists without any divide between its perception and its coming into being. The unity in vision is destroyed by this visitor, the *ab extra* in the case, who "called out" and "detained" the creator in his unfallen state of divine vision. The Preface can thus in itself be read metaphorically as the story of a Fall. Something along these lines has been suggested by Lucy Newlyn:

---

[59] Kathleen Wheeler suggests that "The phrase 'Person from Porlock' could (…) be a designed alliteration of 'Purchas's Pilgrimage', the one marking the beginning, the other the end of the poem" (23). It seems likely.

[60] As Wheeler remarks:"The existence of the preface persona in 'Kubla Khan' is further suggested by the sudden shift from third to first person in the last paragraph of the preface, and the statement of this persona suggests that he is meant to be taken as an editor: 'As a contrast to this vision, I have annexed a fragment of a very different character describing with equal fidelity the dream of pain and disease'. He refers to 'Pains of Sleep'. This last sentence is also frequently left out of the best modern editions, as for example I.A. Richards' edition for Viking Press, or John Beer's Everyman edition." With this kind of critical inability to let things alone, "[o]ne loses the shift from the third to the first person, and by this omission is lost the equally important comment about the 'Pains of Sleep'- namely that it too is called a fragment, and that it too is supposed to described a dream. This puts a very different meaning on the use of the words 'fragment' and 'dream' in the early sentences of the preface, when the terms are used so broadly. For in what sense can one understand 'Pains of Sleep' as a fragment or as a dream poem?"(21) In *Romanticism: An Anthology*, ed. Duncan Wu, the poem is for some reason presented on pp. 514–15, whereas the Preface figures on pp. 577–78.

Coleridge's investment, in describing 'Kubla Khan' as incomplete, is therefore twofold: he succeeds in expressing nostalgia for the unfallen state, and in pointing toward 'the tomorrow [that] is yet to come,' when language will once again be paradisal. But he also claims the poem itself as a product of true symbolic vision. What the interruption from the Person from Porlock suggests is that, once lost, this vision cannot be restored. Rather than fall back on post-lapsarian language, to complete the poem, Coleridge preserves what he has already written as a 'fragment' of higher truth. (235)

The Romantic idea of the fragility of the mind in creation, and of the relation between the very first vision and the final composition, was very well described by Shelley in a manner which serves to elucidate the present discussion:

A man cannot say it; 'I will compose poetry'. The greatest poet even cannot say it: for the mind in creation is as a fading coal, which some invisible influence, like an inconstant wind, awakens to transitory brightness: this power arises from within, like the colour of a flower which fades and changes as it is developed, and the conscious portions of our natures are unprophetic either of its approach or its departure. Could this influence be durable in its original purity and force, it is impossible to predict the greatness of the results: but when composition begins, inspiration is already on the decline, and the most glorious poetry that has ever been communicated to the world is probably a feeble shadow of the original conception of the poet. (503–04)

By contrast, the wholeness of the prelapsarian vision and inspiration is exhibited in the effortless suddenness of Adam's perception (Gen. 2.19–20). In *PL* Adam explains how "[he] named [the animals], as they passed, and understood / Their nature, with such knowledge God endued / [his] sudden apprehension" (VIII. 352–54). In prelapsarian understanding there was no divide between what was perceived and the perceiver. It was believed "that Adam had an angelic understanding, capable of moving through objects to concepts instantly" (St Thomas Aquinas, *Summa Theol.* I xciv 2–4; qtd. in Fowler 415). This also meant that language was pure; that is, every object corresponded to its name without postlapsarian ambiguities and the arbitrariness of "fallen" language. Language and understanding were considered as God-given, complete and undivided, a state shattered by the Fall. Milton metaphorically explains how Sin and Death will destroy and plunder the new creation: "[man's] thoughts, his looks, words, actions all infect" (X. 608). The worst corruption of language is of course the one conveyed in *PL* by the "dismal universal hiss, the sound / Of public scorn" (X. 508–59), which Satan hears on his return to Pandaemonium. An example of the prelapsarian unity and perfection of language is, as John Leonard demonstrates, Eve's love song to Adam (IV. 639–56) (256–57). The idea of a progressive disruption of language as a medium of communication was also traditionally illustrated in the story of Babel; "[w]ith this biblical event the world becomes divided from the thing it signifies, distorting the equivalence of word and understanding" (Swaim 52). Thus the Fall dissolves and divides the thing and its meaning. Language itself becomes ambiguous.

A postlapsarian word can also be used in a prelapsarian context, as a reminder of the Fall, as this line shows: "With mazy error under pendant shades/Ran nectar"(IV. 239–40), referring to the river in Eden, which is finally divided into four rivers. Fowler considers the word "error" as "one of the most resonant key words in the poem. ... The *pendant* shades are not merely convenient hanging trees but also a *proleptic* suggestion of the horrid shadows that impend" (207).[61]

Though this refers to the Edenic river, the Fall is foreshadowed in postlapsarian words. Whatever river we have in *KK*, the same device is used: the river, though "sacred", runs "with a *mazy* motion". The hint of a Fall is there. Another example of an innuendo is mentioned by John Beer. He explains the "sinuous rills" in the poem thus:

> As Coleridge writes of 'sinuous rills', similarly, we are likely to be reminded that Milton's river- fountain went on to water the garden 'with many a rill'; the word 'sinuous' which had not appeared before in Coleridge's poetry or Wordsworth's, was elsewhere used by Milton to describe the worms and serpentlike creatures which for all their attrac-

---

[61] "So parted they, the angel up to heaven / From the thick shade, and Adam to his bower." (*PL*. VIII. 650–51) "'Shade' and 'Shadow' are among the poem's most resonant words: they are gradually transformed from innocence (...) through evil associations (...) back to hope of salvation" (Fowler 432). Thus a word can have both divine and satanic value.

tive colouring were to become pests after the Fall (IV, 481). (1985, 240–41)[62]

Both Milton and Coleridge believed that they were divinely inspired, though fallen poets, writing in a Fallen World. Prelapsarian language had no need for a written language at all. We could maintain that one of the consequences of the Fall is the written language; with it literature came into being and the concomitant difficulty of communicating by means of a text. In this situation we are faced with our desire to see wholeness while only perceiving fragments, and there are barriers not only between the artist and his work, but also between the audience and a work of art. Simplicity and "natural language" were replaced by diversity and sophistication after the Fall.

The Fall had two significant consequences in this respect: "If language speaks for the principle of fallen spirit in its lapse from paradisal oneness with its world, then it also contains the seeds of a possible redemption through consciousness" (Simpson 147). In this connection we can also speak of a Fortunate Fall which, it is true, bars us from paradisiacal simplicity and wholeness, but which has engendered poetry and aroused man's creativity as well as consciousness of problems inherent in communication and our struggle for knowledge. We hence collect fragments of truth; we make choices and judgements and we draw conclusions; and in this active process, we also become aware of complex visions, situations which can, when brought into poetry, be expressed in paradoxes or metaphors. In this dynamic search for knowledge and perception of unity in literature we make use of our memory, frequently appropriating from earlier experience of literature (and criticism) and perhaps arriving, like the fallen Adam in *PL,* at a conclusion by means of a dramatic "interpretative leap". The Fall, however, resulted in freedom of interpretation, the possibility of evolving and expressing different attitudes to art and creativity. As Wheeler very aptly points out, "[r]omantic idealism (...) rejected the notions that the mind is passive and reality is stable and independent of it, or, in aesthetic contexts, that the work of art has a fixed and determinate meaning or truth apart from the experience of and engagement with it" (163). Art in a Romantic context is always to be considered as something in the process of becoming. There is a loss-and-gain process in a Fortunate Fall, a dynamic,

---

[62] *PL.* IV. 481: "Thou following cried'st aloud, Return fair Eve". Beer's reference is apparently erroneous.

transitional state which speaks in the language of fragmentariness. It is in this spirit that we should understand the Preface and the poem.

A vision in a dream – the fragility of art

Dream visions are in fact very common in art, especially in religious litera-ture. As Wheeler points out, "[t]he connection between dream-consciousness and poetic vision is of course an ancient allegory which recurs in medieval dream poetry, and which Shakespeare and then all the Romantics take up" (23). The vision and dream aspects are linked to the Romantic idea of the prophet-poet, the inspired bard, which was already commented on in the general introduction. The poet indicates in the Preface that the poem is "A Vision in a Dream." We can never know whether this is a statement of fact or not, and the issue is of limited importance, as the presence in the text of visionary characteristics stresses the chimerical aspects of the artefact. It should be remembered, though it seems like a truism, that we are concerned with the world of fiction; that is, poetry is not factual, dealing with the 'real world' – its concern is with poetic truth. Deception is part and parcel of fiction, and the Preface belongs to its domain. Poetry is a literary artefact; or, to borrow from Plato, what the artist produces are "phantoms, not reality". Coleridge builds up an illusion of reality by the device of adding some sort of authenticity to both circumstances and persons when describing the poem's coming into being. He is even keen to mention particulars which could invest it with some sense of reality, being precise about place, "lonely farm-house between Porlock and Linton" (7–8), and time, "at the moment that" (11), "three hours in a profound sleep"(16), "during which time he has the most vivid confidence, that he could not have composed less than from two to three hundred lines" (17–19). Other specific details occur as well: the narra-tor was "unfortunately called out by a person on business from Porlock, and detained by him above an hour" (26–27); and finally, when he was about to put into writing the "dim recollection of the general purport of the vision" (30), he was not able to recollect more than "some eight or ten scattered lines and images, all the rest had passed away like the images on the surface of a stream into which a stone has been cast, but, alas! without the after restora-tion of the latter!" (30–34) To illustrate the idea of fragility in creativity as well as the illusive quality of fiction, Coleridge adds a couple of lines:

> Then all the charm
> Is broken – all that phantom-world so fair
> Vanishes, and a thousand circlets spread,
> And each mis-shape[s] the other.

In fact, the Preface instils the idea that we are in the realm of fiction. It also states that visions are easily punctured. The Preface is thus not primarily concerned with the issue of reality; instead it stresses that the poet is constructing a literary artefact, an illusion existing within a phantom-world. It seems to me that the poet succeeded in controlling the element of illusion.[63] The above lines quoted from the Preface reflect the divide between the perceiver and the perceived, as well as the divide between the time when the poet conceived the full vision of his work and the point in time when it was written down. The passage elucidates the creative process. Shelley expressed similar thoughts in the following manner:

> For language is arbitrarily produced by the Imagination and has relation to thoughts alone; but all other materials, instruments, and conditions of art, have relations among each other, *which limit and interpose between conception and expression*. The former is as a mirror which reflects, the latter as a cloud which enfeebles, the light of which both are mediums of communication. (483) (my italics)

The "split speaker" and the audience

A preface always serves to communicate with the audience by creating a kind of externality to a poem. In this case it does so by incorporating the creative ego into the work, as well as an invitation to the reader to partake in the creative process. This creative ego, however, has to be understood as split or divided. Simpson points out that this incorporation of the creative ego can function

> as a public and voiced response to the presence of the hermeneutic

---

[63] As Wheeler says, "[i]t is possible to understand that phrase ['psychological curiosity'] as an indication that the poem is not only interesting poetically, but also as a source of knowledge about the mysterious processes of perception, which it mirrors as an artefact" (30).

circle as it was pointed out by Goethe: 'and so it may be said that we are already theorising at the moment of each attentive glance into the world' ('und so kann man sagen, dass wir schon bei jedem aufmerksamen Blick in die Welt theoretisieren'). (*Werke* XIII 317, qtd. in Simpson 192)

On the other hand, as Jasper points out, "[w]e must be careful to distinguish between the poet who is possessed by a divine frenzy which is not his own, and the self who reflects and recollects" (1985, 46). In the Preface there is a reflection of "the Author", who is called "he", in the third person. This is presumably the voice of the poet who reflects on his creation and his creative ego. This self-reflection was voiced by Coleridge himself, who declared that "[t]he first step to knowledge, or rather the previous condition of all insight into truth, is to dare commune with our very and permanent self" (*The Friend* I Essay XVI 115).

The relation between the author and his characters has often been discussed in the old terms of "the omniscient author" and more, recently "the death of the author". This is, according to Paul Ricoeur, "a game that the author plays. In all cases he remains (...) a 'creator of the universe'" (189). Accordingly, the author can render himself fictitious, or adopt a disguise, "but he can never choose to disappear" (188). Therefore, Ricoeur introduces what he calls "the idea of the 'split speaker'", which can at times imply an "imaginative variation [which] (...) consists in being part of the narrative, in disguising oneself according to the narrative"(188). Hence, "[i]t makes little difference (...) whether a text is written in third or in first person"(189). To fully understand the idea of the split speaker, both the speaker and the reader have to be regarded as playful figures. In hermeneutic understanding, this implies that "the presentation of a world in a work of art and in general in a work of discourse, is a playful presentation" (186). In this playful interdependence, where the reader is appropriating the text, a dialogical situation is developed. The appropriation is thus considered to be a dialogue between the writer and his text, but also between the reader and the text. The appropriation can, according to Ricoeur, be regarded as a dialectical situation which "takes the place of the answer in the dialogical situation, in the way that 'revelation' or 'disclosure' takes the place of ostensive reference in the dialogical situation"(185). Drawing out the extreme consequences of all this, one would find oneself with as many dialogues as players (readers) of a text. Indeed, Coleridge opened a kind of dialogical situation with his poem *KK*, which has elicited so many different interpretations and placed so many critics under pressure to open up a dialogue with it.

If we adopt the idea of the "split speaker", we may assume that the author named in the Preface, in the third person, is the poet himself. This speaker is mentioned in the first person in the poem, before it returns to the third person. All these persons are different voices or disguises of the speaker, the author lurking behind them all. What Coleridge also achieves by using the different voices of a "split speaker" is that he "deliberately establishes a number of narrative levels in (...) in 'Kubla Khan'"(Jasper 1985, 46). In this way "he prompts reflection by an interplay between a number of perspectives or visionary centres" (46). This is of course deliberately achieved by switching from the first to the third person; as Jasper says, the divinely inspired poet is distanced from the first-person narrator who recollects and recreates what he once saw (46). However, another perspective is introduced in line 38, which seems to invoke some vision prior to the one of Xanadu: "once I saw"[64] . Yet another analepsis occurs when "Kubla heard from far / Ancestral voices prophesying war!" (29–30), which could be an echo from Purchas ("but Cubla heard of [the Rebellion; there was a civil war]" (Vol. III ch. 4, 81). To be able to make these shifts between different levels of perspective, the author clearly needs to be in absolute control of his "fragment-dream". *KK* is thus a wilfully conscious creation. The author or his voice in the Preface is aware of the fictitious character of his work. Provoking the "suspension of disbelief", he traps the reader into a fallen perspective, but also into an active and creative response.

Communication

In this final passage on the Preface, attention will be drawn to yet another component in the problem complex of communication which should be borne in mind when reading the Romantics. It is the fact that the Romantic writer is highly self-conscious. He frequently evinces a state of hypersensitivity to the question of audience. This sensitivity is often coupled to a sense of elitism, "fit audience though few", as was discussed in the general intro-

---

[64] Also noted by Simpson: "Once again, the 'once I saw' (l. 38) seems to invoke a time outside of and prior to the vision of Xanadu" (92).

duction to this study. The Romantic artist hence relied on small but "en-lightened" audiences. In the dialectics of communication, the Romantic writer subtly hints and suggests instead of stating. He is thus not an author-itarian writer, but rather an insinuating one by way of fragments and vi-sions. He is aware of the fact that an identical replication (understanding and response) in communication is an impossibility in a Fallen World (as Shelley put it, "truth cannot be communicated until it is perceived"). The Romantic writer's self-consciousness is often manifested in the need to con-trol or direct his readers, directly or by irony. One could claim with Shaffer that even "the apologetical style is a form of Romantic irony"(8). By con-trast, René Wellek claims that "there was no Romantic irony in England, nothing of the detachment of the author, the psychic distance, the irony, the playing with the material" (qtd. in Simpson 33n. 238). Irony is very much concerned with the author's (or his voice's) presence, not only from a distance but from within, using different approaches, playing with his ma-terial. The way in which the Romantic self-consciousness shows itself in the awareness of an audience can be seen in several of Coleridge's statements, like the following one from *The Friend:*

> [T]he Writer wishes (...) to convey not instruction merely, but fun-damental instruction; not so much to shew my Reader this or that fact, as to kindle his own torch for him, and leave it to himself to chuse the particular objects, which he might wish to examine by its light. (I Essay II, 16)

As we have seen, the Fall made communication, including the exchange of information, difficult. With reference to this problem, David Simpson ad-dresses the questions raised by the hermeneutic circle. They cannot be con-clusively answered; but, as he argues, the Romantic poets "themselves thought and created within the shadow of this problem, and (...) their aware-ness of it led them to fashion artifacts wherein the issue is repeated and trans-ferred, in a finer tone, rather than definitively solved" (21).[65] We realize that in the very act of reading and interpreting there are barriers, such as our "precomprehension which expresses the way in which the reader has already understood himself and his world" (Ricoeur 106) as well as limitations im-

---

[65] "All things exist as they are perceived: at least in relation to the percipient"(Shelley 505).

posed by language itself. By writing the Preface, Coleridge conveyed his consciousness of the interval, the "empty space", between inspiration and composition, as explained earlier by Shelley.

However, the artist's self-consciousness in relation to his work and his audience is of course not particular to Romanticism. For instance, it is very much a factor in *PL*, too. Milton declares that his effort is "unattempted yet in prose or rhyme" (I. 16), a claim commented on by Schwarz in the following terms:

> It has often been noted that in the invocation to Book I, even when Milton first boasts that his effort is 'unattempted yet in Prose or Rhyme', he also makes the dark side of that boast explicit: only twenty-eight lines later, he speaks of another 'attempt' and it, he tells us, is vain. He barely concludes the description of his ambition to soar with 'no middle flight', when he speaks of another soaring ambition: the effort of one who aspires 'To set himself in Glory above his peers'. He invokes the aid of the Muse, for his 'adventurous song'.(61)

What Schwartz fails to make clear in this particular case is that Milton's "effort" is not equivalent to an "ambition to soar with 'no middle flight'" or "To set himself in Glory above his peers" – these lines refer to Satan, *not the poet*. In the first book, along with his invocation and his argument (I. 1–5), Milton starts *in medias res* with the presentation of the "revolt" of "the infernal serpent", and of the fallen angels who are "[h]urled headlong flaming from the ethereal sky" (I. 45) to dwell "Confounded though immortal" (I. 53) in "darkness visible" (I. 63). The twenty-eight lines following the poet's declaration that he undertakes things "unattempted yet in Prose or Rhyme" refer to Satan, not Milton:

> The infernal serpent; he it was, whose guile
> Stirred up with envy and revenge, deceived
> The mother of mankind, what time his pride
> Had cast him out from heaven, with all his host
> Of rebel angels, by whose aid aspiring
> To set himself in glory above his peers,
> He trusted to have equalled the most high,
> If he opposed: and with *ambitious aim*
> Against the throne and monarchy of God

Raised impious war in heaven and battle proud
With vain attempt. (I. 34-44) (my italics)

Furthermore, Schwartz is of the opinion that "in the invocation to Book III, the complex interplay of allusions to sight and blindness convey moments of despair"(61) but that Milton finally resumes confidence, expressed in the words: "So much the rather thou celestial Light / Shine inward" (III. 51–52) (61). The self-conscious speaker in these lines is, of course, as Ferry points out, both a "limited human creature whose vision was dimmed by the Fall and an inspired seer whose divine illumination transcends the limits of mortal vision" (qtd. in Swaim 165). Schwartz, however, believes that "confidence in his poetic endeavour dims by the invocations to Book VII" (61). This seems a dubious statement, though, as what the poet invokes is a kind of celestial inspiration, "Up led by thee [Urania] / Into the heaven of heavens I have presumed, / An earthly guest, and drawn empyreal air" (VII. 12–14). Having ascended and even "drawn empyreal air"– that is, received celestial inspiration – he descends to earth, where he writes "still govern thou my song, / Urania, and fit audience find, though few" (VII. 30–31). He is afraid he will fall "on the Aleian field (...) / Erroneous there to wander and forlorn" (VII. 19–20). We could actually comprehend these invocations as references to "the narrator's physical blindness, [which] includes and generalizes the reader's varying and definitely human limitations in receiving light unless divinely aided" (Swaim 165).

Milton makes it clear from the beginning, in the very first lines of his epos, that he will deal with the Fall and its consequences. The very first lines declare that his work will treat: "Of man's first disobedience, and the fruit / Of that forbidden tree, whose mortal taste / Brought death into the world, and all our woe "(I. 1–3). The Fallen World is present from the start, and it is a reality. As a poet writing in a Fallen World Milton continuously asks for help, or as Michael Lieb expresses it:

That is, the poet must confront the uncreative aspects of the fall in order to create positively. ... The poet immediately reveals a self-consciousness about his craft and what he must do as fallen creator to fulfill the exigencies of his craft. He is aware of his limitations as a human being, yet equally aware of his divine obligations as a poet. (37, 38)

This means that the poet is human in himself but divine in his creativity. Milton's invocations thus demonstrate his self-consciousness and attitude in the face of his creation; his description of how human creativity functions reveals that the process can be felt to embody an element of menace: "On evil days though fallen, and evil tongues; / In darkness and with dangers compassed round, / And solitude" (VII. 26–28). A similar feeling can be seen in his final appeal, which is to Urania: "So fail not thou, who thee implores" (38). His creativity is divinely inspired but always threatened by the *ab extra*, to use Coleridge's phrase. In Milton's case that *ab extra* was not only lack of inspiration but also his own precarious situation during the retaliations that followed the Restoration.

KK is like a pageant unfolding before our eyes, a pageant which comes to life when the poem is read or recited. It is an expression of poetic truth and as such an atemporal object; that is, "[t]hat which the poem describes would not be were it not for the poem-as-it-is-read"(Jasper 1985, 46). The Preface prepares the reader for the poem proper. We shall also see how Paradise is partly regained, in that what happens is that the primary vision is transformed into something else. That something else will, however, always be a fragment only, a shadow of the ideal prelapsarian vision.

The Verse

Despite the enormous variety of responses to the poem, literary criticism has obviously failed to find a convincing interpretation which could be generally shared. The pursuit of mythological and literary allusions and echoes will constantly lead us in different directions and towards new perspectives which are tempting and interesting enough in themselves. Unfortunately, though, such investigations often fail to reach the heart of the problem; that is, it proves difficult or impossible to relate our findings to the poem itself. J. S. Hill has expressed the problem in lucid terms:

> In the first place, source-studies (including that of Lowes) generally do little to enhance our understanding or appreciation of 'Kubla Khan'. They treat the poem as a means rather than an end and devote their energies, not to interpretation, but to an often mechanical inventory of verbal parallels and apparent echoes from earlier literature. 'Kubla

Khan' itself serves as a starting-place, almost a pretext, and *the roads lead out from Xanadu, never to return.* (88) (my italics)

As was mentioned in the introduction, the attempts to trace mythological and literary allusions could in part be explained by the poem's power to reach a mythical subconscious, thereby making it difficult for the reader to view the poem from a distance, a critical perspective. However, the variety in interpretation is in itself part of the critical story of the poem, in that its readers and critics not only act as an audience but are in a continuous dialogue with the fifty-four lines which constitute the poem. This fact is quite remarkable in itself. In another critical comment on the pursuit of allusions, Harold Bloom states the following opinion:

> Poetic influence thus reduces to source-study, of the kind performed upon Coleridge by Lowes and later scholars. Coleridge was properly scornful of such study, and I think most critics learn how barren an enterprise it turns out to be. I myself have no use for it as such, and what I mean by the study of poetic influence turns source-study inside out. (1986, 10)

However, source-study can be fruitful when it returns to the poem itself. The many and various studies of *KK* along such lines are also in a sense part of the Coleridge canon. I have not been able to find any substantiation in Coleridge's writings of Bloom's claim that he was "properly scornful of such study".

It is possible, as was suggested above, that readers are particularly apt to be seduced, drawn into a "suspension of disbelief", by this poem. *KK* is, after all, a highly suggestive work. In the very act of "recognising, remembering, realising, recognise connecting, 'which are necessary for allusion to work; and (...) the pleasure these acts involve, by way of analogy with the rediscovery of something familiar which Freud sees as important ingredient in jokes' g", we may be irresistibly induced to this kind of research (Newlyn 15 qts. from Carmela Perri *Poetics* 7, 1978). Maybe "we cannot choose but hear"; and this could actually be regarded as the essential 'psychological curiosity' of the poem, or as a way of appropriating it. What seems to be generally agreed upon among critics is the poem's connection with Paradise and with ideas of poetic creation of some sort, biblical and mythical references or echoes manifesting a strong presence. It is certainly a poem which brings various traditions and mythologies together. [66]

In her book *Kubla Khan and the Fall of Jerusalem*, Shaffer has investigated Coleridge's relation to Higher Criticism and the development of the mythological school of European biblical criticism. As is pointed out elsewhere, one of the ideas of Higher Criticism was to treat the scriptures as a literary text, and not as a repository of absolute truths. A concomitant idea was the notion that Christianity was like other religions, a kind of mythology, fundamentally similar to other oriental religions.

The Romantics were interested in the Apocalypse, and the Book of Revelation fascinated Coleridge in the 1790s. In the circles of Higher Criticism, the authenticity and authorship of that book were also discussed. In relation to *KK*, Shaffer explains the historical background of the Fall of Jerusalem (AD 68–69) in detail, arguing that Coleridge originally conceived the poem as a full-scale epic,

> based, according to neoclassic precepts, on history, though history interpreted in a symbolic way; in the event, he produced something even more radical than a symbolic epic, an apocalyptic one, in which the entire action is concentrated, past and present and future, into one moment of vision expressed in wholly lyrical style. (18)[67]

---

[66] As late as 1985, John Beer writes: "Insofar as the symbolism of *Kubla Khan* can be seen to bring together various strands of mythology and traditions of interpretation from the past, its interest is inevitably limited for a modern reader, who has ceased to assign supreme authority to the Bible as a historical record" (226). We do not believe in the historical records of any myth, so what is the point here?

[67] I have only been able to find three references to "The Destruction of Jerusalem" as an epic poem in Coleridge's writings. One is in a letter to Thomas Wedgwood, 20 October, 1803: "I have since my twentieth year meditated on an heroic poem of the Siege of Jerusalem by Titus – This is the Pride, & the Stronghold of my Hope. But I never think of it except in my best moods". Another is from April 1832: "DESTRUCTION OF JERUSALEM .-EPIC POEM. The destruction of Jerusalem is the only subject now remaining for an epic poem; a subject which, like Milton's Fall of Man, should interest all Christendom, as the Homeric War of Troy interested all Greece. There would be difficulties, as there are in all subjects; and they must be mitigated and thrown into the shade, as Milton has done with the numerous difficulties in the Paradise Lost. But there would be a greater assemblage of grandeur and splendour than can now be found in any other theme. As for the old mythology, *incredulus odi*; and yet there must be a mythology, or a *quasi*-mythology, for an epic poem. Here there would be the completion of the prophecies - the termination of the first revealed national religion under the violent assault of Paganism, itself the immediate forerunner and condition of the spread of revealed mundane religion; and then you would have the character of the Roman and the Jew and the awfulness, the completeness, the justice. I schemed it at twenty-five; but alas! venturum expectat" (*Table Talk II* Appendix 166). Another note on the destruction of Jerusalem is the following from 4 September 1833:"I have already told you that in my opinion the destruction of Jerusalem is the only subject now left for an epic poem of the highest kind. Yet, with all its

This statement illustrates the typological mode with its juxtapositions and flexibility of time-schemes, as well as of events; but it is difficult to interpret *KK* typologically. Shaffer's argument that the poem started out as part of a planned full-scale epic is less than convincing, though she moves cautiously when writing that "Coleridge's notes suggest that 'Kubla Khan' is based on his epic plan, and that his 'dreamwork' condensed the three Acts of the Apocalypse into the climactic moment of the First Act, when the sixth seal is opened"(18). Though her background research on the historical fall of Jerusalem is comprehensive, it only bears an exiguous relation, if any at all, to the poem *KK*. Hers is an interesting book, but she does not "return to Xanadu", to borrow a phrase from Hill. There is no adequate proportion between her extensive research and her subsequent account of the fall of Jerusalem and its relation to the poem.[68] Shaffer maintains:

> But what Coleridge does here is characteristic of the symbolism of "Kubla". First, the three great sacred cities – Jerusalem, Babylon, and Rome – are blended; the symbolism is not sequential, as in Eichhorn's scheme, but simultaneous. Because Rome too must fall, and the city of wickedness is Babylon, the captive demons in Jerusalem may be imprisoned in "the Euphrates". (101)

The cities she refers to can be worked into a typological reading; but some evidence is needed for establishing that what is described in *KK* is Jerusalem, *or* Rome, *or* Babylon. Shaffer makes the above comment in the context of Coleridge's objection against Johann Gottfried Eichhorn's dealing, among

---

great capabilities, it has this grand defect - that, whereas a poem, to be epic, must have a personal interest, – in the destruction of Jerusalem no genius or skill could possibly preserve the interest for the hero from being merged in the interest for the event. The fact is, the event itself is too sublime and overwhelming" (Appendix H 264).

[68] Graham Davidson has this to say about Shaffer's book: "Coleridge's notes suggest that 'Kubla Khan' is based on his epic plan, and that his ' "dreamwork" condensed the three Acts of the Apocalypse into the climactic moment of the First Act, when the Sixth Seal is opened.' If by 'notes' Shaffer means those on Eichhorn, she does not once quote here from the source that she says has formed her central thesis. It seems to me most unlikely that Coleridge himself considered this poem as a collapsed or condensed epic, and what is wanting at the outset of the argument is some glimpse of how the notes on Eichhorn follow a pattern of intellectual activity which runs more or less parallel to the progress of 'Kubla Khan'. But we are given neither those nor a close reading of the poem; and E.S. Shaffer is elsewhere given to magisterial statements the foundations for which she does not reveal to us: 'The shape of romantic poetry, indeed of poetry to the present day, begins to be visible as the eighteenth-century Biblical epic emerges into the lyrical ballad'. Op. cit., 62" (318).

other things, with the fall of Jerusalem. But I fail to see how Coleridge's views on Eichhorn can be profitably linked to the poem *KK*.

It is true that there might be a connection with the temple of Jerusalem: a spring of water will well up from its threshold and become a great river, flowing to the east and making a fountain in Jerusalem (Ezekiel 47). However, the imagery of the Garden of Eden or the New Jerusalem, both located on the top of a hill with an oasis of trees and water, can be found throughout the Bible, as well as the idea of a temple controlling masses of water. That imagery could refer to the idea of "a city or building situated on a hill" which would, as Frye points out, "be a kind of keystone for the world; its removal would release the forces of chaos" (1982, 158). In the Psalms there is a frequent symbolic connection between the temple or city of God and control of the "floods" below it. Psalm 24, for example, mentions a vision of the world "founded upon the seas, and established (...) upon the floods"; and in verse 3 there seems to be some kind of ascent to the temple. The main point is that the image of a sacred place dominating chaos or water is far from uncommon in the Bible and is thus not restricted to the Book of Revelation.

The woman wailing for her demon-lover

Another component in the poem which has drawn the attention of critics is the "woman wailing for her demon-lover." To begin by considering her in a biblical context, the only women who correspond to such a characterization in the Bible are the ones who wail for Tammuz, seen by Ezekiel (8.14) in his vision of the abominations of Jerusalem and also referred to by Milton: "Of Thammuz yearly wounded: the love tale / Infected Sion's daughters with like heat, / Whose wanton passions in the sacred porch / Ezekiel saw" (I. 452–55). It is doubtful whether the woman "wailing for her demon lover" in the poem refers to these biblical women, or to the Great Whore of Babylon in Revelation. Other interpretations or explanations are possible, too. The woman is evoked in association with a landscape where forces of chaos are reigning in a context charged with sexual connotations. She could serve like a device sometimes used in pictorial art, which amounts to placing a small, often ambiguous figure or animal (generally with strong mythical connotations) in a landscape as a clue to a further level of meaning, often transforming our perception of the picture, telling us something else. This could be achieved, for example, by painting a small lurking serpent, as a reminder of evil, into a beautiful landscape, or by placing a frightened little hare in some corner of the picture as a symbol of fear, or by means of the old device of painting a skull in a picture to remind viewers of life's transitoriness. The mention of this woman could be a device for inserting a "savage", "holy" and "enchanted" note into the poem. Piper brings up the "woman wailing for her demon lover" in connection with the biblical women who wailed for Tammuz, as well as with Milton's lines. He declares:

> But if whoredom with a demon was specially chosen by Coleridge as an abomination marking the fallen world – and it is certainly an evocative one – what still needs explaining is the curious romantic tone of the whole passage, caught up in the strange antithetical phrase 'holy and enchanted'. (1987, 65)

Piper comes to the conclusion that

> [e]ven at the end of the eighteenth century it is necessary to be cautious about the extent of approval implied by 'romantic' and 'savage', particularly with Milton's 'grottesque' and 'savage' somewhere behind the words. Nevertheless, there is a real antithesis here, with both 'holy' and 'enchanted' to be given their full force. (1987, 65)

Beer suggests that "The second stanza likewise suggests the disorders of lust (the working of grievous sexual energies, emblematized in the rough chasm and violent fountain, is made manifest in the woman wailing for her daemon-lover)" (1985, 233). But again we are in some way the victims of delusion. This woman who has given rise to so many critical lines is not in fact present in the poem. She is merely alluded to as a phantom, as it were, or simile, in the following passage:

> A savage place! as holy and enchanted
> As e'er beneath a waning moon was haunted
> By woman wailing for her demon-lover!
> (14–16)

The woman is thus evoked in a simile centred on a place which is paradoxically said to be both "savage", "holy" and "enchanted". At the same time, the *KK* lines adumbrate a place frequented or visited by ghosts, all of which takes place beneath a moon on the decline. The quoted lines, 14–16, are admittedly taken out of their context; but the ensuing lines might be taken to suggest that this woman could be related to an Old-Testament-cum-historical background. Moreover, if we recognize the allusive character of this simile, a significance which lies deeper than the similarity of situation will emerge. These are the lines that follow:

> And from this chasm, with ceaseless turmoil seething,
> As if this earth in fast thick pants were breathing,
> A mighty fountain momently was forced:
> Amid whose swift half-intermitted burst
> Huge fragments vaulted like rebounding hail,
> Or chaffy grain beneath the thresher's flail.
> (17–22)

The action which brings forth the fountain thus resembles the process of threshing. It is important to understand the threshing-floor as an altar, that is "a holy place", a notion which occurs in the Old Testament, for instance in II Samuel 24.18–25 and I Chronicles 21.18–22. The threshing-place was at the same time a place of cult and offerings. The "thresher's flail" line with its sexual connotations could be taken to refer to the threshing-grounds of the different pagan tribes in the Old Testament.[69] These tribes were mainly agricultural, and their religions included fertility rites and motifs which were attractive to the Hebrew tribes. Many of the Israelites succumbed to the sexually charged fertility rites, in spite of warnings from their prophets. The cultic ceremonies involved sexual acts between male members of the agricultural communities and sacred harlots (see for instance Hosea). This historical context could, perhaps, have some connection with the wailing woman. In *KK* the stress is on the savage nature of the place, which is *likened to* a place as holy and enchanted and haunted as that where, under a waning moon, a woman wails for her demon-lover. This Old-Testament background could go some way towards explaining the paradoxical attributes used in the description of

---

[69] It could even be adduced that the mention in the Preface of the poet retiring to a "lonely farmhouse", or, for all we know, a barn, where the grain is normally stored and threshed, can be viewed in connection with the "threshing-place/altar" discussed above.

the place in the poem. In *PL* these cult ceremonies, with their blend of 'savage' and 'sacred', are described in the following manner:

> With gay religions full of pomp and gold,
> And devils to adore for deities:
> Then were they known to men by various names,
> And various idols through the heathen world.
> (I. 372–75)
>
> ....

> Their seats long after next the seat of God,
> Their altars by his altar, gods adored
> Among the nations round, and durst abide
> Jehovah thundering out of Sion, throned
> Between the cherubim; yea, often placed
> Within his sanctuary itself their shrines,
> Abominations; and with cursed things
> His holy rites, and solemn feasts profaned,
> And with their darkness durst affront his light.
> (I. 383–91)

In a kind of list, following the above lines from *PL*, Satan's twelve disciples are enumerated and Thammuz is mentioned among them.

On the whole, the indications are too general and vague to establish the "place" in the poem as being Jerusalem, let alone any other typologically related place. What we have, as it were, are gardens with a pleasure-dome, walls and towers, a river, a fountain and a sea. There is a possible Old-Testament and/or Miltonic reference to pagan cult ceremonies. The huge fragments likened to "rebounding hail" and to "chaffy grain" form a description of a chaotic, ongoing phase with sexual connotations. Something has happened in the course of this process, because in the midst of this turbulence the river Alph is "flung up". The full significance of the image of threshing in the poem will be dealt with below in connection with the section called "Creativity and Chaos".

Kubla's gardens

Elaine Shaffer also develops the idea of what she calls "the oriental idyll", feeling that *KK* should be viewed in such a context. While the Oriental in literature is not something particular to the end of the eighteenth century and the beginning of the nineteenth, it emerges "in a new form" at this time, as Shaffer says. She also mentions Salomon Gessner as a pastoral poet, calling his work *Der Tod des Abels* "one of the most charming little epic-idylls of the 18th century" (106).

Concepts such as 'pastoral' or 'garden' are sometimes used with a degree of carelessness. They tend, without sufficient reflection, to be invested with the semantic status of an Eden or a Paradise. This is particularly obvious when we look at how the Romantics' relation to, and invocations of, nature are addressed in critical literature. An article by McFarland supplies a useful example. It starts out by declaring that "[t]here exists a natural and almost inevitable affinity between the Romantic and the pastoral" (5). McFarland then supplies instances taken from several poets. However, he arrives at the conclusion that there is an inherent uncertainty in attempts to define the pastoral along these lines, because "many Romantic invocations of nature perhaps cannot, even by the conception of laminated pastoral, be seen as according with pastoral implication" (14). There are still further restrictions in the pastoral, as McFarland points out; "[a] certain social interaction is necessary to pastoral; the natural landscape is merely the arena for the interplay of a group" (14). He then quotes from Alpers, who argues that the representative pastoral tale "is the lives of the shepherds within the landscape, rather than the landscape itself. Whatever the specific features and emphases (...) it is the representative anecdote of shepherds' lives that makes certain landscapes pastoral" (14).

Applying the above criteria to *KK*, we must conclude that the poem has nothing of the pastoral idyll, unless we regard Kubla himself, the "woman wailing for her demon-lover" (who is only part of a simile) and the Abyssinian maid seen "once in a vision" as shepherds moving around in an idyllic landscape. There are gardens and a landscape in Coleridge's poem, containing traditional elements from the garden-poetry genre and incorporating Edenic and paradisiacal connotations; but there is also, as Hill points out, "the primitive energy of Coleridge's savage chasm, seething fountain, and sacred river that tumbles through measureless caverns and sinks in tumult to a lifeless ocean"(89).

The term "paradisiacal" in itself brings highly traditional garden images to mind. The garden-poetry genre has its conventions. Its recreations of Paradise draw their imagery and descriptive elements from the biblical garden tradition and Christian poets, as well as from the classical tradition, and the genre was well developed during the seventeenth century. The garden in *KK* seems akin to the kind of garden which, at the end of the eighteenth century, broke free from the restrictions of the neoclassical garden "[a]nd here were forests ancient as the hills, / Enfolding sunny spots of greenery" (10–11). The conception of the garden at the end of the eighteenth century, and in the beginning of the nineteenth, differed from seventeenth-century ideas in that it was no longer dominated by the notion of a *hortus conclusus*, or a formal, walled and man-made garden. Instead, the idea of the garden came to include a 'natural' dimension beyond the enclosures. The English garden which broke free from the constraints of the neoclassical garden is certainly germane to the garden-imagery in *KK*.[70]

We are told that "a stately pleasure-dome" is built on the decree of the Khan in Xanadu, a construction scheme "with walls and towers". This pleasure-dome is finally a "shadow" floating "midway on the waves"; but still it is a "miracle of rare device, / A sunny pleasure-dome with caves of ice!" The dome and the caves of ice are evoked in the second part of the poem, as that which the "I" would have liked to build in air. This imagery of the floating pleasure-dome shows us that we are not in Paradise. In fact the only lines out of all fifty-four which could claim any paradisiacal dimensions are the lines "So twice five miles of fertile ground"(6) and "And there were gardens bright with sinuous rills, / Where blossomed many an incense-bearing tree; / And here were forests ancient as the hills, / Enfolding sunny spots of greenery"(8–11) – five lines altogether.

Of pastoral or even Edenic elements there are thus little in the poem. We are misled into looking for particular sources in this respect, as Coleridge assimilates an entire tradition of gardens. While his "Edenic" lines are quite conventional, there are, as we have seen, sufficiently strong hints that we are not in Paradise, but in some kind of attempted recreation of it.

---

[70] As for the garden in *PL*, Charlotte F. Otten has demonstrated that it "is no mere metaphor for spiritual activity or 'dreamlike fantasy', but (...) solidly and exactly grounded in the native English gardening tradition" (qtd. in Swaim 60).

The Oriental elements – the figure of Kubla

As was pointed out above, the occurrence of Oriental features is in no way peculiar to eighteenth-century or for that matter nineteenth-century literature. "What we would label as exotic or the mysterious East, was a recurrent element in Western culture ever since Antiquity, though it appealed strongly to writers and painters of the early nineteenth century" (Honour 12). Seventeenth-century England was also aware of the splendours and the exotic glamour of the East, though its attitude was different from that of the Romantics. As Broadbent points out:

> The 17th century poets were less naive about the values of the oriental civilization. The Ottoman Turks had only just been kept out of western Europe at the siege of Vienna in 1529, when their hegemony finally broke. There was an historical prejudice in favour of the Roman boundaries of peace; and the Middle Eastern powers were seen as the ancestral enemies of Christendom because they had persecuted the Israelites. Thus in his *First Defence* Milton, following classical precedent, cites the Orient in general to exemplify tyranny, slavery and barbarism. (100–01)

Orientalism is present here and there in *PL*. Satan is called "the great Sultan", which would remind Milton's contemporaries of tyranny rather than of splendour.[71] From a Fallen World perspective, the name "Kubla Khan" is relevant in this context. It is only recently that the traditional image of the Mongols as perpetrators of mayhem and bloodshed has been questioned.[72] The name also suggests Cain, whose descendants were Tubal Kain and Jubal, discoverers of the arts of ironwork and music. They are, as Rosamund Tuve has pointed out, "a type of the hammering of Christ on to the Cross with nails" (145), representing a much-cherished motif in religious poetry, that of ingratitude. The various traditional and mythical characteristics evoked by the name Kubla Khan indicate that the naming of the poem could have to do

---

[71] Anthony John Harding has this to say about the orientalism of the poem: "The first thirty-six lines of the poem encapsulate the mythic constructs of the Orient: neither haphazard antiquarianism nor an unprecedented attack of the collective unconscious can be credited with responsibility for this narrative."(1985, 50). He refers to Shaffer's book, chaps. 1-4 *passim*.

[72] See e.g. Morries Rossabi, *Khubilai Khan: His Life and Times*. Berkeley: University of California Press, 1988.

with evil and tyranny; but the name could of course have been chosen for other reasons. But there is yet another Khan to be considered, the one Coleridge himself refers to in his Preface to the poem. This is the Khan who figures in Samuel Purchas's *Haklytus Posthumus or Purchas His Pilgrimes* (ed. of 1625, from now on *Purchas*),[73] where he is presented in the following way:

> In this Booke I purpose to write of all the great and marvellous Acts, of the present *Can* called *Cublai* Can, which is in our Tongue *Lord of Lords,* the greatest Prince in peoples, Cities and Treasures, that ever was in the world ... ruling the people with great wisedom and gravitie. He is a valiant man, exercised in Armes, strong of bodie, and of a prompt mind for the performance of matters, before he attained to the dignitie of the Empire (...) he often shewed himselfe a valiant Souldier in the warres, and carryed himselfe like a wiser and bolder Captaine, then ever the *Tartars* had. But since he swayed the Kingdome, he went but once into the Field, but sends his Sonnes, and other Captains in expeditions.... Cublai is a comeley and faire man of meane stature, of a red and white face, blacke and goodly eyes, well fashioned nose, and all the lineaments of his bodie consisting of a due proportion.(Vol. III ch.V, 81–82) (Purchas's italics)

Having crushed an important rebellion,

> [Cublai Chan] returned (...) with great triumph to *Cambalu,* and stayed there till Easter. On that day he called the Christians before him, and kissed their Gospels, and made his Barons doe the same. The like hee doth in the great Feasts of *Saracens, Iewes,* and *Ethnikes,* that *Sogomamber Can* the God of the Idols, *Mahumet, Moses,* or whosoever is greatest in heaven might helpe him. Yet he made best shew of liking to the Christian Faith but pretended the ignorance of the Professors, and the mightie acts of the Sorcerers, to his not professing it. (82)(Purchas's italics)

Kubla Khan is thus referred to in favourable terms in *Purchas.*
Fruman wishes us to believe that

---

[73] C. Hill tells us that *Purchas* ran to four editions between 1613 and 1626 (1965, 162).

He [Coleridge] cited a very obscure volume, Purchas's Pilgrimage, as the immediate inspiration of this miraculously given poem, but it happens that 'Kubla Khan' also reverberates with echoes of the fourth book of *Paradise Lost*, with Milton's roll-call of earthly paradises. Coleridge must have known this work practically by heart, for he quoted bits of it from memory in letters and imitated a portion of it in his early *Religious Musings*. (1992, 166)

First of all, *Purchas* is very far from being "a very obscure volume". This work – well known to every student of the Renaissance – consists of 4 volumes, each of around 1300 pages, with an extensive introduction and index to every volume. Nor does *KK* reverberate "with echoes of the fourth book" of *PL*. The only place-name that might have suggested Milton is 'Amara' in the Crewe manuscript, but Coleridge could have found that in *Purchas* or Heylyn as well as in Milton.[74] Fowler has the following comments to make on Mount Amara:

> Heylyn describes Mt *Amara* as 'a dayes journey high; the Rock so smooth and even ... that no wall can be more evenly polished'. The summit he says, is compassed with a high wall, within are gardens and palaces where 'the younger sons of the *Emperour* are continually inclosed, to avoid sedition: they enjoy there whatsoever is fit for delight or Princely education' (iv. 64). The province Amara to the west 'stretches towards the Nile'; and it was blessed with 'such ravishing pleasures of all sorts, that some have taken (but mistaken) it for the place of *Paradise*'. (211–12)

Finally, it might be pointed out that Coleridge did not quote "bits" from either *Purchas* nor from *PL*. IV in *Religious Musings*.

Who, then, is the Kubla Khan of the poem? We are told in the very beginning of the work that bears his name as a title that he ordered the building of "A stately pleasure-dome"; then follows the description of the garden and the landscape. The second reference to the eponymous ruler are the lines according to which he "'mid this tumult heard from far / Ancestral voices prophesy-

---

[74] John Heylyn (1600–62), whose works include *Cyprianos Anglicus* 1668, *Histories of the Reformation* 1661 and *Cosmographie* 1658.

ing war". This could be an echo from *Purchas's* reference to Cublai's uncle Naiam's rebellion, which was crushed (Vol. III ch. V, 57). Kubla Khan is, in fact, not a strong presence in the poem at all; rather, he functions as a kind of foreground figure, not unlike the ones painted by the Romantic artist Caspar David Friedrich. A closer comparison with some of Friedrich's paintings could serve to illustrate the idea of the figure in the landscape which comes to mind when reading *KK*. Honour points out that we are usually suspended in mid-air when looking at Friedrich's pictures:

> Friedrich's figures are usually extraneous to the landscape like his 'Wanderer', neither wholly of its world nor of ours, standing on the edge of reality. Motionless, isolated, they seem to be both within and yet somehow outside nature, at once at home in it and estranged symbols of ambiguity and alienation. (81)

As Honour claims, these figures – whether foregrounded or not – do seem to stand on "the edge of reality"(81). Whatever associations or possible sources apply to the choice of the name "Kubla Khan", however, the chief significance of that name in the poem itself seems primarily emblematic.[75]

Piper maintains that "Kubla is not a divine creator, nor even a believer; his dome was decreed for purely human pleasure, and is built among the symbols of a fallen world under judgement" (1976, 157). This is only one of the many attributes given by critics to Kubla Khan in the poem. Kubla in the poem is in fact a creator, and like the orthodox God he creates *ex nihilo*; that is, he decrees, calling things into being by his word.[76]

---

[75] It is also interesting to note that the new attitude or "shift of consciousness" that emerged in the 1790s in Romantic art and literature brought a distinct awareness where the work of art becomes self-validating, self-referential. Even the use of material and techniques was transmuted in pictorial art, as well as the attitude of the artist to his creation. This new consciousness on the part of the artist can be seen in the many self-portraits of the period. There is thus a further step out from anonymity into self-awareness, both as individuals and creators.

[76] George Watson has the following things to say about Kubla: "The authoritarian word 'decree' is not in Purchas, who simply says: '*In Xaindu did Cublai Can build a stately palace...*'[The italicized sentence cannot be found in Purchas.] And the painfully contrived quality of the tyrant's pleasure becomes clearer with every line: in the formal, though not entirely formal, gardens, and the trivial purpose to which the brute strength of the sacred river has been harnessed. The reader is meant to be left with a disagreeable image of the patron himself, congratulating himself on his facile ingenuity in degrading a matchless natural phenomenon to the service of a landscape garden – in itself a very Augustan pleasure – in order to flatter his own megalomaniac dreams" (128–29). The poem does not provide any kind of foundation for such a comment. Watson dogmatically continues, "Certainly the Khan is very like a tyrannical aristocrat as seen

Pleasure

Piper draws attention to the word 'pleasure', arguing that it had a more exalted ring in the eighteenth century than later and that Coleridge used it with reference to his poetic purpose (1976, 157). In addition, he is of the opinion that "*Kubla Khan* is a poem about Eden, that is to say, about pleasure, and the symbolic statement which it makes is a complicated one, encompassing the primal Eden, pleasure in the fallen world, and the second Eden" (157). As has been pointed out above, the garden in the poem is a picture of a garden which is not without Edenic connotations and which conforms to a long tradition of garden poetry; but that does not make *KK* a poem about Eden. However, the word pleasure was – as Piper points out – a word Coleridge used for "his poetic purpose".

The well-known connection between pleasure and poetry has a long history. As Malcolm Heath remarks, "poetry had always excited the wonder which Aristotle sees as the root of philosophical enquiry: the Greeks habitually talked of the intense pleasure to be derived from poetry, and of the bewitching enchantment it could work"(xi). The idea of "pleasure derived from poetry" is quite a traditional western concept. Aristotle regarded poetry and painting as fundamentally similar activities; we derive pleasure from a well-constructed play as we are helped to *understand* why it is good. Even catharsis is connected with pleasure. 'Understand' was a key-word for Aristotle, along with pleasure, since understanding in itself is a source of pleasure. But it is more important to realize that 'pleasure' is a fundamental concept in Romantic literary theory, as are the words 'beauty' and 'truth'. In his first lecture on poetry, Lowth discusses its qualities. His indicator for poetry is 'pleasure', which is connected with concepts such as 'good morals', 'virtue' and 'truth'. Shelley repeatedly returns to the word 'pleasure' in describing poetry, insisting that poetry is always accompanied by pleasure (493).

The word pleasure is thus closely connected with poetry and creativity. A commonplace in Romantic literary theory, it is invested with very favourable connotations and has little to do with erotic pleasure, either in a Romantic

---

through romantic and liberal eyes. This is an aspect of the poem that might easily have seemed too obvious, in the years around 1800, to be worth mentioning, but it needs to be emphasized in an age which finds tyrants engagingly exotic, even to the point of supposing Kubla a model of the creative artist" (126–27). The last quotation reveals Watson's opinion of orientalism, which betrays a degree of ignorance: "The Khan, too, may be something of a barbarous fop. And if this seems a lofty and remote view of the East, it should be recalled that accurate orientalism is an extreme rarity in England before the Victorians" (127–28).

context *or in the poem KK.* The following appraisal by John Beer is thus a puzzling one: "Among other things, this is a poem about sensual pleasure – including erotic pleasure: the delights of vision, sounds and scents in the first stanza convey suggestions such as those which are overtly expressed in the Song of Solomon, where the bride describes herself as a wall, her breasts like towers, and promises to be a spice-laden garden to her lover" (1985, 233).[77] The Song of Solomon 4.12–15 referred to by Beer has nothing at all to do with the Bride describing herself, let alone with *KK,* nor does the Song of Solomon 8.10.[78] The pleasure-dome could be regarded as some kind of poetical emblem which might have come to Coleridge's mind when reading *Purchas,* but considering the garden landscape in the poem, which recalls the newly 'liberated' English garden, the pleasure-dome could be envisaged as one of those pleasure-houses, admittedly small, which could be found in an English garden at that time, but which were often constructed with orientally inspired architecture, to please the eye.

Mount Abora and Xanadu

An examination of the place-names Coleridge chose tells us something about the kind of poetic place we are dealing with. Why Mount Abora, Xanadu and the river Alph? Looking at the Crewe manuscript it seems, but it is not at all certain, that Coleridge first wrote "Mount Amora" and then changed it to "Mount Amara". The final name he opted for was "Abora". Fruman comments:

> Finally let us glance at a concealment so successful that it led John Livingston Lowes (and many others) to pore over innumerable old maps and to peruse numberless volumes, all in the hope of locating the elusive 'Mount Abora' of Kubla Khan 'unknown to any map', Lowes reluctantly concluded, 'since time began'. When the only known man-

---

[77] In n. 30 p. 260 of his article, a reference is given to "the Song of Solomon 4:12-15, 16; 8:10" (quoted in *Coleridge the Visionary* (270–71).

[78] "A garden inclosed is my sister, my spouse; a spring shut up, a fountain sealed. Thy plants are an orchard of pomegranates, with pleasant fruits; camphire, with spikenard, /Spikenard and saffron; calamus and cinnamon, with all trees of frankincense; myrrh and aloes, with all the chief spices: / A fountain of gardens, a well of living waters, and streams from Lebanon" (Song of Songs, 4.12–15). "I am a wall, and my breasts like towers: then was I in his eyes as one that found favour" (Song of Songs, 8.10).

uscript of 'Kubla Khan' came to light in 1934, the famous passage proved to read as follows: A Damsel with a Dulcimer / In a Vision once I saw / It was an Abyssinian Maid, / And on her Dulcimer she played, / Singing of Mount Amara. Or possibly Amora, for the place-name in Coleridge's handwriting, has a heavy stroke from the top of the a to the r, thus changing the letter to an o. Why should STC have wished to do this? The obvious reasons are aesthetic. Amara does not establish even a decent assonance with *Dulcimer* or *saw*, let alone an acceptible rime. (1992, 165–66)

The reason for Coleridge's undertaking these changes has been a matter for speculation. In the Crewe manuscript, the first version might read Amora which means "Gomorra" in Hebrew – a name which certainly does not carry any paradisiacal connotations. The "change" from an 'o' to an 'a', that is from Amora to Amara, could just be a slip of the pen, too. The different variants Amora and Amara have the same root in the Hebrew. "Amara" appears, as has been pointed out, in *PL*. It is mentioned in a list of names of false paradises or invented ones. The "real" Eden is thus not the paradise of Ethiopia: "Nor where Abassin Kings their issue guard, / Mount Amara, though this by some supposed / True Paradise under the Ethiop line" (IV. 280–82). So Mount Amara belongs to the idea of a false Paradise. There is a description of the Kingdom of Amara in *Purchas* (Vol. II ch. X), suggesting that Coleridge could have derived the name from *Purchas* as well as from Milton or Heylyn. In any case, the Kingdom of Amara is a mythological name lost in the mists of history (but clearly well-known to seventeenth-century geographers). Fruman's contention that Coleridge, suffering from "self-doubt", was "anxious to obscure or deny his intellectual obligations" (165) is difficult to understand. Coleridge did not conceal anything; he tells us that he was reading *Purchas*, where we not only find a description of Mount Amara but also of Mount Tabor. Mount Amara was the name used in the autumn of 1797; but there was a 19-year gap from that time until the publication of *KK* in 1816, during which period there were ample opportunities for Coleridge to reconsider the name in the poem.

The final name he adopted, "Abora", should be the most interesting for the critic, however. *Purchas* outlines Mount Tabor, which means the "sacred mountain", "they call this Mount *Tabor*, in *Italian*, Monte Santo, that is, the

Holy Mountain" (Vol. II. ch. 9, 1351) (Purchas's italics). This, in the world of *Purchas,* is the mountain of Transfiguration (Mark 9) where Jesus Christ showed himself in all his glory. There is actually little difference between Mount Tabor and Mount Abora. The name 'Abora' can easily come into being by means of an elision of a 't' between the two words 'Mount' and 'Tabor' in English. According to the general rule for words consisting of two or more syllables, the stress should be on the first 'a' in 'Abora'. This would also adhere to a rhythmic principle, and the final 'a' would, in consequence of reduction, become almost inaudible (Johansson 73, 75, 89 and 94). It seems clear that Mount Abora has both biblical and religious connotations.

Coleridge's Khan resided in Xanadu, wheras Milton chose Cambalu as the residence of the Cathaian Khan:

> City of old or modern fame, the seat
> Of mightiest empire, from the destined walls
> Of Cambalu, seat of Cathaian khan[.]
> (XI. 386–88)

Referring to Coleridge's Xanadu, John Beer maintains that "the memory of Cambalu here probably helped to transform Purchas's 'Xamdu' into Coleridge's trisyllabic 'Xanadu'" (1971 62); but that seems less than likely. In *Purchas* the Khan is said to have two palaces, one in Xa*n*du (my italic) and the other in Cambalu. Both palaces are described, with their splendour and gardens. Near his palace in Xandu, the Khan built "In the middest in a faire Wood (...) a royal House on pillars gilded and vernished", and a gloss in the margin of *Purchas* reads "A goodly house of pleasure" (Vol. III ch. 4, 80).[79]

It should moreover be remembered that in Coleridge's time poetry was written with the aim of being recited aloud; therefore the name 'Xandu' was made into 'Xanadu' for the sake of rhythm. Furthermore, for the sake of both rhythm and sonority, 'Abora' should be recited with the stress on the first syllable, that is Ábora, instead of Abóra, which is the way the word is generally pronounced nowadays.

---

[79] This is what Purchas tells us about Xandu: "(...) the Citie Xandu, which the great Chan Cublay now raigning, built; erecting therein a marvellous and artificiall Palace of Marble and other stones (...). He included sixteene miles within the circuit of the wall ... In this inclosure or Parke are goodly meadows, springs, rivers ... In the middest in a faire Wood hee hath built a royall House on pillars gilded and vernished"(Vol. III ch. 4, 80).

The river Alph

The river Alph, called "the sacred river ", is presented as early as in the third line of the poem. The name strongly suggests the river *Aleph*, the stream of origination, as well as a derivation from the Greek river *Alpheus*, in classical mythology the river "that defies metamorphosis as stasis; the thwarted stream [which] goes underground, still pursuing, still flowing, so that sexual conflict ends not in degenerated immobility but in the regenerated stream" (Brisman 1975, 475). Beer argues that Alph's running down to the sunless sea rather than returning as a fountain suggests that there is a "flaw in this paradise" (1971, 62).This is a reference to the tradition that the Edenic river divided before the Fall, one part returning to well up at the Tree of Life. This circumstance contributes to showing us that we are not dealing with a Paradise garden in *KK*.

Shaffer has presented the following idea of the river:

> Especially characteristic of 'Kubla' is the way the river expands at a touch into a sea – size is as immaterial as place and time – while retaining all the connotations of that particular named river and acquiring all those of the sea. Both river and sea are prominent in the Apocalypse. Babylon's seat is also 'upon many waters'(Jeremiah 51,13) ... The sea is of course, as Lowth put it, the 'place where the wicked after death were supposed to be confined; and which, from the destruction of the old world by the deluge, the covering of the Asphaltic vale with the Dead Sea, etc. was believed to be situated *under the waters.* (101) (Shaffer's italics)

River and sea images are not prominent in the Revelation, but they recur throughout the Bible as a whole. However, we should also remember – as was stated above – that the Khan in *Purchas* has two palaces: one in Cambalu, which is seated on a great river; the other in Xandu, close to "springs, river" (Vol. III ch. 4, 81, 83). There is thus no reason to attach specific importance to either biblical or apocalyptic watercourses in the context of *KK*.

The Dead Sea is also described in *Purchas*:"the Valley where Sodom and Gomorrha were destroyed (...) is now the great Lake Asfalti, which they call the Dead Sea" (Vol. III ch. 2, 1205). The Dead Sea in *Purchas* is said to be watered by the River Jordan, which is certainly *the* sacred river in the Bible. It is therefore difficult to feel sure that the river in *KK* is an apocalyptic river, any more than a paradisiacal one. It is clearly stated in the beginning of the poem that the river runs "Through caverns measureless to man / Down to a sunless sea" (4–5). On its way to the sea, it is "flung up momently (...) / Five miles meandering with a mazy motion" (24–25). The poem repeats that it finally reaches "the caverns measureless to man", to sink eventually "in tumult to a lifeless ocean" (27–28). This suggests, as Brisman points out, that "unthwarted by Coleridgean caverns measureless to man, Alpheus just goes on" (475). Milton refers to Alpheus in "Lycidas", where the tradition of the ongoing flow of the stream directs attention to the blockage that has taken place: "Return Alpheus, the dread voice is past / That shrunk thy streams, return Sicilian muse." Brisman is of the opinion that the renewed continuity of the stream in "Lycidas" represents poetic continuity. The river in *KK* seems to suggest some ongoing process, and the resemblance of its name to that of Alpheus in classical mythology supports Brisman's view. As the Preface to the poem explains, the renewed continuity of inspiration is metaphorized in a stream image: "all the charm / Is broken, all that phantom-world so fair / Vanishes"; but in spite of this, "[t]he stream will soon renew its smoothness, soon / The visions will return!"

In his article, Brisman expands his identification of the river with Alpheus. However, he also implies that the river Alph could be seen as "the Aleph, stream of origination" (475). Labelling the river Alph the "stream of origination" would be appropriate, as the poem gives us to understand that it has no ordinary source: though flung up by the mighty fountain, it simply exists, and it can in this sense also be an Aleph, symbolizing inception.

The river Alph's analogy to Aleph has been overlooked by most critics – Brisman is one of a small number of exceptions – and it is certainly worth considering. In order to illustrate this possibility, I wish to refer to one of Jorge Luis Borges's most famous short stories, "El Aleph". Borges's tale deals with poetry, creation and the subconscious; it describes the epiphany when the *ubi et cuando* is revealed. If we are to be able to perceive Alph as Aleph, though, we also need to know what Aleph stands for in the Cabbala.

For the purpose of the following discussion, a short summary of some of the ideas in the Cabbala will be provided. The Cabbala is a system which tries to define man's relation to God. Magical significance is given to numbers and the letters of the alphabet. As Borges writes, "El Aleph es la primera letra del alfabeto de la lengua sagrada" (173)[80]. The letter signifies "el Ensoph, la ilim-

---

[80]"The Aleph is the first letter of the alphabet of the sacred language" (my transl).

itada y pura divinidad".[81] One of the most influential books in this system is *The Zohar* (*Book of Brightness*), created in the thirteenth century in Gerona, Spain. *The Zohar* is a kind of compilation of the whole of the Cabbala which also develops it; gnosticism, neo-Platonism and other metaphysical doctrines are fused in it. What Borges mentions as the Ensoph is explained by Stemberger in the following terms: "Dem unerkennbaren Dunkel Gottes, des En Soph (des Unendlichen), entspricht in dynamischer Verbindung die Lichtwelt seiner Attribute, der zehn Sefirot, in denen Gott erkennbar ist" (130). These Sefirot are thus so to speak emanations from God. The problem of evil is explained as a result of the world being divided into one divine and one demonic part, opposed since the begining of Creation. Evil is thus not primarily associated with the sin of mankind, but with a destruction of connections, and man may attempt to balance it by prayer and adherence to the Torah (131). There is thus no notion of original sin here, though apparently the fragmentariness, the lack of any perceived wholeness, is explained as a consequence of evil.

This division into a divine and demonic world could be held to be relevant to Coleridge's poem. Its topography is significant in this context: it carries occasional reminiscences of Paradise, but it is demonic, too; the poem clearly states that the place where Alph is flung up is "savage" as well as "holy" and "enchanted"; and it is a place where the tumultuous forces of chaos dwell. Another circumstance mentioned by Stemberger is relevant: "Die Schöpfung ist nicht eine *creatio ex nihilo*", as in orthodox Christian belief, "sondern eine natürliche Entwicklung der in Gott tätigen Kräfte" (131).

The name Aleph leads us directly to the Cabbala, with which Coleridge was well acquainted, as was stated in the chapter on *AM*. In a letter to his son in August 1820, he wrote that "[t]he Aleph, say the Rabbinical Philologists, is no Letter; but that in and with which all Letters are or become" (*CL* V, 1246). Why should we relate the river in *KK* to the river Aleph? There is the obvious resemblance of their names, of course, which is the natural starting-point. Furthermore, the river Alph is said to be "sacred", as is the nature of Aleph, since it leads to the Ensoph which, as was mentioned above, is considered a kind of divine active principle or, as Borges puts it, "the limitless and pure divinity." Arguably, too, the Alph which runs through the poem transforms the "lifeless ocean"; as will be shown, the river in the poem could therefore

---

[81] "[T]he limitless and pure divinity" (my transl).

metaphorically be seen as an emanation from God, or from the divine. As we saw, the Cabbala describes Creation as a natural expansion and growth of the divine powers. The river Alph might therefore be a metaphor for the expansion of the divine power as a stream of origination, recalling the conception of creation set forth in the Cabbala.

Regardless of whether this dimension is deemed relevant to *KK,* there is reason to consider a question asked by Borges: "Por increíble que parezca, yo creo (o que hubo) otro Aleph" (173).[82] There is always "another" Alph, because the river Alph acts as all rivers do. That is, the river Alph could be the river Aleph, the river Alpheus, or any river; but it is still the river in the poem *KK.* It could represent all rivers, as well as the individual river whose movements nothing can hinder, which whirls and is never at peace, undermining the earth, forming caves, acting as a mighty force, pushing any obstacle aside, always in the direction which will lead it towards rejoining its element, the sea. There could hardly be a more apt metaphorical representation of the process of becoming, an image of creation itself. Thus the sacred river Alph could be a conflation of Aleph, which stands for origination and divine inspiration, and the river Alpheus, the stream of regeneration and of poetic continuity. In both those manifestations Alph, though rising to the surface among fragments, could be regarded as a force counteracting chaos.

The image of water as a life-giving force is a conventional one, and the river Alph could also metaphorically convey an image of the subconscious mind in the process of creating: it is "flung up" in a burst of uncontrolled movement; meandering in its motion it runs, presumably peacefully, through forests and plantations; and after reaching the caverns measureless to man, it sinks with all the burden of its tumultuous passage into a lifeless ocean. It could be argued that the river transforms or makes something happen to this lifeless sea, since the shadow of the dome of pleasure appears floating "on the waves", where even "the mingled measure / From the fountain and the caves", which are also part of Alph's transit, are echoed:

> The shadow of the dome of pleasure
> Floated midway on the waves;
> Where was heard the mingled measure
> From the fountain and the caves.

---

[82] "Though it seems incredible, I think there is (or was) another Aleph" (my transl).

It was a miracle of rare device,
A sunny pleasure-dome with caves of ice!
(31–36)

Speaking about the whole of the poem, Ashton points out that "[it] is hard to know where to lay the interpretative stress when contemplating 'Kubla Khan'"(115). The above lines could be regarded as the core of the poem, the chief focus of any interpretative approaches to it. This shadow-dome could be seen to illustrate the fragility of poetic activity, which from the first divinely inspired primary imagination emerges as an Aleph, and which, in spite of obstructions, comes – as Coleridge writes – "trembling back to unite", then like an Alpheus, which can be regarded as standing for "poetic continuity." If the poet could, as he says, revive the symphony and song of the maid singing of Mount Abora, which is the Mountain of Transfiguration, he would even be able to build that dome in air. In the Preface he explains the fragility inherent in the act of composition, and the shadowy pleasure-dome may be seen as a representation of it, bearing the characteristics of the unreal, the delusive and the insubstantial.

Shaffer has emphasized that it is a shadow we are dealing with, not with an actual dome, reflecting on that shadow's precise location: "We have to do now not with the dome itself, but with its 'shadow', the dome's double. The shadow 'floats' – but yet it is exactly placed: 'midway on the waves'. Midway vertically or horizontally or both?"(165) With regard to the lines on the "floating shadow-dome", Piper claims that the image possesses

(…) a touch of surrealism that makes any interpretation speculative, but something may be attempted by examining the symbolic or allegoric significances of these paradisal images. The relation is first made through the shadow of the dome of pleasure floating on the water: the connection is oblique and is not made easier to interpret by the ambiguity of the word 'shadow'. The lines have been taken to mean that a second spectral dome was floating midway between the banks; the solid-seeming caves of ice are no absolute bar to this for, after all, the visionary temple which Saint John saw in the heavens contained a sea of glass, *but there seems no real need or reason to introduce this specter dome.* The logical sense of the lines is that the dome was alongside the river in the middle of its course, so that its shadow or reflection could be seen on the surface of the water, perhaps with patches of clear or gleaming water to suggest the ice. The relationship is an immaterial one and the two entities do not react physically, but in this relationship it is the water which supports the immaterial aspect of the pleasure-dome; in this place the roar of the divine fountain and the tumult full of prophetic and threatening voices have become a harmony, a mingled measure. (1987, 67) (my italics)

The shadow of the dome can be regarded as the "shadow of the substance", and as such as a mere reflection of the primary imagination, a sort of spectral form or a phantom, a kind of copy of the primary imagination. A copy is never the same as the original, but it will always in some way incorporate elements from the original. Here primary imagination is metaphorically evoked and echoed by "the mingled measure from the fountain and the caves". In this way the copy, secondary imagination, is given traces of or material from the first imagination.

That is all that human imagination – 'secondary imagination' as Coleridge called it – is able to achieve. Even so, imagination is a process which confers, adds and abstracts, and a new existence is created in this process. Wordsworth calls imagination the "endowing or modifying power" which also "shapes and creates – and how?" (Preface *Poems* 1815) (Wordworth's italics) He answers his question in the following way:

> By innumerable processes, and in none does it more delight than in that of consolidating numbers into unity, and dissolving and separating unity into number – alternations proceeding from, and governed by, a sublime consciousness of the soul in her own mighty and almost divine powers.

Here Wordsworth uses verbs such as consolidate, dissolve and separate, all of them referring to a process where he declares that the soul employs "her own mighty and almost divine powers". The Romantics believed creation (the exercise of creativity) to be an active process in which the mind collects fragments and then recollects them. This action requires an adjustment or ordering of the fragments, of that which has been divided, into a kind of realignment; it was suggested above that Alph as Alpheus, the regenerated stream, could serve as an emblem of such poetic continuity. The secondary imagination chooses its own way of manifesting itself, as a shadow, a paradox, a metaphor, a line in a poem or a whole poem. In *KK* its manifestation emerges as a shadow of what has or could have been, with paradoxical characteristics. As Wheeler says, the shadow "has Platonic undertones of relations of shadow to substance with the correspondent reversal of the reality of each" (37), then related to shadow as 'type'; but I am more inclined to see the word 'shadow' here as standing for something insubstantial, illusory and fragile, which can only choose to manifest itself as a shadowy reflection.

In his discussion on imagination, Wordsworth draws on some examples from Milton (*PL* II. 636–43). They might enhance the understanding of the poetic process as rendered in *KK*:

> As when far off at sea a fleet descried
> *Hangs* in the clouds, by equinoxial winds
> Close sailing from Bengala or the Isles
> Of Ternate or Tydore, whence merchants bring
> Their spicy drugs; they on the trading flood
> Through the wide Ethiopian to the Cape
> Ply, stemming nightly toward the pole. So seemed
> Far off the flying fiend.

On these lines, Wordsworth comments: "'So seemed': and to whom 'seemed'? To the heavenly muse who dictates the poem, to the eye of the poet's mind, and to that of the reader, present at one moment in the wide Ethiopian, and the next in the solitudes, then first broken in upon, of the infernal regions!"(Preface *Poems* 1815) This statement is important. It declares that we are allowed to participate in the poet's imagination, which is divinely inspired, at the same time suggesting that we are in the world of fiction with its own laws, which are not the same as those in real life. It goes without saying that there is an undermining of reality in fiction, but curiously also of the illusory, which means that great art is not allusive to anything but to itself. It stands alone. As readers we conceive of the shadow of the dome of pleasure as it presents itself, since we can experience the mysterious, the enigmatic, the invisible only as it "chooses" to manifest itself. In other words, "[w]e know a thing not by its essence, but by the way it is perceived" (Prickett 1989, 121). "The shadow of the dome of pleasure" could also be expressed as "the associated objects of human experience [which] are perceived in ever-sharper clarity as 'not-self'; to be appreciated fully only when they are separated from the undifferentiated matrix of primary perception" (121). Coleridge's shadow is like Milton's Pandaemonium which rises, as Broadbent points out, "like the machinery of a masque – artificial, temporary, illusory" (178). It is insubstantial, elusive, mystifying: "Anon out of the earth a fabric huge / Rose like an exhalation, with the sound / Of dulcet symphonies and voices sweet"(I. 710–12).

All is fluidity, and the outcome of poetic creativity is presented as a pageant in *KK*. The transient, the ephemeral and the illusory in imagination are all evinced in the very word "shadow" and in the paradox of "a sunny pleasure-dome with caves of ice". In connection with this "shadow-dome of pleasure", the following lines from Mircea Eliade might be quoted. They formulate the idea of creation very clearly and could be taken to illustrate the preceding discussion:

> The waters symbolize the universal sum of virtualities; they are *fons et origo*, "spring and origin", the reservoir of all the possibilities of existence, they precede every form and *support* every creation. One of the paradigmatic images of creation is the island that suddenly manifests itself in the midst of the waves. (130) (Eliade's italics)

Similarly, the shadow of the dome on the water will dissolve into its element, which is water – the substance which preceded creation and supports it.

The Abyssinian maid

Critics have commonly regarded the "Abyssinian maid" as a representative of a force for good, a kind of paradisiacal muse, with few exceptions. One of those exceptions is Burke, who comments on her in less than rapturous terms:

> [T]he vision of the 'Abyssinian maid' is clearly *beatific*, yet the beholder of the vision (as presented in terms of the poem) is also to be identified with *sinister* connotations (as with those that explicitly emerge just after a recurrent reference to the 'caves of ice'). I refer to the cry, 'Beware! Beware!' – and to the development that transforms malignly the principle of encirclement (introduced benignly in Stanza One) (...)

Derive her [the Abyssinian maid] as you will along the lines of sources in other books, there's still a tonal likelihood that the lady is 'Abyssinian' because, among other things, as so designated she contains within this name for her essence the syllables that spell 'abyss'. (Burke 47)

Burke's reflections are particularly apt: the "beatific" and sinister characteristics, as well as the maid's relation to the "Abyss" or to the "chasm" in the poem, illustrate Coleridge's manner of conflating the divine and the demonic. His initial choice of presenting the maid as singing of Mount Amora could be held to be relevant here. The sinister, demonic counterpart of the Mountain of Transfiguration (Mount Tabor or Mount Abora), where Christ showed himself in his glory, is the Assyrian mount of degradation, where Uriel witnessed the disfigured Satan: "on the Assyrian mount / [Uriel] saw him disfigured"(*PL.* IV. 126–27). Besides, play on a dulcimer need not carry any favourable connotations at all; indeed it could rather be held to function as a demonic counterpart to heavenly music. We recall that Pandaemonium rose to the music "Of *dulcet* symphonies and voices *sweet*" (*PL.* I. 713) (my italics). As Fowler points out, "we are probably ment to see the rising of Pandaemonium as a grotesque travesty of the rising of earth out of chaos at the Creation" (84–85). In other words, Coleridge refers to the Mount of Transfiguration and possibly to the Assyrian mount of degradation, accompanied by music with both divine and satanic overtones. If we wish to invest the maid's musical instrument with any biblical connotations, they would come from Daniel 3.5–6, the only place in the Bible where a dulcimer is mentioned. There it is used in pagan idolatry, i.e. for worshipping "the golden image that Nebuchadnezzar the king hath set up". What we have to understand from these paradoxical fusions is that the poet in his creative activity is both divine and demonic; he conflates both divine Creation and the Fall; he constructs some kind of Paradise, but since Eden is lost, he must recreate it. According to Shelley, the poet creates a paradise out of the wrecks of Eden (497). The last lines of the poem emphasize this dual, divine-demonic nature of the poet-maker:

> Beware! Beware!
> His flashing eyes, his floating hair!
> Weave a circle round him thrice,

And close your eyes with holy dread,
For he on honey-dew hath fed,
And drunk the milk of Paradise.
(49–54)

In his poetic/creative capacity, the poet is "beyond good and evil". Thus, poetic creation does not necessarily involve any moral consideration, as Shelley also declared: "A poet therefore would do ill to embody his own conceptions of right and wrong, which are usually those of his place and time, in his poetic creations, which participate in neither" (488).

The "beatific" and the "sinister" qualities possess a "common substance"; but they are opposites, as Burke remarks. This way of conflating opposites or linking apparently disconnected ideas is one of Coleridge's devices, and as Prickett points out "this conflation of two (or, in effect, three) meanings to 'imagination' is central to the development of his mature thought "(1989, 143).

Before we leave the last lines of the poem, the word "dew" calls for some clarification. Burke argues that we should look for the uses of a given term "in other works *by Coleridge* rather than asking (...) about possible sources in *other* writers" (34) (Burke's italics). Though it can be fruitful to look into a poet's 'nomenclature', one must avoid the fallacy of presuming that he always uses the same word with the same meaning. However, in *Religious Musings* some analogue to the honey-dew in *KK* can be found: "Of dewy glitter gems each plant and tree"(11). Dew is a traditional image of grace and it lends itself very well to *KK,* since the poet in his creativity is divine and a recipient of grace.

Creativity and chaos

A few more words on the 'landscape' in the poem should be added, as it is relevant to the subsequent discussion of creativity and chaos. A comment of Shaffer's supplies a useful starting point:

> What 'spot' is it we actually see in 'Kubla' at the pregnant visionary moment? The landscape of Revelation is there, certainly: the sacred river, the fountain, the sea where the forces of darkness are imprisoned, the woman both holy and demonic, the sacred enclosure of the Temple. But the immediate impression is of course primarily pastoral, par-

adisiacal, and Oriental, and the imagery has always been felt, rightly, to have been displaced from the undeniable Biblical base. (106)

As we have seen, the landscape in *KK* cannot be said to be "[undeniably] Biblical". The mention of a pleasure-dome, walls and towers tells us that we are dealing with a man-made garden. If we wish to impart biblical significance to it, that significance would reside in the idea that towers and walls, representing the civilized world, are to be found, for instance, in Isaiah (2.13–18), along with a a number of lofty objects in general which are doomed to ultimate destruction. A "stately pleasure-dome" would be another example of a tall man-made object, as would a "Tower of Babel". Other lofty things which will finally be destroyed are cedars, oaks, high mountains and "all the hills that are lifted up".

Nor is there, as was pointed out above, any foundation at all for the belief that the sacred river called Alph constitues a parallel to the river in Revelation. River imagery in the Bible is multifaceted, as is that of the fountain; and both usually have advantageous connotations. Another Isaiah passage might be quoted by way of example: "I will open rivers in high places, and fountains in the midst of the valleys. I will make the wilderness a pool of water, and the dry land springs of water" (41.18). Revelation's "living fountains of waters" (7.17) is another instance. However, the fountain in *KK* seems more like a demonic counterpart of the fountain-imagery in the Bible:

> And from this chasm, with ceaseless turmoil seething,
> As if this earth in fast thick pants were breathing,
> A mighty fountain momently was forced:
> Amid whose swift half-intermitted burst
> Huge fragments vaulted like rebounding hail,
> Or chaffy grain beneath the thresher's flail:
> (17–22)

At a first reading , these lines suggest the idea of something that is in a state of becoming, though in a violent, tormented way. The process is full of agitation and unrest. As was pointed out above, the quoted lines suggest a possible sexual dimension; but the main point is that these "huge fragments", though forceful "like rebounding hail", are still likened to "chaffy grain beneath the thresher's flail". In these lines both divine and demonic implications are, again, conflated.[83] Introducing one of his central images of fecundity, Isaiah portrays the future emerging as a seed (44.3). In another image he presents God as "a travailing woman" crying as she gives birth (42.14). The implication is that "God pregnant with the future, is going to bring forth a new time, in a new creation" (Schökel 178). As we shall see, the Creation, the Fall and the Last Judgement are violently yoked together in the lines quoted above.

To express the idea of some sort of disarray, Coleridge makes use of a simile: "this earth" breathes "in fast thick pants". This derangement might be compared with Nature's reaction at the Fall in *PL*:

> [S]he plucked, she ate:
> Earth felt the wound, and nature from her seat
> Sighing through all her works gave signs of woe
> That all was lost.
> (IX. 781–84)

A second groan ensues when Adam falls (IX. 1000–01). The notion of Nature's change through the Fall is a traditional one. The essentially platonic idea that the whole "creation groaneth and travaileth in pain" also goes back to Rom. 8.2. The idea of earth breathing in "fast thick pants" could be regarded as indicating sexual connotations, but the main idea conveyed here is that of a Fall, which in turn brings something creative into being, a Creation as it were, as discussed above. The conjunction of a creation and a Fall may, typologically, be taken to foreshadow the Last Judgement, because, as Fowler points out, "[n]ature's sigh is only a *sign* (portent) of mutability, because the changes themselves will not take place until man's case has been heard and judged" (484) (Fowler's italics).

The threshing image may be related to biblical contexts. Threshing was, as Fowler says, "a very familiar metaphor for divine judgement" (251) (Jer. 51.33, Hab. 3.12). Another good example is found in Psalm I. It can also be found in Christ's parable of the Last Judgement, which is likened to separating the wheat and the chaff (Matt. 13. 38–40). Metaphorically, of course, the threshing process illustrates the separation of good and evil and is as such a very effective symbol of the Last Judgement. For the Romantics, creation was

---

[83] Burke is of the opinion that "Coleridge could just as well have given us a fountain *without* chaff" (44).

a process constantly threatened by the forces of Chaos. When something comes into being, there is always "chaffy grain", or a residue, left over. Man's frail and elusive belief in a once-and-for-all fixed reason was abandoned: instead there was passion, the personal sensibility of the artist, and the view of the object of art as something self-validating. Consequently, many of the poems written during the Romantic period are concerned with the making of poetry and with presenting poets as attempting the unattainable, a kind of perpetual aspiration which can be understood as a key element in the so-called Romantic longing or yearning.

In an examination of Coleridge's use of particular metaphors in relation to creativity and chaos, a closer look at Milton could help, though his method is basically different from Coleridge's. Whereas Milton carries his poetics of creation on a dialectical level in his treatment of Chaos, Coleridge conflates the divine and the demonic. Milton in *PL* argues, albeit poetically, in order to put his "great argument" across. He conveys the relation between creativity and Chaos in words and concepts which carry dialectical or antithetical patterns. (As an example of a commonplace contrast, there is the parody of the holy Trinity of God, Son, and Spirit in the demonic Trinity of Satan, Sin and Death, or the building of Pandaemonium, which is a parody of "how the Heavens and Earth rose out of Chaos".) Even so, we should note the ambivalent qualities of Chaos, as Michael Lieb indicates: "The chaotic realm is imbued with the potentiality for glorious production and inglorious destruction"(16); that is, destruction or demonic creativity lies in dangerous proximity to the divine. They are both an outcome of Chaos. Chaos is formless and unmanifested but still full of possibilities, a potential for good or for evil. Therefore, as Lieb writes, "Chaos becomes the referent through which the powers of God and Satan, of creative Deity and destructive anti-deity, work their way" (16).

Milton thus argues dialectically, whereas Coleridge does not; instead he fuses heavenly and infernal dimensions and phenomena. This peculiar technique has led to many delusions in the interpretative story of *KK*, but they have a useful function in that they illustrate the richness of the poem's interpretative potential. A good example of Coleridge's conflation of the divine and the demonic is the metaphor of the thresher's flail, which carries both negative and positive connotations; it is heavenly and hellish, both prelapsarian and postlapsarian, possessed of a life-giving creative force which is also tumultuous and destructive.

Poetry as understood by the Romantics embodies both creativity and destruction, both Creation and Fall. Moral considerations as to what could be factual or delusive, good or evil, divine or demonic are not always appropriate. The poet-maker is almighty; he "decrees", as it were, and his poetic creation does not engage with distinguishing between good and evil.

As was mentioned by way of introduction, the ironic undermining of both reality and the illusory in the Preface and the poem suggests that *KK* is not allusive to anything but itself. This means that it is neither dependent nor independent on reality or on the functioning of allusions, as source-hunting has shown. In fact *KK* students find themselves facing a kind of "interdependent state". Despite allusions and references which might strike us as apparent, even leading us into pages on possible references or background research (as is certainly the case in the present book), the great challenge remains: once the different elements, allusions or possible allusions and echoes are identified, we are still outside the poem.

Great art claims an attitude from the audience; it invites interpretation. What has been achieved is a critical history of *KK* which could also be regarded as part of the poem. This two-hundred-year-long story has brought forth a plethora of different responses, ranging from broodings upon the Preface to speculations as to how opium affects the possibility to create. An enormous amount of interest and work has been devoted to and invested in tracing allusive elements and references. There are the soundly scholarly interpretations and the more fanciful ones; there are the innocent, the observant, the intelligent, the scornful, the imaginative, the resourceful readers. What do all these responses have in common? The answer is an easy one: the poem *KK*, which has proved itself to be an atemporal non-fixed object which has created an audience. We have been deluded many times in our interpretations, projecting our expectations to fill in empty spaces; we have let our imagination run in many directions in order to make sense of the poem. The technique used by Coleridge in *KK* is very similar to that of painting, for instance to Turner's, whose paintings became progressively more fluid and mysterious, or to techniques where the painter leaves out areas of the canvas. This is also the device of the fragment: suggestivenesss through incompleteness. Art transforms, changes and metaphorizes reality. All art is a metamorphosis of some sort, and poetry is very much about the impossibilities present in the real world. Coleridge built his dome in air.

Postscript

This study has argued that the motif of the Fallen World plays an important role in Coleridge's poetry. While a brief summary of early poems – which also explore the notion of a Fallen World – was presented, Coleridge's major poems *The Rime of the Ancient Mariner, Christabel* and *Kubla Khan* have been the main object of the book. Milton's *Paradise Lost* has served as an intertextual tool. In this intertextuality – which could be seen as an "establishment of a creative interaction between texts, each making the other exist", to use Jasper's words (1992, 83) – the text itself has been the focus of interest and the starting-point of explorations. Using *Paradise Lost* as an intertextual foil throughout allowed themes and metaphors inherent in a Fallen World to emerge clearly in Coleridge's poetry. It has been my wish to expose contextual and existential situations and dimensions in the text, too. By considering a text against a certain convention, we might perceive not only its allegiance or similarity to such a tradition; its newness or 'otherness' might be discovered, too. Such dimensions can – as has been pointed out – only be perceived if we possess some knowledge of the given, an acquaintance which is essential particularly if we aspire to deconstruct a text. The attitudes, terminologies and formulations of methods for approaching a text that are current today could be labelled hermeneutic in a wide sense, in that they are engaged with the understanding of a text. In a more narrow sense, however, the hermeneutic approach has to do with factors involved at the moment we set about interpreting a text. Perception, familiarity with the given and self-knowledge are elements in any interpretation. However, our perception and self-knowledge are subjective; in a fallen world, the outcome of any interpretation will hence be fragmentary and only partly adequate. We might be tempted to resort to some sort of cultural relativism or, at the other extreme, anxiously embrace a complete hermeneutic solution. This last resort leads to the freezing of an *objet d'art* into something static.

Before the Fall, no questions were asked since there were no problems to be solved, no decisions to make. In a fallen world, questioning becomes part of our exploration of the world and ourselves. Questions and answers always lead to some appreciation (cognizance) of self and others. Endeavouring to get behind/beyond the Fall does not entail being in possesion of the truth; instead, it amounts to a yearning towards an understanding. The outcome of our explorations also depends on where our wandering vanity takes us. Part of our task – and obligation – should consist in attempting an assemblage of the given and inquiring whether it has any bearing on the work of art in question. This could be seen as a process of reflection on the work, the subject of our investigation. Thus, in any theoretical approach to a work of art, especially when it involves using a deconstructive gesture – acknowledging the gaps in the relations between poet, work and reader, as well as the instability of these three components – it is not possible to arrive at a consideration or interpretation in a void. Even if our self-satisfied musings take us to different locations, we can never evade the given.

Art makes a generous gesture in that it allows for different interpretative voices. This condition, however, also exposes it to preying fingers. A certain degree of self-searching should be part of all intellectual activities, including what I called the process of reflection. For instance, *pseudo*-Freudian speculations on a text – which reveal a lack of knowledge not only of the given, but unfortunately also of the psychoanalytical school itself – will sometimes be the only contact a student will have with literary criticism. If we believe that we know the poet and his work better than he/she, our wandering vanity has led us into the wilderness – particularly if our expositions are imbued with anxiety, even hatred, stating inaccurate "facts" *a priori* in support of our opinions. The problem with such "literary doorkeepers", to use a phrase from Coleridge, was addressed by him in the following terms: "But how are we to guard against the herd of promiscuous Readers? Can we bid our books be silent in the presence of the unworthy?" (*The Friend* I. 51). This Coleridge quotation betrays a kind of elitist thinking; but as has been argued elsewhere, such ideas were inherent in Romantic literature. Without going into the particular situation in which this statement was made, we could instead argue that a poem might in fact remain silent in front of some readers. Whether the "promiscuous Readers" are "unworthy" or not is not in our power to judge; the point I wish to stress by means of this Coleridge quotation is that a a text may in fact remain silent in that it does not surrender when criticism turns abusive.

In my examination of the poem *KK*, I stressed the idea of dialogue in literary criticism, or what was referred to as a sort of 'audience' for a text in the course of time. The critic is – at least if he/she has not interrupted the dialogue by abusing both the poet and his text – a representative of fallen man who listens and asks questions, participating in a hermeneutic community. The abusive critic silences the text which then becomes as a Christabel, failing to communicate what has happened, or – when trying to tell – yielding a confused narration. Even so, you cannot kill a powerful text; in the attempt it might, sooner or later, turn into something else, perhaps metaphorizing itself into a singing bird, as an image of "the viewless wings of Poesy" (Keats, "Ode to a Nightingale", IV), telling us of beauty but also reminding us of both ancient and recent wrongs.

In the poems discussed here, particularly in *AM,* Nature comes forward as something separate, apart from man. Fallen Nature does not explain how things ought to be; it does not provide an ordered system where the universe can be explained; and it does not yield to questions, such as how and why. Nature as separated from man reveals its own manifestations, according to its own choice, as a whirlwind or in a soft thin voice. Nature does not deal with self. It excludes itself from our need for evidence: instead, it evokes the need for revelation. In this it leads us into a subjective and active construction of our impressions which could be regarded as a Fortunate Fall: the creation of the individual, who constructs his/her reality, which is both flexible and inconsistent, building trembling wholes out of fragments, filling in, when considering it necessary, gaps and details. With the Romantic emphasis on the individual, the world becomes private. In this separateness, inwardness and consciousness of self, the creation of art will always be an individual thing as perception and self-consciousness will vary from one person to the next. Even Wordsworth's relation to Nature, which could be taken as a pantheist position, is in point of fact only used as a starting-point for his own musings, in the course of which he looks into his own heart and feelings. As Willey very aptly points out when discussing Wordsworth's later poetry in relation to Nature: "The 'philosophic mind' is but consolation; it is a poor substitute for the splendour in the grass and glory in the flower"

(1940, 286). The sense of loss is sublimated into a philosophic quality.

If we were to make an attempt to state what Romanticism stands for, it would be this awareness of a self and the legitimacy of emotion. Reality is not regarded as something which can only be described as a construct with exact and immutably fixed formulas. When adapting emotion to art, the Romantic artist can be considered as perceiving truth, or in Keats's words: "'Beauty is truth, truth beauty,' – that is all / Ye know on earth, and all ye need to know."

In *AM*, Nature is presented as something that is not only apart from man, but even vengeful and demonic. The vision of Nature in *AM* may be labelled schizoid. Interest in the human heart and in psychology led the Romantics to deal with different states of mind, including their explorations of madness. It is in the context of this interest in man's internal world, his soul as it were, that the interest in madness should be considered. The word alienation was mentioned in connection with the concept of 'inner hell'. In this alienation from self and others, man creates his own hell within and without, suffering from a quasi-schizophrenic state with serious consequences for his will and emotional responses, as can be studied in the character of the Mariner. This interest in psychology, in pursuing the personality or identity of a character, is displayed in the many portraits and self-portraits of artists during this period.

It is, of course, natural for contextual circumstances to influence any human expression. The Romantic period was a time of social upheaval and repression. A special kind of optimism was abroad, a hope for a better future. When faced with the French Revolution, its aftermath and the continental wars as well as with the abuses, indifference and heartlessness of different authorities, that optimism turned into pessimism. This circumstance could be viewed as a Fall in itself. When they were too overpowering to be fought, the outward evils might persuade man to look into himself, exploring what values are still there. When evil seems to lurk in the wilderness of the Fallen World, man turns inward: the loss, admittedly sad, of a community of feeling forces him to look into his own consciousness.

The separation of man from Nature is even more apparent in Coleridge's later poetry, which unfortunately has not received attention in any substantial study. Boulger is a partial exception; he dedicated the last chapter in his book to Coleridge's later poetry. The stress on Coleridge as a prose writer has resulted in a "longstanding neglect of his poetic texts as texts" (Stillinger 5). I would maintain that this neglect can also be felt in readings of his poems, not as texts only but as poetry. Some explanation for considering man and Nature as separate could be derived from Coleridge's readings of Kant, as mentioned in my introduction. Boulger also points out that "the semidualism he inherited from Kant, served as a force denying him the possibility of becoming a Christian poet in the traditional sense" (206).

Of course, this semidualism does not suffice as an explanation of that disturbed relationship between man and Nature in a Fallen World which pervades Coleridge's poetry. More disquieting, though, is the fact that the normal consolations of a Christian – for instance joy – are largely absent from his major poems and later poetry. For a Christian, even the Fallen World is mitigated by the belief in the relief of redemptive powers, powers which are not related to Nature but belong to man's spiritual inheritance, his soul. In Coleridge's later poetry, for instance in "Human Life. On the Denial of Immortality" (publ. in *Sibylline Leaves*, 1817), man is explained as "Surplus of Nature's dread activity"(10), "Blank accident! nothing's anomaly!" (14). This poem, as Boulger remarks, shows "a breakdown between spirit and Nature [as] complete" (208). The poems "Constancy to an Ideal Object" (publ. 1825) and "Work without Hope" publ. 1828), the separation between spirit and Nature is complete. Later poems dispense with relationships between man, spirit, thought and Nature. In "Baptismal Birthday" there is a complete surrender of personality and will, or, as Boulger remarks: "a complete surrender to the extreme Calvinistic position" (215). There are terms such as "Christ my all", "Eternal Thou and everlasting we", "In Christ we live". Boulger is of the opinion that the lack of structure and tension in this poem "shows that Coleridge has not been able to turn his religious interest into good poetry" (216).

It is apparent that Coleridge's poetry draws heavily on Christian tradition and biblical associations. As mentioned, an important dimension in Christian life is joy; so is the belief in redemption and in a transcendentally good God. Coleridge presents Nature separated from man and spirit by some evil entity. When he uses the idea of a Fortunate Fall, his Nature is drawn from the shadows reflected by imagination. We have seen how imagination works in the poem *KK*. The *tertium aliquid*, a product of the secondary imagination, is also discussed by Coleridge in the following way: "In short, what I had supposed substances were thinned away into shadows, while every where shadows were deepened into substances:

'If substance may be call'd what shadow seem'd,
For each seem'd either! '

> Milton.

(*Biographia Literaria* ch. 13, 301)
(*PL* II. 669–70 in Fowler's ed. reads as follows: "Or substance might be called that shadow seemed, / For each seemed either".)

The quoted lines from *Paradise Lost* are a description of Death. There seems to be little in the way of Christian consolation in Coleridge's poetry. The Fallen World is left unredeemed.

Coleridge wrote on theology and religious matters, it is true; but his protean oeuvre also includes writings on philosophy, psychology, politics, literature, literary criticism, history, and journalism, and they are as comprehensive as his religious or theological works. In order to try to comprehend Coleridge's position, the connection between belief and poetry in general could be considered. This connection has been studied by Jasper, who considers four kinds of relationships. With regard to the second relationship, he quotes Yeats and Kipling as examples illustrating his position. Jasper states that both poets draw heavily on biblical associations and Christian tradition as sources for their poetry. This kind of poetry requires the particular elements of doctrine and its imagery, as Jasper points out:

> Clearly doctrine and symbolism remain powerful for Yeats and Kipling (...) because they are so deeply embedded in the culture in which they lived. Their poetry required this particular element if it was to plumb the depths of the human society which was its concern; for it remains a profoundly formative element in our society, even if it is one which we may choose to challenge, reject or ignore. (1992, 16,17)

Thus, Christian tradition – including its dogmas, terminologies and imagery – can be put to use as a contrivance not primarily for stressing or defining what is religious, but for comprehending man's situation and relation to Nature, exploring man's ontological status or as a comment on or standpoint in respect of current situations. The last statement could, as was argued above, be germane to the poem *CH*.

Coleridge's later poetry, though only superficially reviewed here, hence also shows an adherence to the Fallen World motif. However, in connection with later poetry, the poem "To Nature" (publ. 1836) should be included. It is at variance with other poems from the same period. Here Nature gives solace, "inward joy", and "lessons of love and earnest piety".

The Fallen World is incontestably present in Coleridge's poetry. In an attempt to understand why evil is prominent and forceful in Coleridge's Fallen World, I would like to quote from Willey's discussion of Joseph Butler, as it might shed some light on Coleridge's standpoint:

> In passing from Shaftesbury to Butler we pass from an optimistic to a relatively pessimistic theory of the world. It is not strange that the champion of orthodoxy should be more pessimistic than the heretic, for the Christian tradition had always been associated rather with a sense of the imperfection of Nature and of man, in their present state, than with any optimism of the eighteenth century type. (1940, 78)

But then again, pessimism is a pervading mood in Romanticism and in no way particular for Coleridge.

At this point, one wonders if it is the critic's province to determine a poet's denominational habitat, which is something quite different from examining the text's relation to a certain religion or belief, or from the attempt to establish or define the religious or Christian elements in his/her verse. This problem is raised by Jasper in his discussion of Hans Urs van Balthasar's *Herrlichkeit*. According to Jasper,

> the crux of the matter is not whether a poet can be defined as 'Christian' or categorized by his belief or worldview, but rather the way in which the poet makes use of the sacred, and how, in series of specified writers (…) a genuine dialogue is established between the divine and the human, the theological and the literary. Dialogue and not identification of the two spheres is the key to the discussion. (1992, 75)

In Coleridge's case, critics have even assigned dates to his different "beliefs". Such critical exercises as categorizing and dating someone's "beliefs" may not only amount to trespassing into a domain which belongs to "the holiness of the heart's affection", to use a phrase from Keats (*Letters*, 22 Nov. 1817, 36); it might also easily lead to the fallacy of concluding that the poet or writer belongs to the critic's own party.

However, when discussing Butler's relation to evil, Willey considers that Butler "looks [evil] more directly in the face, and with a more disillusioned eye, than the optimists of the time" (78). This is exactly what Coleridge did, or dared to do: look evil "in the face".

In October 1803, Coleridge wrote :

> To return to the Question of Evil – woe to the man, to whom it is an uninteresting Question – tho' many a mind, overwearied by it, may shun it with Dread / and here, N.B. scourge with deserved & lofty Scorn those Critics who laugh at the discussion of old Questions – God, Right & Wrong, necessity & Arbitrement – Evil, &c – No! forsooth! – the Question must be new, *new spicy hot* Gingerbread (*Notebooks I*, 1622 , 21. 379)

We may as Coleridge puts it, "shun [Evil] with Dread" when "overwearied by it"; but it does not disappear even if we attempt to turn it into something else by using different defensive strategies or excuses, thereby closing our eyes to its presence.

Unwillingness to confront evil has often had an unfavourable influence on *CH* criticism. Evil might be considered fascinating, even be regarded as fashionable, in some quarters; but since it is obscene and offensive, it is not fit for the drawing-room. This could go some way towards explaining why *CH*, although a central poem in English literature, has not been given proper critical attention before. A close intertextual reading with *PL* confirms that evil is at work in Coleridge's texts.

The element of exaggeration which we might find in some of Coleridge's images – images which were also common in English seventeenth-century poets – moves the reader towards an emotional response. A similar factor can be seen to operate in the works of some seventeenth-century poets, particularly religious ones. Our attention is drawn to a particular state of affairs; an emotional response is engendered; at the same time, some sort of spiritual truth is conveyed: consequently, these images support the belief that art might change the reader/spectator. In a typological reading – never before applied to Coleridge's poetry, as far as I know – the abuses of an actual Fallen World appear. In a time agitated by conflicts and doubts, this way of presenting evil and crisis could also be seen as a yearning if not for peace and redemption, then for illumination or revelation. Spiritual drought and unfavourable external circumstances might, strangely enough, be conducive to inner progress, or in Keats's words: "Until we are sick, we understand not" (*Letters* 3 May 1818, 93). When secular and spiritual powers fail and betray us, and human existence is undermined by non-improvement and disillusionment, man turns inward; in the 1790s people were looking forward to a Second Coming and to the Final Judgement. This is one factor enabling us to refer to Romanticism as a kind of religious movement.

It was argued that *KK* could be read as a Romantic manifesto. Preface and verse should be read together. The poem demonstrates the poetic process and adheres to the idea of a Fortunate Fall: thanks to a Fall, that is, man creates, though his creations are fragile. The poem also reveals how we as individuals behave in front of a piece of art. By and large, the reference to *Purchas* generously supplied by Coleridge has either been ignored or subjected to ironic comment. The place-names in the poem have too often led to critical confusion. My examination was also intent on showing that we should listen to and trust the poem.

Each period has its own terminologies, formulations and methods; but it is astonishing how similar the polemics, concepts and approaches are from one time to another. (It seems that what differs are just the terminologies and the formulations of theory.) We could affirm that modern literary criticism started during Romanticism, stressing the individuality in interpretation as well as the contextual situation of a text. On the other hand, the ancient concept of a Fallen World has great affinities with both Romantic literary theory and modern literary theory in its approach to, and method of understanding a text.

The text is the assignment; it is the only entity which can present some sort of stability, though, admittedly, it still varies and moves according to the reader's response to it. However, system-builders and literary doorkeepers of whatever kind come and go, according to fashion; what prevails is the text, the poet and the reader – though not always in a stable relation. The legacy of a Fall is, paradoxically, both hope and despair. In our wrestle with ourselves and the text, we arrive at an acceptance of limitations as well as at a hope for redemption, experiencing both despair, revolt and longing for prelapsarian unity and perfection. This tension between hope and despair is expressed in the very last lines of *PL*:

> Some natural tears they dropped, but wiped them
>> soon;
> The world was all before them, where to choose
> Their place of rest, and providence their guide:
> They hand in hand with wandering steps and slow,
> Through Eden took their solitary way.

Bibliography

Abrams, M.H. *The Mirror and the Lamp: Romantic Theory and the Critical Tradition*. Oxford University Press, 1953.

– *A Glossary of Literary Terms*. Holt–Saunders International Editions, 1984.

Alter, Robert and Frank Kermode. "General Introduction." *The Literary Guide to the Bible*. Eds. R. Alter and F. Kermode. London: F. Fontana Press, 1987, 1–8.

Aristotle. *Poetics*. Ed. M. Heath. Penguin Books, 1996.

Ashton, Rosemary. *The Life of Samuel Taylor Coleridge*. Oxford: Blackwell, 1996.

Auden, W. H. *The Enchafed Flood or Romantic Iconography of the Sea*. New York: Random House, 1950.

Auerbach, Erich. *Scenes from the Drama of European Literature*. New York: Meridian Books, 1959.

Barnes, Robert and Stephen Prickett. Eds. *The Bible*. Cambridge University Press, 1991.

Barth, Robert, S.J. *Coleridge and Christian Doctrine*. Cambridge/Mass.: Harvard University Press, 1969.

– "Coleridge and the Church of England. " Gravil and Lefebure 291–307.

Beddoes, Thomas Lovell. *Works*. Ed. H.W. Donner. Oxford University Press, 1935.

Beer, John. *Coleridge the Visionary*. London: Chatto & Windus, 1959.

– "Coleridge and the Poems of the Supernatural." Brett 45–90.

– ed. *Coleridge's Variety – Bicentenary Studies*. University of Pittsburgh Press,1974.

– "The Languages of Kubla Khan." Gravil, Newlyn and Roe 221–259.

Bennett, Jack A.W. *Poetry of the Passion: Studies in Twelve Centuries of English Verse*. Oxford: Clarendon Press, 1982.

Berkeley, George. *Principles of Human Knowledge: Three Dialogues*. The World's Classics. Oxford University Press, 1996.

Berkoben, Lawrence. "Christabel: A Variety of Evil Experience." *Modern Language Quarterly* 25 (1964): 400–11.

The Bible. King James's Version. The Cambridge Standard Text Edition. Cambridge University Press [1986].

Bicknell, E.J. *A Theological Introduction to the Thirty–Nine Articles of the Church of England* . London: Longmans, Green and Co., 1925.

Bloom, Harold. *The Visionary Company: A Reading of English Romantic Poetry.* Ithaca & London: Cornell University Press, 1971.

– ed. and introd. *Modern Critical Views: John Milton.* New York: Chelsea House Publishers, 1986.

– ed. and introd. *Modern Critical Views: Samuel Taylor Coleridge.* New York: Chelsea House Publishers, 1986.

Bodkin, Maud. *Archetypal Patterns in Poetry: Psychological Studies of Imagination.* Oxford University Press 1934. New York: Vintage Books,1958.

Boettner, Lorraine. *The Reformed Doctrine of Predestination.* Grand Rapids, Michigan: W.M. B. Eerdmans Publishing Co., 1960.

Borges, Jorge Luis. *El Aleph.* Buenos Aires: Emece Editores, S.A., 1985.

Bostetter, Edward. "The Nightmare World of the Ancient Mariner. " Coburn 65–77.

Boulger, James D. *Coleridge as Religious Thinker.* New Haven: Yale University Press, 1961.

Bredvold, Louis I. Introd. *Coleridge on the Seventeenth Century.* Brinkley 1968.

Brett, R.L. Ed. *Writers and Their Background: Samuel Taylor Coleridge.* London: G. Bell and Sons, 1971.

Brinkley, Roberta Florence. Ed. *Coleridge on the Seventeenth Century.* New York: Greenwood Press, 1968.

– and Keith Hanley. Eds. *Romantic Revisions.* Cambridge University Press,1992.

Brisman, Leslie. "Coleridge and the Ancestral Voices." *The Georgia Review* 29 (1975): 469–498.

– "Edenic Time." Bloom (*Milton*) 1986, 149–161.

Broadbent, J.B. *Some Graver Subject: An Essay on Paradise Lost.* London: Chatto & Windus , 1960.

Brooks, Colin. "England 1782–1832: the historical context." Prickett 1981, 15–76.

Burke, Kenneth. "Kubla Khan: Proto–Surrealist Poem." Bloom (*Coleridge*)1986, 33–52.

Bush, Douglas. *English Literature in the Earlier Seventeenth Century.* Oxford: Clarendon Press, 1945.

Byatt, A.S. *Unruly Times: Wordsworth and Coleridge in their Time.* London: The Hogarth Press, 1970.

Byron, George Gordon, Lord. *The Complete Poetical Works.* Ed. Jerome J. McGann. Oxford: Clarendon Press, 1980, 1981, 1991.

– *Letters and Journals.* 6 vols. Ed. Rowland E. Prothero. London: John Murray, 1901.

Calvino, Italo. *Invisible Cities.* Trans. William Weaver. London: Vintage, 1997.

Coleridge, Samuel Taylor. *The Notebooks.* Text and Notes, 4 vols. Ed. Kathleen Coburn, 1957, 1961.

– *Coleridge Complete Poetical Works.* Ed. Ernest Hartley Coleridge. Oxford: Clarendon Press, 1912, reprint Oxford University Press,1969.

– *Collected Letters of Samuel Taylor Coleridge.* 6 vols. Ed. E.L. Griggs, Oxford: Clarendon Press 1958, 1971.

The following works are from *The Collected Works of Samuel Taylor Coleridge*, Routledge and Kegan Paul, Bollingen Series, Princeton University Press:

– *Lectures 1795 : On Politics and Religion.* Eds. Lewis Patton and Peter Mann, 1971.

– *The Watchman*. Ed. Lewis Patton, 1970.

– *The Friend*. 2 vols. Ed. Barbara E. Rooke, 1969.

– *Lectures 1808–1819: On Literature*. 2 vols. Ed. R.A. Foakes, 1987.

– *Lay Sermons*. Ed. R. J. White, 1972.

– *Biographia Literaria, or Biographical Sketches of My Literary Life and Opinions*. 2 vols. Eds. James Engell and W. Jackson Bate, 1983.

– *Aids to Reflection*. Ed. John Beer, 1993.

– *Marginalia*. 3 vols. Eds. H.J. Jackson and George Whalley, 1992.

– *Table Talk*. 2 vols. Recorded by Henry Nelson Coleridge (and John Taylor Coleridge). Ed. Carl Woodring, 1990.

Chamber, Alma Jane. "Christabel in Context". Dissertation, University of North Carolina at Chapel Hill, 1983.

Coburn, Kathleen. Ed. *A Collection of Critical Essays*. Englewood Cliffs, N.Y.: Prentice–Hall, 1960.

Crashaw, Richard. *Poetical Works*. Ed. L.C. Martin. Oxford: Clarendon Press, 1927.

Cruz, San Juan de la. *Poesías Completas*. Ed. and introd. by Cristobal Cuevas. Barcelona: Bruguera, 1981.

St John of the Cross. *Poems*. Trans. by Roy Campbell. Ed. E.V. Rieu. The Penguin Classics, 1960.

Cuddon, J.A. *Dictionary of Literary Terms*. Penguin Books, 1991.

Cunnar, Eugene R. "Crashaw's 'Sancta Maria Dolorum'. " Roberts 99–126.

Daley, Morton and Tim Fulford. Eds. *Coleridge's Visionary Languages*. Cambridge: D.S Brewer, 1993.

Daniélou, Jean. *From Shadows to Reality: Studies in the Biblical Typology of the Fathers*. Trans. Wulstan Hibberd. London: Burns & Oates,1960.

Danielson, Dennis. *Milton's Good God: A Study in Literary Theodicy*. Cambridge University Press, 1982.

– ed. *The Cambridge Companion to Milton*. Cambridge University Press,1989.

Dante Alighieri. *The Divine Comedy*. Transl. Dorothy L. Sayers. Penguin Classics 1988 edition.

Davidson, Graham. *Coleridge's Career*. London: Macmillan, 1990.

Deconinck-Brossard, Françoise. "England and France in the Eighteenth Century." Prickett 1991, 136–181.

Dix, Dom Gregory. *The Shape of the Liturgy*. First publ. in 1945. Repr. by A & C Black, London 1993.

Downing, Taylor and Maggie Millman. Eds. *Civil War*. London: Collins and Brown, 1992.

Donne, John. *Works*. The Wordsworth Poetry Library, 1994 edition.

Eliade, Mircea. *The Sacred and the Profane*. San Diego, New York and London: Harcourt Brace,1957, repr. in 1987.

Eliot, T.S. "The Metaphysical Poets." *TLS*, 1031, 20 October 1921: 669–70.

– "Tradition and the Individual Talent." *Selected Essays,* 3rd ed. London: Faber and Faber, 1951.

Elmen, Paul. "Jeremy Taylor and the Fall of Man. "*Modern Language Quarterly* 14, June 1953: 139–148.

Empson, William. "Heaven." Bloom (*Milton*) 1986, 39–60.

Evans, J.M. *Paradise Lost and the Genesis Tradition.* Oxford: Clarendon Press, 1968.

Freeman, Rosemary. *English Emblem Books.* London: Chatto & Windus, 1967.

Fruman, Norman. *The Damaged Archangel.* New York: Braziller, 1971.

– "On Editing Coleridge: Creative Process and Concealment in Coleridge's Poetry." Brinkley and Hanley 154–168.

Frye, Northrop. *Anatomy of Criticism: Four Essays.* Princeton University Press, 1957; Penguin ed. 1997.

– *The Great Code. The Bible and Literature.* London:Routledge and Kegan Paul, 1982.

– *Words with Power, Being a Second Study of the Bible and Literature.* San Diego, New York and London: Harcourt Brace Jovanovich, 1990.

Fulford, Tim. *Coleridge's Figurative Language.* London: Macmillan, 1991.

– and Morton Daley. Eds. *Coleridge's Visionary Languages.* Cambridge: D.S. Brewer, 1993.

Gerber, Richard. "Onomastic Symbolism in Coleridge's 'Christabel.' "*Studien zur englischen und amerikanischen Literatur,* Neumünster (1974): 188–194.

Gravil, Richard, Lucy Newlyn and Nicholas Roe. Eds. *Coleridge's Imagination. Essays in Memory of Peter Laver.* Cambridge University Press, 1985.

Gravil, Richard and Molly Lefebure. Eds. *The Coleridge Connection: Essays for Thomas McFarland.* London: Macmillan, 1990.

Gravil, Richard. "Introduction and Orientation." Richard Gravil and Lefebure, 1990. 1–23.

Greenberg, Moshe. "Job". Alter and Kermode 283–304.

Hanley, Keith and Roberta Florence Brinkley. Eds. *Romantic Revisions.* Cambridge University Press, 1992.

Harding, Anthony John. *Coleridge and the Idea of Love.* Cambridge University Press, 1974.

Havens, Raymond Dexter. *The Influence of Milton on English Poetry.* Cambridge/Mass.: Harvard University Press, 1922.

Hawthorn, Jeremy. *A Concise Glossary of Contemporary Literary Theory.* 2nd ed. London: Edward Arnold, 1996.

Healy, Thomas. "Crashaw and The Sense of History." Roberts 49–65.

Herbert, George. *The Complete English Poems.* Ed. John Tobin. Penguin Books, 1991.

Hill, J. E. Christopher. *The Intellectual Origins of the English Revolution.* Oxford: Clarendon Press, 1965.

– *Milton and the English Revolution.* London: Faber and Faber, 1977.

Hill, John Spencer. *A Coleridge Companion: An Introduction to the Major Poems and the Biographia Literaria.* London: Macmillan Press, 1983.

Holmes, Richard. *Coleridge: Early Visions.* London: Penguin Books, 1990.

Honour, Hugh. *Romanticism.* London: Butler & Tanner, 1979.

Irvine, Christopher. Ed. *Worship Resources for Easter to Pentecost.* London: Mowbray, 1996.

Jasper, David. *Coleridge as Poet and Religious Thinker.* London: Macmillan, 1985.

– *The Study of Literature and Religion.* First publ. in 1989. Repr. London: Macmillan, 1992.

Johansson, Stig. *Kort lärobok i engelsk fonetik.* Lund: Studentlitteratur, 1972.

Johnson, Lee M. "Milton's Epic Style: the invocations in *Paradise Lost.* " Danielson 65–78.

Keats, John. *Poetical Works.* Ed.H.W. Garrod. Oxford University Press, 1987.

– *Letters*. Ed. Robert Gittings. Oxford University Press, 1987.

Kelsey McColley, Diane. *A Gust for Paradise, Milton's Eden and the Visual Arts*. Urbana and Chicago:University of Illinois Press, 1993.

Kermode, Frank and R. Alter. Eds. *The Literary Guide to the Bible*. London: F. Fontana Press, 1987.

Knight, G. Wilson. *The Starlit Dome*. London: Methuen, 1959.

Landry, Francis. "The Song of Songs. " Alter and Kermode 305–319.

Lampe, G. W. H, and K. J. Woolcombe. "The Reasonableness of Typology. " *Essays on Typology: Studies in Biblical Theology* 22. London: SCM Press, 1957, 9–38.

Lefebure, Molly and R. Gravil. Eds. *The Coleridge Connection: Essays for Thomas McFarland*. London: Macmillan, 1990.

Leonard, John. *Naming in Paradise: Milton and the Language of Adam and Eve*. Oxford: Clarendon Press, 1990.

Levere, Trevor H. *Poetry Realized in Nature: Samuel Taylor Coleridge and Early Nineteenth Century Science*. Cambridge University Press, 1981.

Lewalski, Barbara Kiefer. *Protestant Poetics and the Seventeenth-Century Religious Lyric*. Princeton University Press, 1979.

Lewis, C.S. "A Preface to Paradise Lost." The Ballard Matthews Lectures delivered at University College, North Wales 1941. Oxford University Press, 1942.

Lieb, Michael. *The Dialectics of Creation: Patterns of Birth and Regeneration in Paradise Lost*. [Amherst]: University of Massachusetts Press, 1970.

Logan, Beryl. Ed. *Immanuel Kant Prolegomena to Any Future Metaphysics*. London and New York: Routledge, 1996.

Longley, John Lewis, Jr. Ed. *R. P. Warren – A Collection of Critical Essays*. New York University Press, 1965.

Lowes, John Livingston. *The Road to Xanadu*. London and Cambridge/Mass.: Constable, 1927.

Lowth, Robert. *Lectures on the Sacred Poetry of the Hebrews*. Trans. G. Gregory. London, 1787.

MacCaffrey, Isabel G. "Satan's Voyage." Bloom (*Milton*) 1986, 19–38.

Madsén, William G. *From Shadowy Types to Truth*. New Haven and London: Yale University Press, 1968.

Marigny, Jean. *Le Vampire dans la littérature Anglo-Saxonne*. Paris: Didier Erudition,1985.

Marshall, Walker. *A Vision Earned*. Edinburgh: Paul Harris, 1979.

Martin, John Rupert. *Baroque*. New York: Harper and Row, 1977.

Martz, Louis L. *The Poetry of Meditation: A Study in English Religious Literature of the Seventeenth Century*. New Haven and London: Yale University Press, 1954.

McFarland, Thomas. *Coleridge and the Pantheist Tradition*. Oxford: Clarendon Press, 1969.

– *Romanticism and the Forms of Ruin: Wordsworth, Coleridge, and Modalities of Fragmentation*. Princeton University Press, 1981.

– "Romantic imagination, nature, and the pastoral ideal." Gravil, Newlyn and Roe 5–21.

McGinn, Bernard. "Revelation." Alter and Kermode 523–541.

Millman, Maggie and Taylor Downing. Eds. *Civil War*. Repr. by A & C Black, London 1993.

Milton, John. *Paradise Lost*. Ed. Alastair Fowler. London: Longman, ed. 1971.

Newlyn, Lucy, R. Gravil and N. Roe. Eds. *Coleridge's Imagination: Essays in Memory of Peter Laver*. Cambridge University Press, 1985.

Newlyn, Lucy. *Paradise Lost and the Romantic Reader*. Oxford University Press, 1992.

Olsson, Bernt. *Spegels Guds Werk och Hwila. Stockholm:* Natur och Kultur, 1963.

Otten, Charlotte F. "'My native Element': Milton's Paradise and English Gardens." *Milton Studies* 5 (1973): 249–267.

Paglia, Camille. *Sexual Personae – Art and Decadence from Nefertiti to Emily Dickinson.* Penguin Books, 1991.

Patrides, C.A. "Renaissance and Modern Views on Hell." *The Harvard Theological Review* 57 (1964): 217–235.

– *Milton and the Christian Tradition.* Oxford: Clarendon Press, 1966.

– "Something like Prophetic Strain: Apocalyptic Configurations in Milton." *English Language Notes* 19. 3, March 1982:193–207.

Peterfreund, Stuart. "The Way of Immanence: Coleridge and the Problem of Evil." *ELH* 55. 1, Spring 1988:125–149.

Piper, H.W. *The Active Universe.* London: Athlone Press, 1962.

– "The Two Paradises in Kubla Khan". *Review of English Studies* 27 (1976): 148–158.

– *The Singing of Mount Abora.* London and Toronto: Associated University Press, 1987.

– "The Unitarian Consensus. " Gravil and Lefebure 273–290.

Praz, Mario. Introd. *Three Gothic Novels.* Penguin Classics, 1986.

Prickett, Stephen. Ed. *The Context of English Literature. The Romantics.* London: Methuen, 1981.

– ed. *Reading the Text: Biblical Criticism and Literary Theory.* Oxford: Blackwell, 1991.

– "The Ache in the Missing Limb: Coleridge and the Amputation of Meaning." Fulford and Daley 123–135.

– *Words and the Word: Language, Poetics and Biblical Interpretation.* First publ. in1986. Cambridge University Press, 1989.

– *Origins of Narrative. The Romantic Appropriation of the Bible.* Cambridge University Press, 1996.

Prickett, Stephen and Robert Barnes. *The Bible.* Cambridge University Press, 1991.

Purchas, Samuel. *Haklytus' Posthumus or Purchas His Pilgrimes.* 1625 edition.

Rajan, B. *Paradise Lost and The Seventeenth Century Reader.* London: Chatto and Windus, 1947.

Revard, Stella P. "Crashaw and the Diva." Roberts 80–98.

Roberts, Lorraine and John Roberts. "Crashavian Criticism." *New Perspectives on the Life and Art of Richard Crashaw.* Ed. John Roberts. Columbia and London: University of Missouri Press 1990. 1–29.

Roberts, Lorraine. "Crashaw's Sacred Voice. " Roberts 66–79.

Roe, Nicholas, R. Gravil and Lucy Newlyn. Eds. *Coleridge's Imagination: Esays in Memory of Peter Laver.* Cambridge University Press, 1985.

Ricoeur, Paul. *Hermeneutics and the Human Sciences.* Ed. and trans. John B. Thompson. Cambridge University Press, 1995.

Rossabi, Morries. *Khubilai Khan: His Life and Times.* Berkeley: University of California Press, 1988.

Schaar, Claes. *The Full Voic'd Quire Below: Vertical Context Systems in Paradise Lost.* Lund Studies in English 60: C.W.K. Gleerup, 1982.

– "A Note on Paradise Lost VIII, 42–47." *English Studies* 4 (1987): 313–315.

Schneider, Elisabeth. "The Unknown Reviewer of *Christabel:* Jeffrey, Hazlitt, Tom Moore." *Publications of the Modern Language Association of America.* Ed. William Riley Parker, 70 (1955): 417–432.

– "Tom Moore and the Edinburgh Review of Christabel." *Publications of the Modern Language Assocation of America.* Ed. George Winchester Stone Jr. Vol. 77 (1962): 71–77.

Schökel, Luis Alonso. "Isaiah. " Alter and Kermode 165–183.

Shaffer, E.S. *Kubla Khan and The Fall of Jerusalem: The Mythological School in Biblical Criticism and Secular Literature 1770–1880.* Cambridge University Press, 1980.

– "The Hermeneutic Community: Coleridge and Schleiermacher." Gravil and Lefebure 200–229.

Schwartz, Regina M. *Remembering and Repeating Biblical Creation in Paradise Lost.* Cambridge University Press, 1988.

Shawcross, John T. *John Milton, The Self and the World.* Lexington, K.Y.: University Press of Kentucky, 1993.

Shelley, P. B. *Poetry and Prose.* Eds. Donald H Reiman and Sharon B. Powers. A Norton Critical Edition. New York and London, 1977.

Shoaf, R.A. *Milton, Poet of Duality: A Study of Semiosis in the Poetry and the Prose.* New Haven and London: Yale University Press, 1985.

Sinfield, Alan. *Literature in Protestant England 1560–1660.* London: Croom Helm, 1973.

Simpson, David. *Irony and Authority in Romantic Poetry.* London: Macmillan, 1979.

– *Romanticism, Nationalism and the Revolt against Theory.* Chicago and London: University of Chicago Press, 1993.

Sims, James H. *The Bible in Milton's Epic.* Gainesville: University of Florida Press, 1962.

Smith, Eric. *Some Versions of the Fall: The Myth of the Fall of Man in English Literature.* London: Croom Helm, 1973.

Stemberger, Günter. *Geschichte der jüdischen Literatur. Eine Einführung.* München: Becksche Elementarbücher Verlag C.H. Beck, 1977.

Stewart, Herbert L. "The Place of Coleridge in English Theology". *Harvard Theological Review* 11.1 (1918):1–31.

Stillinger, Jack. *Coleridge and Textual Instability: The Multiple Versions of the Major Poems.* Oxford University Press, 1994.

Stock, R.D. *The Holy and the Daemonic from Sir Thomas Browne to William Blake.* Princeton University Press, 1982.

Sultana, Donald. Ed. *New Approaches to Coleridge.* London: Vision & Barnes & Noble, 1981.

Swaim, Kathleen M. *Before and After the Fall: Contrasting Modes in Paradise Lost.* Amherst: University of Massachusetts Press, 1986.

Tennant, Frederick Robert. *The Sources of the Doctrines of the Fall and Original Sin.* Cambridge University Press, 1903.

Thormählen, Marianne. "Rochester and *The Fall* : The Roots of Discontent." *English Studies* 69. 5, October 1988:396–409.

Trimmer, Sarah. *Help to the Unlearned in the Study of the Holy Scriptures.* Printed by T. Bensley, Bolt Court, 1805.

Tuve, Rosamund. *A Reading of George Herbert*. University of Chicago Press, 1952.

– *Images and Themes in Five Poems by Milton*. Cambridge/Mass.: Harvard University Press, 1957.

Tsuchiya, Kiyoshi. "Coleridge's Phantom and Fact: Two Natures, Trinitarian Resolution, and the Formation of the Pentad to 1825". Dissertation, Glasgow University, 1994.

Wallerstein, Ruth. *Studies in Seventeenth-Century Poetic*. Wisconsin University Press, 1950.

Warren, Robert Penn. "A Poem of Pure Imagination. " *Selected Essays*. Random House (1945–1946), 1958 edition.

– *Audubon: A Vision*. The Norton Anthology of American Literature, 4th ed., vol. 2. New York and London, 1979 edition.

Watson, George. *Coleridge the Poet*. London: Routledge and Kegan Paul, 1966.

Vaughan, Henry. *Works*. 2 vols. Ed. L.C. Martin. Oxford: Clarendon Press, 1914.

Venuti, Lawrence. "The Ideology of the Individual in Anglo–American Criticism: The Example of Coleridge and Eliot." *Boundary*, Fall– Winter 1985–1986: 161–193.

Werkmeister, Lucyle. "The Early Coleridge: His Rage for Metaphysics." *The Harvard Theological Review*. 54 (1961): 99–123.

Whalley, George. "The Bristol Library Borrowings of Southey and Coleridge, 1793–1798." *The Library* 4, Sept. 1949: 114–131.

Wheeler, Kathleen. *The Creative Mind in Coleridge's Poetry*. London: Heinemann Educational Books Ltd., 1981.

Willey, Basil. *Nineteenth Century Studies: Coleridge to Matthew Arnold*. Penguin Book in assoc. with Chatto and Windus, 1949, 1964 edition.

– *The Seventeenth Century Background*. First publ. in 1934. Penguin ed., 1962.

– *The English Moralists*. London: Chatto & Windus, 1964.

– "Coleridge and Religion." Brett 221– 245.

Williams, Norman Powell. *The Ideas of the Fall and of Original Sin: a Historical and Critical Study*. [Bampton Lectures 1924] London: Longmans & Co., 1927.

Woolcombe, K.J. "The Biblical Origins and Patristic Development of Typology." *Essays on Typology, Studies in Biblical Theology 22* (1957): 39–75.

Wordsworth, William. *The Poetical Works*. 5 vols. Ed. E. de Selincourt, Oxford: Clarendon Press 1940, 1941.

– *The Prose Works*. 3 vols. Ed. W. J. B. Owen and J.W. Smyser. Oxford: Clarendon Press, 1974.

The Letters of William and Dorothy Wordsworth. 7 vols. Rev., arr. and ed. by Alan G. Hill. From the first ed. by E. de Selincourt. Oxford: Clarendon Press 1978, 1988.

Wu, Duncan. *Romanticism: An Anthology*. Oxford: Blackwell, 1994.

Young, R.V., Jr. "Crashaw and Biblical poetics." Roberts 30–48.

Zim, Rivkah. "The Reformation: the Trial of God's Word." Prickett 1991, 64–135.

Index

Index of Names

Index of References to Coleridge's Works

Prose

Poetry

"Reason", 184
"My Baptismal Birth-day", 236

Zapolya, 97,
Osorio, n.143

Index of References to Paradise Lost

Index of References to the Bible

Old Testament

New Testament

LUND STUDIES IN ENGLISH

Founded by Eilert Ekwall

Editors: Marianne Thormählen and Beatrice Warren

1 BERTIL WEMAN. 1933. Old English Semantic Analysis and Theory. With Special Reference to Verbs Denoting Locomotion. 187 pp.

2 HILDING BÄCK. 1934. The Synonyms for *child, boy, girl* in Old English. An Etymological-Semasiological Investigation. xvi + 273 pp.

3 GUSTAV FRANSSON. 1935. Middle English Surnames of Occupation. With an Excursus on Toponymical Surnames. 217 pp.

4 GUSTAV HOFSTRAND. 1936. *The Seege of Troye.* A Study in the Intertextual Relations of the Middle English Romance *The Seege or Batayle of Troye.* xv + 205 pp.

5 URBAN OHLANDER. 1936. Studies on Coordinate Expressions in Middle English. 213 pp.

6 VIKTOR ENGBLOM. 1938. On the Origin and Early Development of the Auxiliary Do. 169 pp.

7 IVAR DAHL. 1938. Substantival Inflexion in Early Old English. Vocalic Stems. xvi + 206 pp.

8 HILMER STRÖM. 1939. Old English Personal Names in Bede's History. An Etymological-Phonological Investigation. xliii + 180 pp.

9 UNO PHILIPSON. 1941. Political Slang 1759–1850. xvi + 314 pp.

10 ARTHUR H. KING. 1941. The Language of Satirized Characters in PoÉtaster. A Socio-Stylistic Analysis 1579–1602. xxxiv + 258 pp.

11 MATTIAS T. LÖFVENBERG. 1942. Studies on Middle English Local Surnames. xlv + 225 pp.

12 JOHANNES HEDBERG. 1945. The Syncope of the Old English Present Endings. A Dialect Criterion. 310 pp.

13 ALARIK RYNELL. 1948. The Rivalry of Scandinavian and Native Synonyms in Middle English, especially *taken* and *nimen.* With an Excursus on *nema* and *taka* in Old Scandinavian. 431 pp.

14 HENNING HALLQVIST. 1948. Studies in Old English Fractured *ea.* 167 pp.

15 GÖSTA FORSSTRÖM. 1948. The Verb *to be* in Middle English. A Survey of the Forms. 236 pp.

16 BERTIL WIDÉN. 1949. Studies on the Dorset Dialect. 179 pp.

17 CLAES SCHAAR. 1949. Critical Studies in the Cynewulf Group. 337 pp.

18 BERTIL SUNDBY. 1950. The Dialect and Provenance of the Middle English Poem *The Owl and the Nightingale.* A Linguistic Study. 218 pp.

19 BERTIL THURESSON. 1950. Middle English Occupational Terms. 285 pp.

20 KARL-GUNNAR LINDKVIST. 1950. Studies on the Local Sense of the Prepositions *in, at, on,* and *to,* in Modern English. 429 pp.

21 SVEN RUBIN. 1951. The Phonology of the Middle English Dialect of Sussex. 235 pp.

22 BERTIL SUNDBY. 1953. Christopher Cooper's *English Teacher* (1687). cxvi + 10* + 123 pp.

23 BJÖRN WALLNER. 1954. An Exposition of *Qui Habitat* and *Bonum Est* in English. lxxi + 122 pp.

24 RUDOLF MAGNUSSON. 1954. Studies in the Theory of the Parts of Speech. viii + 120 pp.

25 CLAES SCHAAR. 1954. Some Types of Narrative in Chaucer's Poetry. 293 pp.

26 BÖRJE HOLMBERG. 1956. James Douglas on English Pronunciation c. 1740. 354 pp.

27 EILERT EKWALL. 1959. Etymological Notes on English Place-Names. 108 pp.

28 CLAES SCHAAR. 1960. An Elizabethan Sonnet Problem. Shakespeare's Sonnets, Daniel's *Delia*, and their Literary Background. 190 pp.

29 ELIS FRIDNER. 1961. An English Fourteenth Century Apocalypse Version with a Prose Commentary. Edited from MS Harley 874 and Ten Other MSS. lviii + 290 pp.

30 The Published Writings of Eilert Ekwall. A Bibliography Compiled by Olof von Feilitzen. 1961. 52 pp.

31 ULF JACOBSSON. 1962. Phonological Dialect Constituents in the Vocabulary of Standard English. 335 pp.

32 CLAES SCHAAR. 1962. Elizabethan Sonnet Themes and the Dating of Shakespeare's Sonnets. 200 pp.

33 EILERT EKWALL. 1963. Selected Papers. 172 pp.

34 ARNE ZETTERSTEN. 1965. Studies in the Dialect and Vocabulary of the *Ancrene Riwle*. 331 pp.

35 GILLIS KRISTENSSON. 1967. A Survey of Middle English Dialects 1290–1350. The Six Northern Counties and Lincolnshire. xxii + 299 pp.

36 OLOF ARNGART. 1968. The Middle English *Genesis* and *Exodus*. Re-edited from MS. C.C.C.C. 444 with Introduction, Notes and Glossary. 277 pp.

37 ARNE ZETTERSTEN. 1969. The English of Tristan da Cunha. 180 pp.

38 ELLEN ALWALL. 1970. The Religious Trend in Secular Scottish School-Books 1858–1861 and 1873–1882. With a Survey of the Debate on Education in Scotland in the Middle and Late 19th Century. 177 pp.

39 CLAES SCHAAR. 1971. Marino and Crashaw. *Sospetto d'Herode*. A Commentary. 300 pp.

40 SVEN BÄCKMAN. 1971. This Singular Tale. A Study of *The Vicar of Wakefield* and its Literary Background. 281 pp.

41 CHRISTER PÅHLSSON. 1972. The Northumbrian Burr. A Sociolinguistic Study. 309 pp.

42 KARL-GUSTAV EK. 1972. The Development of OE *y* and *eo* in South-Eastern Middle English. 133 pp.

43 BO SELTÉN. 1972. The Anglo-Saxon Heritage in Middle English Personal Names. East Anglia 1100–1399. 187 pp.

44   KERSTIN ASSARSSON-RIZZI. 1972. *Friar Bacon and Friar Bungay.* A Structural and Thematic Analysis of Robert Greene's Play. 164 pp.

45   ARNE ZETTERSTEN. 1974. A Critical Facsimile Edition of Thomas Batchelor, *An Orthoëpical Analysis of the English Language* and *An Orthoëpical Analysis of the Dialect of Bedfordshire*(1809). Part I. 260 pp.

46   ERIK INGVAR THURIN. 1974. The Universal Autobiography of Ralph Waldo Emerson. xii + 288 pp.

47   HARRIET BJÖRK. 1974. The Language of Truth. Charlotte Brontë, the Woman Question, and the Novel. 152 pp.

48   ANDERS DALLBY. 1974. The Anatomy of Evil. A Study of John Webster's *The White Devil.* 236 pp.

49   GILLIS KRISTENSSON. 1974. John Mirk's *Instructions for Parish Priests.* Edited from MS Cotton Claudius A II and Six Other Manuscripts with Introduction, Notes and Glossary. 287 pp.

50   STIG JOHANSSON. 1975. Papers in Contrastive Linguistics and Language Testing. 179 pp.

51   BENGT ELLENBERGER. 1977. The Latin Element in the Vocabulary of the Earlier Makars Henryson and Dunbar. 163 pp.

52   MARIANNE THORMÄHLEN. 1978. *The Waste Land.* A Fragmentary Wholeness. 248 pp.

53   LARS HERMERÉN. 1978. On Modality in English. A Study of the Semantics of the Modals. 195 pp.

54   SVEN BÄCKMAN. 1979. Tradition Transformed. Studies in the Poetry of Wilfred Owen. 206 pp.

55   JAN JÖNSJÖ. 1979. Studies on Middle English Nicknames. I: Compounds. 227 pp.

56   JAN SVARTVIK & RANDOLPH QUIRK (eds). 1980. A Corpus of English Conversation. 893 pp.

57   LARS-HÅKAN SVENSSON. 1980. Silent Art. Rhetorical and Thematic Patterns in Samuel Daniel's *Delia.* 392 pp.

58   INGRID MÅRDH. 1980. Headlinese. On the Grammar of English Front Page Headlines. 200 pp.

59   STIG JOHANSSON. 1980. Plural Attributive Nouns in Present-Day English. x + 136 pp.

60   CLAES SCHAAR. 1982. The Full Voic'd Quire Below. Vertical Context Systems in *Paradise Lost.* 354 pp.

61   GUNILLA FLORBY. 1982. The Painful Passage to Virtue. A Study of George Chapman's *The Tragedy of Bussy D'Ambois* and *The Revenge of Bussy D'Ambois.* 266 pp.

62   BENGT ALTENBERG. 1982. The Genitive v. the *of*-Construction. A Study of Syntactic Variation in 17th Century English. 320 pp.

63 JAN SVARTVIK, MATS EEG-OLOFSSON, OSCAR FORSHEDEN, BENGT OR-ESTRÖM & CECILIA THAVENIUS. 1982. Survey of Spoken English. Report on Research 1975–81. 112 pp.

64 CECILIA THAVENIUS. 1983. Referential Pronouns in English Conversation. 194 pp.

65 NILS WRANDER. 1983. English Place-Names in the Dative Plural. 172 pp.

66 BENGT ORESTRÖM. 1983. Turn-Taking in English Conversation. 195 pp.

67 EVA JARRING CORONES. 1983. The Portrayal of Women in the Fiction of Henry Handel Richardson. 183 pp.

68 ANNA-BRITA STENSTRÖM. 1984. Questions and Responses in English Conversation. x + 296 pp.

69 KARIN HANSSON. 1984. The Warped Universe. A Study of Imagery and Structure in Seven Novels by Patrick White. 271 pp.

70 MARIANNE THORMÄHLEN. 1984. Eliot's Animals. 197 pp.

71 EVERT ANDERSSON. 1985. On Verb Complementation in Written English. 293 pp.

72 WIVECA SOTTO. 1985. The Rounded Rite. A Study of Wole Soyinka's Play *The Bacchae of Euripides.* 187 pp.

73 ULLA THAGG FISHER. 1985. The Sweet Sound of Concord. A Study of Swedish Learners' Concord Problems in English. xii + 212 pp.

74 MOIRA LINNARUD. 1986. Lexis in Composition. A Performance Analysis of Swedish Learners' Written English. x + 136 pp.

75 LARS WOLLIN & HANS LINDQUIST (eds). 1986. Translation Studies in Scandinavia. Proceedings from The Scandinavian Symposium on Translation Theory (SSOTT) II. 149 pp.

76 BENGT ALTENBERG. 1987. Prosodic Patterns in Spoken English. Studies in the Correlation between Prosody and Grammar for Text-to-Speech Conversion. 229 pp.

77 ÖRJAN SVENSSON. 1987. Saxon Place-Names in East Cornwall. xii + 192 pp.

78 JØRN CARLSEN & BENGT STREIJFFERT (eds). 1988. Canada and the Nordic Countries. 416 pp.

79 STIG CARLSSON. 1989. Studies on Middle English Local Bynames in East Anglia. 193 pp.

80 HANS LINDQUIST. 1989. English Adverbials in Translation. A Corpus Study of Swedish Renderings. 184 pp.

81 ERIK INGVAR THURIN. 1990. The Humanization of Willa Cather. Classicism in an American Classic. 406 pp.

82 JAN SVARTVIK (ed). 1990. The London-Lund Corpus of Spoken English. Description and Research. 350 pp.

83 KARIN HANSSON. 1991. Sheer Edge. Aspects of Identity in David Malouf's Writing. 170 pp.

84 BIRGITTA BERGLUND. 1993. Woman's Whole Existence. The House as an Image in the Novels of Ann Radcliffe, Mary Wollstonecraft and Jane Austen. 244 pp.

85 NANCY D. HARGROVE. 1994. The Journey Toward *Ariel.* Sylvia Plath's Poems of 1956–1959. 293 pp.

86 MARIANNE THORMÄHLEN (ed). 1994. T. S. Eliot at the Turn of the Century. 244 pp.

87 KARIN HANSSON. 1996. The Unstable Manifold. Janet Frame's Challenge to Determinism. 149 pp.

88 KARIN AIJMER, BENGT ALTENBERG & MATS JOHANSSON (eds). 1996. Languages in Contrast. Papers from a Symposium on Text-based Cross-linguistic Studies Lund. 200 pp.

89 CECILIA BJÖRKÉN. 1996. Into the Isle of Self. Nietzschean Patterns and Contrasts in D. H. Lawrence's *The Trespasser.* 247 pp.

90 MARJA PALMER. 1996. Men and Women in T. S. Eliot's Early Poetry. 243 pp.

91 KEITH COMER. 1996. Strange Meetings: Walt Whitman, Wilfred Owen and Poetry of War. 205 pp.

92 CARITA PARADIS. 1997. Degree Modifiers of Adjectives in Spoken British English. 189 pp.

93 GUNILLA FLORBY. 1997. The Margin Speaks. A Study of Margaret Laurence and Robert Kroetsch from a Post-Colonial Point of View. 252 pp.

94 JEAN HUDSON. 1998. Perspectives on fixedness: applied and theoretical. 177pp.

95 MARIE KÄLLKVIST. 1998. Form-Class and Task-Type Effects in Learner English: A Study of Advanced Swedish Learners. xii + 226 pp.

96 AGNETA LINDGREN. 1999. The Fallen World in Coleridge's Poetry. 264 pp.